3000 800011 40818
St. Louis Community College

D1776510

```
659.2 S596p                          F V
SIMON
PUBLIC RELATIONS MANAGEMENT :
A CASEBOOK
                           19.95
```

St. Louis Community College

Library

5801 Wilson Avenue
St. Louis, Missouri **63110**

PUBLIC RELATIONS MANAGEMENT: A CASEBOOK

Raymond Simon

Professor Emeritus of Public Relations
Utica College of Syracuse University
Utica, New York

Publishing Horizons, Inc., Columbus, Ohio

©COPYRIGHT 1986, PUBLISHING HORIZONS, INC.
    2950 North High Street
    P.O. Box 02190
    Columbus, Ohio 43202

ALL RIGHTS RESERVED. No part of this publication may be reproduced, stored in a retrieval system, or transmitted, in any form or by any means, electronic, mechanical, photocopying, recording or otherwise, without prior written permission of the copyright holder.

Printed in the United States

    1 2 3 4   7 6 5 4

Library of Congress Cataloging-in-Publication Data

Simon, Raymond.
   Public relations management.

   1. Public relations—Management—Case studies.
I. Title.
HD59.S457   1986   659.2   86-3274
ISBN 0-942280-22-9

Dedicated

*In fond memory of these students who ask why,
Including those marked "68 - Nice Try"*

CONTENTS

Introduction..vi

Part 1: Non-Profit Organizations

Case 1.	Brooke College - A	3
Case 2.	Brooke College - B	8
Case 3.	Brooke College - C	9
	Excerpt For Discussion: J. Carroll Bateman's Credo	17
Case 4.	Metro Transit Review Commission - A	18
Case 5.	Metro Transit Review Commission - B	23
	Excerpt For Discussion: Working With Management	26
Case 6.	Metro College - A	33
Case 7.	Metro College - B	45
Case 8.	Heywood Hospital	54
	Excerpt For Discussion: A Model Public Relations Performance ...	63

Part 2. Business and Industry

Case 9.	Eager Instrumatics, Inc. - A	71
Case 10.	Eager Instrumatics, Inc. - B	77
	Excerpt For Discussion: P & G Licking Its Wounds	84
Case 11.	A.H. Robins And The Dalkon Shield	89

Excerpt For Discussion: An Interview With Kal Druck 97
Case 12. Basic Chemicals International - A 101
Case 13. Basic Chemicals International - B 110
  Excerpt For Discussion: Some Considerations In Dealing
    With Public Opinion 122
Case 14. Empire Enterprises 132
  Excerpt For Discussion: An Interview With George Hammond ... 137
Case 15. Bruce Canfield Is Given The Word - A 141
Case 16. Bruce Canfield Is Given The Word - B 149
Case 17. Norton Chemicals 151
  Excerpt For Discussion: Inside The Amoral World of
    Public Relations 159

Part 3. Counseling

Case 18. A Letter From Peter Gantor 173
Case 19. A Talk On Measuring Publicity Effectiveness 178
  Excerpt For Discussion: Protesting Preferential Treatment 190
Case 20. A Search For Public Relations Counsel - A 196
Case 21. A Search For Public Relations Counsel - B 220
Case 22. A Search For Public Relations Counsel - C 228
Case 23 Ruder & Finn Conference On
    Professional Responsibility - A 237
Case 24. Ruder & Finn Conference On
    Professional Responsibility - B 254
  Excerpt For Discussion: S. Africa: A Thorny Ethics Problem 266

Part 4. Appendix

PRSA Code Of Professional Standards With Official Interpretations ... 273

INTRODUCTION

This third edition of a book of public relations cases has evolved from two prior editions which have been used by students and teachers in more than one hundred colleges and universities in the United States and abroad. Its main purpose remains the same as that of its predecessors: to provide a teaching and learning resource for upper-level and graduate courses in public relations and for practitioner seminars and continuing education programs. After more than three decades of public relations practice and teaching I have concluded that the ability to deal effectively with public relations problems is the mark of the most successful practitioners. Realistic cases, developed from actual situations which have faced practitioners, provide students with the opportunity to come to grips with the kinds of problems they will face when they enter the field. Discussion of case situations enables students to develop thoughtful insights and judgments. It is not expected that the situations depicted in the cases of this book will ever be duplicated exactly as described. It follows, therefore, that one should not consider there are "right" and "wrong" answers to the cases, but rather that there are right and wrong perceptions, insights, and judgments.

To enable those using this book to sharpen their perceptions, insights, and judgments, I have assembled a wide variety of cases encompassing a range of public relations activities within business and industry, non-profit organizations, and counseling firms. The cases are concerned with public relations people at all levels of management. They examine practical and ethical questions, and their scope ranges from the very personal problems of a middle-management practitioner facing a career change to the impersonal problems of large business firms and trade associations.

The cases present a set of facts relating to situations that faced practitioners who had to deal with these facts in handling a particular public relations problem or set of problems. People described in the cases make statements and respond in certain ways to remarks made by others in the cases. Decisions are made and actions taken. It is expected that students will act as a group in going through the process of analyzing and considering each case and exchanging ideas about the case situations and the people in them. At times one or several students will be asked to play the role of participants in dealing with an unfolding situation in which they are placed. Those playing roles in these simulations will be required to make statements, engage in conversations, and either take action or state what action they intend to take in handling a specific set of public relations problems.

Discussion of the cases will be most fruitful if participants read the cases carefully in advance. Such close reading should enable participants to come to the discussion sessions thoroughly briefed and aware of the stated facts in each case. These facts should not be memorized - on the contrary, students should openly use the text during each discussion - but the text should be used chiefly as the raw material for discussion. In some instances there will even be differences of opinion about case "facts," and in such instances the early stages of discussion should be utilized for clarification of these facts.

As the class goes through each case discussion, students will begin to come to grips with the very real problems faced by those who play the main roles in the cases. Class members should, in effect, try to see the case through the eyes and mind of those involved, and to note and comment about the validity and soundness of assumptions which have been made and actions which have been taken. Students will also find it valuable to analyze remarks made by people in the cases, and to comment on the wisdom of these remarks. Finally, class members should consider what steps they would take, what remarks they would make, were they faced with a situation similar to the case itself. Most of the cases present either one or a set of problems, either explicit or implied, and these problems demand solutions. It is expected that class members will have conclusions of their own about the problems and their solutions, and it is further expected that they will be willing to match them with others put forth by those in the discussion group.

In the end analysis, both the cases and simulations should serve as catalytic agents. To be most effective they should trigger among the class members a series of responses which will, in turn, trigger further responses from the participants. The class will find that someone has seen an important nuance which others have overlooked; that someone will question a case item which has been taken for granted; that someone has an "answer" which is totally at variance with other "answers." It is hoped that those participating in the discussion will find that the cases and discussion will have helped to clarify each student's thinking and will provide each class member with new insights about the field of public relations.

Some of the cases in this book were first prepared for the Public Relations Society of America and were used in advance professional courses and conferences. I wish to express my appreciation to the Society for permission to use such cases in this book. I also deeply appreciate the comments and responses I have received from teachers and students who used the first two editions and whose ideas about the cases led to change in this third edition. Their reactions have been instrumental in the decision to drop some cases and replace them with new ones, and also to make changes to bring cases up-to-date in regard to current data. I hope that the retention of the most challenging cases from the earlier editions and the addition of the new ones in this edition will provide continuing challenges for those now in the field and those who intend to enter it.

At various points throughout this book of cases I have included as "Excerpts for Discussion" reprints of articles, interviews, and comments by leading public relations practitioners and by those writing and reporting about the American public relations scene. The excerpts are generally not as long or as involved as the cases, and are meant to serve as alternative focal points for discussion. Some teachers prefer to assign excerpts in advance, and some prefer to bring them to class attention following discussion of a case. As with the cases, the excerpts are meant to serve as catalytic agents for student discussion and exchange of ideas and thinking about public relations concepts and practices.

Finally, I want to express my warm appreciation to those who have provided the material and data for the cases in this book and for those who granted me permission to reprint the comments and observations in the excerpts. A special not of appreciation is extended to Kirk and Maria Starczewski for their contribution to the production of this book, and to Lyn, Melissa, and Karen for their constant encouragement, support, and forbearance.

Raymond Simon
Professor Emeritus of Public Relations

Utica College of Syracuse University
Utica, New York

Part 1: Non-Profit Organizations

Case 1.   Brooke College - A
Case 2.   Brooke College - B
Case 3.   Brooke College - C
   Excerpt For Discussion: J. Carroll Bateman's Credo
Case 4.   Metro Transit Review Commission - A
Case 5.   Metro Transit Review Commission - B
   Excerpt For Discussion: Working With Management
Case 6.   Metro College - A
Case 7.   Metro College - B
Case 8.   Heywood Hospital
   Excerpt For Discussion: A Model Public Relations Performance

Case 1

BROOKE COLLEGE - A*

Brooke College, a small, private, liberal arts college for women, was established in 1893 in the downtown section of the capital city of one of the Northeastern states. In 1946 the college moved to a new campus on 300 wooded acres in Swanwick (pop. 10,000), 16 miles west of the capital.

In 1985, when this case was written, the college had an enrollment of 1060 students: 342 in the first year class; 286 sophomores; 246 juniors; and 186 seniors. A total of 338 Brooke students came from the state in which the college was located and 466 came from eight adjoining states. The remaining students came from 32 other states and from 26 foreign countries. A total of 70 percent of the student body had graduated from public schools, the remaining 30 percent from private schools.

Brooke offered degree programs of study in 15 fields and in four interdisciplinary areas. Most of the programs were in the traditional liberal arts and sciences, but the college also offered programs in the performing, visual, and creative arts; education; computer science; and public health.

The campus, which was heavily wooded on its outer fringes, contained three large classroom/science buildings; a library of 240,000 volumes; a College Center housing the main administration offices, bookstore, snack bar, and lounge; a 650-seat hall for the performing arts; the Athletic Center; riding stable; and 14 resident houses organized into four main clusters. The professional resident staff consisted of the resident life director, three resident assistants, and 20 floor advisors.

At about 1:30 a.m. on Wednesday, September 20, a 19-year-old Brooke College sophomore named Heather Domstedder was assaulted and

---

* *All names, dates, and places in this case have been disguised.*

raped some 200 yards from the college's Valley Road entrance. The victim reported the rape to the city police but did not file charges and no arrest was made in connection with the attack.

President Maxwell Pondexter was given the above information when he received a phone call at home at 8 a.m. from the college's director of security. The director informed the president that his contact at the police department told him that the victim told the police that her assailant attacked her from behind, pulled her hard by the hair, punched her, threw her to the ground, and then forced himself on her. According to the director, Domstedder had undergone an examination at Swanwick Hospital which had confirmed the rape. After being treated for bruises and shock, said the security director, the coed was given a ride back to the college. She refused to go to the infirmary, but instead went directly to her room.

One of the actions that President Pondexter considered taking when he got to his office was to call the regional editor of the *Gazette*, the daily newspaper published in the state's capital city. The *Gazette* had a circulation of 120,000, was read throughout the state, and reached 6,000 readers in Swanwick. The president did not know the regional editor personally, but the president knew that he was the editor responsible for coverage of Swanwick news in the *Gazette* and the president thought it would help if he told the editor the steps the college had taken to prevent such incidents as the Domstedder attack. (These are included in the letter subsequently sent out by the president to parents and reprinted later in this case). After some thought, however, the president decided that it would probably be wiser not to call, hence he did not follow through with a call to the regional editor. Later that morning he and the school nurse visited with Heather Domstedder in her room, and while there, the three of them talked to Heather's parents in a phone call put through by the president.

Thursday's *Gazette* carried this story on page 1 of its second, or regional, section:

NOTES

Swanwick Police Investigate Rape

Swanwick police are investigating the assault and rape of a 19-year-old Brooke College sophomore which took place early Wednesday morning 200 yards from the college entrance on Valley Road. According to Sergeant Mort Lux, no charges have been filed and no arrests have been made in connection with the report made to the police by the victim, who underwent an examination at Swanwick Hospital after the incident.

After reading this story the president considered calling Elaine Fox, the editor of the Brooke College *Call*, the college weekly which was distributed on campus every Wednesday. At this time in the semester the president had not had the opportunity to have Fox in for the informal chat he made it a habit of having each year with the new editor. The paper had published only one issue, and as that issue had not contained any editorials, the president had no way of knowing how Fox viewed issues crucial to college students. He thought of asking Fox to stop by, asking her to be discreet in handling the story, and explaining to her the steps the college had taken to prevent such incidents as the Domstedder attack, but in the end he decided not to do so. The issue of September 28 carried the following 24-point headline and story on its front page:

Brooke Sophomore Attacked And Raped

Police in Swanwick are investigating the brutal and vicious attack and rape of a 19-year-old Brooke College sophomore which took place in the early morning hours last Wednesday.

In the attack, which occurred 200 yards from the college entrance on Valley Road, the Brookie was first beaten and assaulted.

"Her assailant," said a police department source, "attacked her from behind, pulled her hard by the hair, punched her, and then threw her to the ground and forced himself on her."

NOTES

A passing motorist took the victim to Swanwick Hospital, and there she was examined and treated. Confirming that the Brookie has been raped, the hospital said she was treated for bruises and shock and later transported back to her dorm.

According to *Call* files, there were no cases of reported rape of Brooke College students last year, but two were reported the previous year, as were several cases of exhibitionism.

President Pondexter felt that Fox had not handled the story in a discreet manner, but he decided not to say anything to her nor to write a letter to the editor expressing his feelings about the way the paper had treated the incident. On October 10, the president sent the following letter to all Brooke College parents:

> Office of the President
> Brooke College
> Swanwick, (State)
> 214-547-6723
>
> October 10, 1985
>
> Dear Brooke Parents:
>
> As many of you have perhaps heard by now, on Wednesday, September 20, at 1:30 a.m. a Brooke student was raped just off the campus grounds near the Valley Road gate.
>
> I am writing you to ask your help in convincing your daughter that she should take all precautions necessary to assure her own safety. While we do not wish our students to be fearful of leaving their dormitories, we do want them to realize that they must exercise caution. As you know, the campus is large and heavily wooded and it is impossible for us to provide security coverage for all of it at all times. Our security people regularly patrol the roads and walkways through the campus, but they cannot keep all the property under surveillance constantly.

NOTES

Our students have been repeatedly told:

1. Not to walk or jog alone at night.

2. To be careful in the woods during the day and stay out of them at night.

3. To travel in groups of three or more at night.

4. To keep their dormitory rooms locked and not prop open exit doors.

As a matter of fact, the very week of the rape, a notice was sent to all students reporting an afternoon incidence of exhibitionism and warning them to take the above precautions.

However, some students assume that "it can't happen to me." We hope it will not. As has always been the case, our security officers and residential living staff are trying to help assure that it does not by patrolling, counseling, speaking to students privately and in groups. But we need your help and the cooperation of the students as well.

Sincerely,

(signed)

Maxwell P. Pondexter
President

NOTES

Case 2

BROOKE COLLEGE - B*

Several months after the incident and letter described in this case, President Pondexter decided to add a director of public relations to the college staff, a decision he had been considering for some time. You are one of three finalist applicants who have been invited to the college for personal interviews. Your present job as editorial assistant of an alumni publication in a large university pays $17,500, and you have learned via your interviews that the Brooke position pays $25,000 and the successful applicant will be responsible for a staff of two full-time employees and two interns. Your last interview of the day is with President Pondexter and has been going well; you've been chatting for almost an hour now and you think you've been making a good impression.

"I would like your opinion about a situation which took place a few months ago," President Pondexter says, and he thereupon provides you with the information set forth in the fact pattern of this case. "I've always felt that the best way to test professional public relations judgment is to measure it against an actual case, so I decided to ask all three of you applicants for your reactions. I'd be glad to answer any questions you may have, but I am primarily interested in knowing your professional opinion about the way I handled the situation."

---

*All names and places in this case have been disguised

Case 3

BROOKE COLLEGE - C*

Shortly after the interview cited in "Brooke College-B," President Pondexter hired Dawn Tomane to fill the school's newly-created director of public relations position. Tomane, 26, had served two years on the PR staff of the Kodak Company and two years as a university assistant public information officer.

Two years after Tomane joined the Brooke staff, President Pondexter held a series of meeting with Betty Baron, 40, the school's athletic director for the past ten years. As a result of these meetings in mid-June Pondexter made the decision to upgrade all Brooke sports from Division III to Division II. Concurrently, Tomane was given permission to hire a full-time Sports Information Director, someone aggressive enough to place Brooke's name in various media outlets, serve as a media liaison, and devise and implement game-night promotions in an effort to maximize home attendance. Up to this time, sports information was handled by a student intern who worked out of the athletic office and reported to Baron for overall supervision.

In late July, therefore, Pondexter appointed Tomane and Baron as a two-person search committee, and the three agreed on a yearly salary of $18,500. Pondexter told the two that the new SID would now report to both Tomane and Baron.

"I'm not sure that's the way to go with this," Tomane immediately said. "Sports information is a PR function, and it should be under the PR department, where the goals would be the same."

"Why change?" Baron countered. "The SID intern has always worked for the athletic department. I don't see any reason to tamper with success."

"Look, this is a new situation for the school," Pondexter cut in. "I think it's best to have two administrators judging the success of the SID

---

* All names and places in this case have been changed.

function at the same time. If it doesn't work out, fine, we'll do something about it." Both Tomane and Baron let the issue drop.

After screening 50 applications, Tomane and Baron brought two applicants to the campus for interviews. The first applicant declined the position after learning the salary.

On August 26, Baron and Tomane interviewed Nancy Adler, the second applicant. Adler, 25, had three years experience as a sports writer on a small daily, and had seen Brooke's ad in *Editor and Publisher* at the same time that she was beginning to question where she was going in journalism.

"Why do you think you're especially qualified to be SID at Brooke?" Tomane asked to open the interview.

"Well, I've always been interested in sports, but as a sportswriter you really don't get that feeling of being on a team, so to speak, like I think you do in sports PR," Adler replied. "Also I'm excited about the move to Division II, and I hope I can be a part of it."

"Just looking at your resume," Baron said, "it appears you have no experience in sports information. How will you overcome that lack of experience?"

"Well," Adler replied, "as a sportswriter, I've worked regularly with SIDs, so I know what the position entails. In addition, my knowledge of the journalism field will aid me in sports PR. I'll be very conscious of the media's needs, because they were once my needs."

After the interview continued for about 20 more minutes, Tomane asked Adler if she had any questions.

"Yes," she said, "I'm wondering who I answer to in terms of the day-to-day routine?"

"Both of us, really," Tomane said after a pause.

"Yes, the two of us," Baron agreed, almost inaudibly.

Adler was disturbed by their responses. They seemed not to want to talk about the issue of direct authority over the SID. But she decided not to press the issue, since it was apparently their desire not to discuss it.

After Tomane said she had no further questions, Baron suddenly said to Adler, "This is a hard job, a thankless job. Often it's a gopher position.

NOTES

You're going to have to make signs to promote games, or go pick up a banner, or announce the games when certain people don't show up. You'll have to do what has to be done. I do what has to be done. We don't have a big staff. Everyone helps out."

"Well, Betty," Tomane said to Baron, though she was looking straight ahead, "that's the way it was when we had a student intern, but since the SID will also be under the PR department this year, she shouldn't have to make signs or announce games. The SID is supposed to act as media liaison first and foremost."

Baron didn't respond and the interview ended shortly thereafter.

Three days later, Baron called to tell Adler she had been selected, and asked her to visit the campus the next day. Her day ended with a meeting with President Pondexter. Toward the end of their 45-minute meeting, Pondexter asked Adler if she had any questions.

"Yes," she said. "In terms of the day-to-day routine, who do I answer to, who do I work for?"

"You work for both Dawn Tomane and Betty Baron," Pondexter said after a brief pause. "Of course, they both have their departments to run, but when the need arises, that's who you go to see, one of them."

Adler decided not to pursue the matter further. She assumed Pondexter meant she would be her own boss, except in extreme cases. But she felt she would be better off not to press the matter because she suspected, given their remarks during the first interview, that Tomane and Barone either didn't have this new arrangement worked out or didn't like it.

Reporting to work on Monday, September 3, Adler found out for the first time that her office was a small cubicle located in the athletic complex. She had assumed her office would be located in the administration building - clear across campus - where the PR office was, but she never thought to ask during her interviews.

Early in September Adler found plenty of work to do. She wrote a well-received 1,500-word article profiling the fall sports season for the first issue of the *Alumni News* magazine, a monthly publication edited by Tomane. She also started working on the basketball yearbook, which would

NOTES

be sold at all home games. (The basketball season would begin November 22). The copy deadline for the book was Monday, October 22. Finally, the fall sports schedule got off to a solid start.

Adler's workload increased as September gave way to October. Basketball season was fast approaching, since Tom Duncan's team officially opened practice on Monday, October 15.

And Brooke's field hockey team, coached by Baron, was enjoying a successful fall campaign. On Friday, October 5, Baron came to Adler's cubicle.

"Nancy, since the field hockey team is doing so well, I'd like to have the games announced, so the fans know who the players are," she said. "I'd like you to come to Tuesday's game and do the announcing. I've rented a bull-horn and I could show you how to work it."

"I see," Adler replied. "That's Tuesday afternoon at 3, right?"

"Yes, it should only take a couple of hours."

Adler was unsure how to respond. She didn't mind handling the announcing, but she knew it would take time away from projects like the basketball yearbook. "I'll have to get back to you on it, Betty," she decided to say. "I think I may have an appointment Tuesday afternoon."

Baron frowned. "I really need you for this," she said. As soon as Baron left, Adler called Tomane and explained the situation.

"Well, here's how we can handle it," Tomane said. "Tell Baron you can't make it to Tuesday's game because you have an all-afternoon meeting with me. Tell her I'm conducting a workshop for everyone affiliated with the PR office on the correct way to write publicity, or something like that."

Adler did not feel comfortable being told to lie to one of her bosses. "Are you sure we should handle it that way?" she asked.

"Absolutely," Tomane responded. "Believe me, she'll forget all about it in a few days."

Adler did as Tomane said, and Baron ended up finding a student to announce the game.

On Monday, October 8, Adler met with Coach Duncan at Duncan's request. She was very familiar with the coach's reputation as a college star, a

NOTES

professional player, and a scrappy, tough competitor. As a coach, Duncan had compiled an outstanding record at Brooke and brought it to national ranking. He was known to be somewhat stubborn and tough on people who work for him.

Adler felt she was prepared for the meeting because three weeks earlier she had called on Joe Casey, the *Gazette's* sports editor, and had what she considered to be an excellent talk with him. The enthusiastic Casey told Adler that the Division III Brooke cagers had received some of the best publicity in town, but now that they were in Division II he wanted to make them the "only show in town."

Adler figured the meeting would be related to the start of the basketball season and she had already thought about the PR strategy for the opening day of practice. She planned to call Casey within the next couple of days and ask for a photographer to be on hand. In addition, Adler planned to call the local TV and radio stations and try to arrange interviews.

To Adler's surprise, Duncan had more elaborate plans. "I'm sure you know we open our practice a week from today," Duncan said. "I think we should get a nice spread in the *Gazette*, with player pictures, profiles and articles, that type of thing."

"Well, I'll try and get a photographer here," Adler said.

"Only a photographer?" exclaimed Duncan. "This deserves more than a photographer. We should make a big deal about this day, have some sort of spread, a big spread."

It's still a month and a half before the season starts, Adler thought to herself, and I don't want to ask for too much from the media too early. But she didn't want to say that to Duncan; it would be better to talk first to Casey and see how he viewed the situation. "Well," she decided to say, "I'll speak to Casey and see what I can do." Duncan nodded his head in approval, and the meeting was over shortly thereafter.

On October 12, Adler spoke to Casey, but all he could promise was one or two pictures. "It's baseball playoff time, college football is hot, pro basketball and hockey are starting up; there's just too damn much going on to

NOTES

devote a whole lot of space to the beginning of a team's practice," Casey said. "Every team in America opens up practice at some time, so it's really not that unusual. But don't worry Nancy, I'll get a good photo or two in there."

True to his word, Casey ran two action photographs in Tuesday morning's (Oct. 16) paper. All three local TV stations showed up and interviewed Duncan and shot action footage of the practice. Four area radio stations were present too, getting sound bites from Duncan and some of the players. All in all, Adler felt the opening of practice was a good kick-off to the season, but she wasn't sure about Duncan's reaction to the coverage.

Adler found on Tuesday morning that she had a problem from another source, that being Betty Baron. Adler was sitting behind her desk when Baron entered Adler's cubicle.

"We've got a big field hockey game on Friday," Baron said. "I'd like you to do the announcing for it."

At that point, before Adler could respond, her phone rang and Baron left, saying "Meet me in my office Thursday morning at 10. We'll work out the details and I'll show you how to use the bull-horn." Adler nodded her head in agreement as Baron walked away.

The next morning (Wednesday) the bull-horn question was Adler's biggest problem. But not for long. When she got to her office, she received a phone call from Tomane.

"I'm sorry about the short notice, Nancy, but we need a piece from you for the *Alumni News* by Friday," Tomane said. "I'm just laying the magazine out now, and we have some space. I'll need about 1,000 words."

"Well, that might be a problem," Adler responded. She was shocked Tomane would ask for 1,000 words in just two days. "My deadline for the basketball yearbook is Monday, and I've really got to work on that. I'd like to have the layout done by Friday, so I can take it and some of the copy to the printers right away."

"Look, I'm on a tighter deadline with the magazine than you are with your book," Tomane replied curtly, clearly annoyed. "I don't have time to

NOTES

argue about this. I need 1,000 words by Friday. Have it on my desk." Tomane hung up.

Adler was surprised at the hostility from Tomane. In fact, she was so taken aback that she forgot to tell Tomane about Baron's latest request to announce Friday's field hockey game. Furthermore, Adler thought, Tomane's attitude over the phone suggested that perhaps she ought to handle Baron herself.

However, she wasn't able to do anything about Baron because at that point Coach Duncan called and asked Adler to come to his office.

"Look at this," Duncan said, pointing to pages from two newspapers. "Two sports sections from yesterday, and they both have major features on the opening of practices. We get two lousy pictures!"

Looking at the clips, Adler saw that one was from Spring City, a town 50 miles to the east, and the other from Penrod, about 30 miles west. Both sports sections contained player profiles, an abundance of pictures, and feature sidebars. Adler didn't know what to say.

"This really tees me off and I want that damn paper to know it," Duncan fumed. "In fact, I've made an appointment with Martin Fisk for lunch today. I'm sure you know Fisk, he's the publisher of the *Gazette*."

"Well, that would be your choice," Adler said. She thought to herself that this lunch would be ill-advised. She had established a good rapport with Casey, and she didn't want that destroyed a month and a half before the season started. However, given the angered state of the coach, Adler felt she ought to keep her objections to herself.

Adler had some errands to run and she returned to her office at 3:30. She immediately went into Duncan's office, and the coach was obviously in better spirits.

"Fisk is a great guy," Duncan told Adler. "He supports what we're trying to do here. He wants you to send him copies of all the releases we distribute, so he can know when Casey doesn't pick up on something we send out. He told me he's behind us 100%. He promises we'll get increased coverage."

Adler was flabbergasted. Everything she ever learned in any

NOTES

journalism class told her that publishers kept their hands off the editorial side. Yet Fisk seemed to have aligned himself with Duncan.

"I'm glad Fisk was so positive," Adler replied. "But I'm still worried we might make Casey angry, especially if we send his boss copies of everything he gets."

"All I know is that Fisk said we'll get the big spreads that we should've been getting all along, and that's what I'm concerned about," Duncan said.

"Well, I hope everything turns out okay," Adler said before leaving Duncan's office.

Adler returned to her office at 4 p.m., in time to answer her ringing telephone. It was Casey.

"Nancy, I'd like to know what the hell is going on," Casey said immediately, obviously perturbed. "I just got called on the carpet by Fisk about our winter coverage and the winter season hasn't really begun yet. What the hell's going on?"

"Well," Adler said, "I think we've got a problem."

"What do you mean, 'we've got a problem'"? Casey began to shout. "**We** don't have any problem - **you've** got the problem!"

There was a pause at the other end, and Adler heard a click. A dial tone followed.

Adler was stunned. So much for the great relationship with Casey, she thought. She decided to mull over the problems that faced her: first, she had to meet with Baron in the morning about announcing Friday's field hockey game. Second, she had to write the 1,000-word piece for Tomane by Friday. Third, she had to somehow deal with Casey's anger. Finally, she had to have the copy for the yearbook done by Monday, though she wanted to have the layout done by Friday.

She looked at her watch. It was 4:15. She decided to go home and mull over her situation.

Brooke College-C was drafted by Larry Platt, a former student SID whose experiences paralleled many of those faced by Nancy Adler.

NOTES

An Excerpt For Discussion

J. Carroll Bateman's Credo*

I believe that public relations is a profession which should concern itself not with the manipulation of people, but with their continuing enlightenment. I believe that public relations practice should strive to elevate its audiences rather than to degrade them and that our communications should be addressed to reason and judgment, rather than to emotion and prejudice. I believe that sound public relations comprises policies and deeds as well as words; that it must seek to clarify the issues of our times rather than confuse them and while I may undertake to present one point of view for public consideration, I believe in the inalienable right of those with opposing points of view to present their cases also, for I recognize that my right to speak can be secured only if the guarantee exists for all, including those whose cases are unpopular. I believe that the democratic process must prevail in the marketplace of ideas as well as in political and economic affairs. I believe that the public interest takes precedence over the interests of those I represent, and I conceive my function as being to assist in conforming the interests of those I represent to the interests of the public when the two do not coincide.

I recognize that the consequences of my actions are effected in the minds of men, and because the human mind has unmeasurable potentials for good and evil, I must approach my task in reverence and awe and with overriding respect for the inviolable right of the individual to make his own judgments.

---

* The late J. Carroll Bateman, former president of the Insurance Information Institute and of the Public Relations Society of America, set forth his beliefs about public relations in this credo. He expressed it in his inaugural address as president of the PRSA in November, 1966, and at the opening of the seventh Public Relations World Congress in August, 1976.

Case 4

METRO TRANSIT REVIEW COMMISSION - A*

Nearing the end of his second consecutive two-year term as mayor of the midwestern city of Metro, Republican Mayor Karl Dorfman foresaw that the privately-owned Metro Transit Company would likely become a campaign issue in the coming fall election.

Metro (population 120,000) was served by a bus company which had been operating at a loss for the past five years, despite increases in fares and a cost-cutting campaign. Two years ago the head of the company offered to sell it, but had no takers. His latest year-end report, which received extensive media coverage, stated that the company would be forced to go out of business unless there was a turnabout in revenues or unless the city provided a subsidy. Neither the turnabout nor the subsidy had become a reality. Anticipating there could be campaign problems related to the transit company, the mayor decided to set up a Transit Review Commission.

Late in May, therefore, the mayor asked for and received from the Republican-dominated Common Council approval of his commission proposal. He then established a seven-member Transit Review Commission with four Republicans and three Democrats. Only one member held a position in city government and all were fairly well known citizens of Metro. The commission was charged with the task of conducting an exhaustive review of the transit situation and recommending proposals for dealing effectively with the transit problem. The mayor set a mid-December date for submission to him (and subsequently to the Common Council) of the commission's report and recommendations.

At its first meeting early in June, the commission elected Tad Goodwin, 30, chairperson of the commission. The only son of Stanley Goodwin, president of Goodwin Insurance Company and one of the city's

---

* *All names, dates, and places in this case have been disguised.*

leading businessmen, Tad Goodwin was head of the city's Planning Department, a position to which he was appointed three years ago by the mayor. A Northwestern Law School graduate, Goodwin had never practiced law. He joined the legal department of Goodwin Insurance Company after graduation and worked there for several years before taking his present position with the city. Both he and his father were registered Republicans. Stanley Goodwin, 63, was a life-long friend of the publisher of the *Courier*, an afternoon daily, and both served on the governing board of the city's most prestigious club and lunched there every weekday.

After his election to the chairperson's position and with the concurrence of the commission members, Tad Goodwin contracted with Paula Martin Associates to handle public relations for the commission on an hourly basis, with out-of-pocket expenses paid at cost. The firm, formed three years ago by Martin, 28, had a number of accounts on an annual retainer basis - including its major account, the Goodwin Insurance Company - and it handled assignments from time to time billed either on an hourly or straight fee basis. Paula Martin, who had graduated seven years ago from a midwestern university with a degree in public relations, worked for four years after graduation with a large Chicago public relations counseling firm as a trainee, assistant account executive, account executive, and account supervisor before opening her firm in Metro. The firm consisted of Martin, a secretary/assistant, and free-lancers hired on a need basis.

The Transit Review Commission also signed a $5,000 contract with Professor Robert Blanchfield. A transportation specialist on the faculty of Metro College, Dr. Blanchfield was to conduct research on private and city-run transit bodies and to submit to the commission by late November recommendations for handling the Metro transit problem. As his research assistant, Professor Blanchfield engaged Susan Gray, a graduate student who had worked her way through undergraduate school as a summer graphics and page-makeup replacement on the *Courier*. (Media in Metro included the *Courier* with a circulation of 84,000 and the morning *Bulletin* with a circulation of 54,000; two television stations; five AM and five FM

NOTES

radio stations. The two newspapers and the electronic media were separately owned and highly competitive.)

Under the terms of his agreement with the commission, Dr. Blanchfield agreed to submit to the commission chairperson a first draft of his report by October 10, to meet subsequently with the commission to discuss various aspects of the proposal, and to submit a final report by November 25. The parties to the agreement fully understood that Dr. Blanchfield's report was to serve the commission only as a working paper from which the commission would prepare the final document to be submitted to the mayor and the Common Council by December 15.

Paula Martin Associates carried out a nominal number of assignments for the commission during the summer. These consisted chiefly of press releases to the local media and guest appearances by Tad Goodwin on Metro radio and television talk shows. Goodwin felt that matters were proceeding according to plan, and at a meeting with Martin on October 1 he told her that he expected Professor Blanchfield's first draft in the very near future. He also told Martin that he was pleased to have it come in at that time because this would give the commissioners time to digest the report and discuss its contents. In responding, Martin suggested that receipt of the first draft would serve as an excellent means of getting out to the public the first solid news of the commission's work. She explained that nothing had been reported about the commission since Goodwin was named chairperson, that a press conference could be held to announce receipt of Professor Blanchfield's first draft and to have the professor available to answer media questions. She also said that it could be clearly explained the draft was only a working paper for the commission's further deliberations. To her surprise, Goodwin said he disagreed with her suggestions.

"I'm sure I need not remind you that we are in the middle of an election campaign and therefore this is not the proper time to air Dr. Blanchfield's first draft," said Goodwin. "I hope you can keep the media off our backs until we agree to release the report at a time of our own choosing. Is that clear?"

NOTES

Not wanting to get into an argument with Goodwin at the time, Martin simply nodded. She felt that Goodwin was wrong, but she decided she could make her point more clearly when the professor's first draft was delivered. She therefore suggested that the two of them might be wise to discuss the matter in more detail some other time, perhaps when the report was actually delivered. Goodwin made no response but changed the discussion to talk about football.

Having worked diligently throughout the closing weeks of summer, Professor Blanchfield and his assistant completed the first draft and submitted it to Goodwin the evening of October 10, five days before a scheduled October 15 meeting of the commission. Goodwin spent the next evening reading through the 65-page report. At 4 p.m. on October 12 Goodwin received a telephone call from Howard Platt, public affairs writer for the *Courier*. Platt advised Goodwin that he had learned of Professor Blanchfield's report and intended to write a story about its major provisions. Goodwin told Platt that his call came just as he was on the way to an appointment - which was not true - and he promised to call back within an hour.

"That's fine," said Platt, "so long as I get a chance to go over the essentials of Professor Blanchfield's report with you."

"Oh?" replied Goodwin. "And what if you don't?"

"Well, then I'll simply report the facts and information I have on hand: the first draft has been delivered to you, but you refuse to reveal its contents. My lead, in such circumstances, would probably go like this: 'The chairperson of Metro Transit Review Commission, Tad Goodwin, has declined to make public a $5,000 consultant's 60-page report which recommends that the city buy and operate the Metro transit system and eliminate certain routes which have proven to be unprofitable. Among the latter, it has been learned, are Route C, serving Metro City Hospital, Route F serving North Metro, and Route G serving lower income South Metro."

"I'm late for that appointment, Mr. Platt," Gooodwin replied coldly, reflecting at the same time that Platt's facts were correct with two exceptions: the report was 65 pages long and Blanchfield did not

NOTES

recommend elimination of Route G. "I'll call you back in an hour."

Goodwin then hung up. He called Martin's office and was informed that she was out of the city and not expected to return until late the next afternoon.

NOTES

Case 5

METRO TRANSIT REVIEW COMMISSION - B*

Keeping his word to Howard Platt, Tad Goodwin called the *Courier* writer at 5 p.m. on October 12. He told Platt that his original decision stood.

"Professor Blanchfield's proposal is merely a rough draft," he said. "The commission hasn't even had a chance to read it, much less review its contents. When the proper time comes, we'll give you information about the proposal, not now."

"Suit yourself, Mr. Goodwin," said Platt, "but I think you're making a mistake."

"That may well be," he replied, " but I do not intend to make the report public at this time. It's not complete and, as I said, it's just a rough draft. We expect to get more information and clarification on some of the sections."

Asked when this would occur, Goodwin told Platt he could not say. He said it would depend on a meeting with the researchers, and he didn't know at this time when that meeting would take place. Although Platt did not ask him when the full commission was scheduled to meet, Goodwin volunteered the information that it would be meeting in three days. Platt thanked him and suggested that he read the next day's *Courier*. His story, carried the next day on the first page of the second, or local, section of the paper, and ran as follows:

---

* *All names, dates, and places in this case have been disguised.*

TRANSIT REVIEW GROUP WON'T RELEASE STUDY

The Metro Transit Review Commission yesterday refused to make public a $5,000 consultant's 60-page report which suggests sweeping changes in the city's transit system.

The report was submitted to Mr. Tad Goodwin, commission chairperson, three days ago and is scheduled to be discussed at a meeting of the full commission on October 15.

Mr. Goodwin said the report would not be made public at this time "because it is incomplete and because we expect to have some of the sections clarified."

Asked when the report would be made public, Mr. Goodwin said "it depends on meetings with the researchers. I can't say when these will be held. They are not definitely scheduled at this time."

Reliable sources indicate that a major recommendation in the report is to have the city buy and operate the transit system and to eliminate certain routes which have proven unprofitable. Among the latter, it has been learned, are Route C, serving Metro City Hospital, Route F serving North Metro, and Route G serving lower-income South Metro.

The consultants are Professor Robert Blanchfield of Metro College and Susan Kane, a graduate assistant.

(See editorial, page 6)

The lead editorial in the same edition of the *Courier* ran as follows:

NOTES

THE PEOPLE HAVE THE RIGHT TO KNOW

We cannot make sense of the decision of Mr. Tad Goodwin, chairperson of the Transit Review Commission, to decline to make public the report of its consultant's research study.

The commission should be aware that it wants and needs public backing, and for this reason it shouldn't hold back news about proposals for change. If Mr. Goodwin is worried that controversy will impede final acceptance of the commission's report, he fails to understand the value that can come of full and frank discussion. And if he feels that public debate at this time will be diverting, then he does not truly recognize the public's interest and right to know.

So let's hope that Mr. Goodwin's decision to withhold news is a temporary one. If it isn't, then let's hear what the consultant, Professor Robert Blanchfield, has to say. We would also be interested in hearing what Mayor Dorfman has to say about the decision of the chairperson he appointed. The commission's chairperson is doing Metro residents a disservice by withholding information of so valuable a nature.

- - -

Paula Martin, who had to leave Metro the day before to keep an appointment in another city, read the above-cited *Courier* story and editorial when she returned to her office at 5:50. Awaiting her were several notes left by her secretary.

One note read: "Tad Goodwin called at 4:00 p.m. He would like you to call him as soon as you return. He said it's very urgent."

A second note read: "Mr. Goodwin called again at 5 p.m. He wanted to know if you had returned and if you had received a call from his father. He said he would be in his office until 6 and can be reached after 7:30 at his father's house. He sounded very upset."

A third note read: "Joe Lightfoot (city editor of the *Bulletin*) called at 4:50. He did not leave a message, but would appreciate a call from you."

The final note read: "Mr. Stanley Goodwin called at 5:10. When I told him you were out of the city but due back, he said he would appreciate it if you would call him as soon as you returned. He said he would be in his office until 6 and can be reached at home after 7:30."

NOTES

An Excerpt For Discussion:

Working With Management*
by Earl Newsom

The "general subject" we have been asked to discuss is: Considerations in Dealing with Public Opinion.

As all of you can testify, there are so many, many considerations constantly in our minds as we go about our daily chores, that it would take volumes to cover them properly. I have therefore chosen for these opening remarks only a segment of the general subject. I would like to discuss some considerations in dealing with managements. I was tempted to use the title, "The Care and Feeding of Bosses," but I have chosen instead the simpler, "Working with Management."

I have chosen this piece of the problem for reasons which I will give you in the form of a syllogism:

Public confidence in the institutions for which we work - whether the Air Force or a well-known corporation - depends in large part, of course, upon how expertly we report the decisions, actions and statements of the managements of these institutions - the bosses we serve. This is in itself an exacting task, requiring high professional competence.

But we know that this is only half the story. What people think about these institutions depends fundamentally upon the actions and statements of our bosses themselves as they may appear to affect the public interest. You and I cannot make the Air Force, or any other American institution, look good if it acts badly.

We cannot, therefore, do our full duty in achieving public confidence in the institutions for which we work unless we can help our bosses to act wisely in matters affecting the public interest.

---

*From a talk given at the third annual seminar of the 9215th Air Reserve Squadron, New York City, October 10, 1957. Reprinted with permission of the author, the founder and head of the counseling firm of Earl Newsom & Company.

But our bosses will not turn to us for such help if they do not have confidence in our ability to help them!

I can short-cut this roundabout syllogism in one sentence: We cannot do our full duty to the institutions we serve unless the bosses of these institutions feel the need for turning to us, among others in management, when decisions important to the public interest are being taken.

In the few minutes allotted to me here, I should like, then, to face up with you to a pertinent questions: "Just why and under what circumstances will our bosses tend to seek our point of view in the process of decision-making?"

Well, in the first place, I assume that all of you know what is news and what is not news; that you are expert in the proper timing of reporting; that you are aware of the variety of techniques in our modern systems of communication for news and feature reporting; that you are familiar with the requirements to be met as we consider each technique. Some of you may do some of these things better than others, but all of us profess competence in the whole area of technical proficiency.

And it is an important area. It is the solid ground on which good craftsmanship rests. Furthermore, real technical expertness will in itself promote the boss's confidence in us - a feeling that we are as good as what he may think we are supposed to do .

The trouble is that too often our bosses think that our job starts after decisions are made, and consists solely of going out and making people like what has been done.

How often have you and I, in the privacy of our own offices, mumbled to ourselves that if the boss had asked our advice before he did what he did, he would not now be in the mess he wants us to get him out of!

Clearly, we must bring to the care and feeding of bosses far more than experienced craftsmanship in reporting. We need to have them feel that our point of view and judgment are sound and helpful in decisions on matters affecting the public interest.

Now, how can such a happy working relationship be brought about?

NOTES

On this question I can only remind you of some things that seem to me important after working for many good bosses during the past twenty-five years or so.

In the first place, we have to recognize that our point of view - yours and mine - is only one among many that have to be considered in the process of decision-making. It is not our job to run the institutions for which we work, and we should not thrash about and attempt to do so. That is the boss's job.

We can, however, be increasingly helpful to him if we try always to bring to discussions on matters which worry him thoughtful and meticulous preparation and the point of view of objective, knowledgeable people - progressively aware of public trends and of the problems plaguing our fellow citizens; sharp in our judgments of what is news and what is not news - and why; having a sure sense of those things that contribute to the long-term health of this Republic and those things with dangerous implications for all of us; quick to spot the thing that seems small but is in reality so significant in human relationships that its smallness can, by a kind of centrifugal force, fly out to catch the attention of millions of people.

Second, we must constantly remember that the point of view we bring to these discussions is somewhat foreign to traditional patterns of American management.

In fact, to many of our teammates we may seem - at first anyway - to be the odd ones in the family. They may be strangely uncomfortable in discussing important problems with us. They are used to thinking in tangible - what they are apt to call "practical" - terms. We tend to move in a world of ideas and human reactions and convictions and beliefs. Our bosses may give us credit for being bright people, but carry around with them the feeling that our judgments should be checked by "sound" people.

Our bosses in time come to share our point of view. They discover that an idea in the minds of a million fellow citizens can be just as tangible - and quite as practical - as a production schedule or an audited statement or a piece of machinery. But in the meantime we have that painful feeling of

NOTES

looking at the same set of circumstances with an entirely different pair of glasses.

It is not strange that this should be so. The American economy is a highly competitive economy. And managements of private - as well as public - enterprises are accustomed to looking upon all matters affecting people and consumers in terms of promotion. Whether you call it "the hard sell" or "the soft sell," managements in our modern economy know that expanding the mass market for what they produce can make all the difference between profit and loss. Expansion of this market, they know, must be made in the teeth of expert competition focused upon the same dollars in the same consumer's pocketbooks.

We should not be surprised, then, if our bosses - who, after all, are smart enough to have become bosses - tend to look upon all matters of public opinion through promotional glasses.

It should not shock us if they assume that our job is to be proficient in the art of "selling" millions of people that the institutions they head are altogether perfect and that they themselves are really not only exceptional human beings but nice and friendly ones - with their hearts in the right place.

On the other hand, you and I have had to learn to throw away our "promotion" glasses as we look at the world about us. We know that while our fellow citizens expect business enterprises to be promotionally competitive in the things they sell, these same promotional techniques - whether the soft sell or the hard sell - don't seem to work when we try to reveal the nature of our institutions as corporate citizens of this Republic.

The fact is that you and I move in what can only be described as a political world, and many of our associates at the decision-making table have become accustomed to living in a competitively promotional world.

Now, the considerations in moving about in a political world are entirely different from those essential to successful survival in a competitively promotional world. Our posture as we face events is entirely different.

NOTES

We have learned the hard way that no institution can persuade people to like it - that, on the contrary, people resist this kind of self-serving persuasion as propaganda. We have learned that people as a whole judge our institutions by the way our bosses handle themselves when the spotlight of public attention is turned upon them - whether we invite the spotlight or whether it just happens by fate to fall upon them.

Now, as I have said, our bosses in time come to see all of this. They become used to looking through our glasses. They even become professionally adept at dealing gracefully with problems involving human attitudes and public opinion. This is the way it should be, because, after all, it is a part of their job. We are there only to help them.

In the meantime, our job is to be patient. If we are, we learn a great deal about the other points of view, and our judgments are enriched thereby. Unfortunately, we too often become impatient and resort to preaching. And this only complicates the problem and ostracizes us from the decision-making round table.

If the problems on which our judgments can be most helpful are those involving the attitudes of large numbers of people, and therefore essentially political problems, then we naturally want to help our bosses to deal with such matters as statesmen - not as opportunistic politicians. For it is vital to the health and progress of this nation that people have confidence in the leadership of our free institutions.

My third reminder, therefore, is that we must always remember that there is a certain cadence in action and statement which statesmen adopt in their political art. This cadence, if you have studied it, is much less hasty and frenetic than the tempo of a competitive world. We learn to temper our instinct for action to the rise and fall of waves on a constantly turbulent sea. Big events do not develop quickly, but are like the ground swells of the ocean. The timing of what we do and say becomes a new art for us.

We cannot read history or observe the world about us without noting this cadence of statesmanship. It was a key to the wisdom of Abraham Lincoln and the wartime leadership of Winston Churchill.

NOTES

This cadence of statesmanship - as we deal with matters in which public opinion is involved - requires of you and me a certain discipline. We can help our bosses to avoid hasty, hotheaded reply when our institutions are criticized. We can help them to avoid public arguments. A battle of name-calling in the public press does not resolve issues and settle questions - it only creates public uncertainty and distrust of both parties. In this day of tensions - with the fear of the ultimate tension, atomic war, hanging over the heads of all of us - people are puzzled and distrustful when leaders of institutions serving them seem unable to resolve their differences privately.

My fourth reminder is that there is a manner of statesmanship, too, which must become second nature to us as we help to deal with these matters.

The language of promotion is pressured - high or low. It is insistent - often abrasive - sometimes blatant. The language of statesmanship is thoughtful, considerate, patient and understanding. It is not self-serving because the language of statesmanship must reflect our desire to serve interests outside ourselves - the interests of the public good.

So the official statements of the institutions we serve - the manner in which they are made, the language in which they are couched - should enable all people of all walks of life who have faith in this country to endorse them as their own.

If, as we voice our point of view day after day at the table of management decisions, we can enable our bosses and our associates to see what we see; if we can lead them to put on a different pair of glasses when we are considering matters of public opinion, we will have achieved our objective. We will have helped our bosses to become what they want to be - statesmen in an increasingly political world.

I have a fifth reminder if our goal is to lead our bosses to seek our point of view, namely that the problems which interest us are usually not simple ones, and we must learn to avoid preaching a simple generality as their solution.

Modern management is at the center of pressures on all sides - each in its own way legitimate. Our bosses must constantly be aware of the points

NOTES

of view of majority and minority stockholders, of employees, of competitors, of organized minority groups, of state and federal governments, of bankers and lawyers.

The fact is that most judgments in this complicated, intensely, competitive world must, in the end, be compromises between what it would be theoretically ideal to do and what it is practically possible to do under the circumstances.

This means, of course, that we cannot always expect to have our own way. It means something else, too, which I am sure you learned from experience; that often when we start from a feeling that we must persuade our bosses to agree with us we end up by learning instead of teaching. And as this process goes on day after day we gradually pick up a little wisdom, if we are not all fools to start with. And as we learn a little wisdom, our presence at the table where decisions are made is sought.

For if we are to be sure of ourselves in our jobs, we must forget ourselves and keep our eyes constantly alert to discern what is best for the institutions we serve and fore the democracy of which we are a part.

NOTES

Case 6

METRO COLLEGE - A*

You are Steve Cady, a 25-year-old navy veteran who completed his service commitment several months ago. You have an undergraduate degree in public relations from one of the schools recognized as a leader in public relations education. You spent one year as a general assignment reporter on a large city daily before going into the service.

Upon receiving your honorable discharge you were interviewed for several public relations positions. You consider yourself fortunate in securing a job in public relations at Metro College as assistant to the director of public relations, Donald Bock.

You were interviewed for the vacancy on Bock's staff last month when you met with Bock, President Angus Euclid, other officials of the college and various members of Bock's department. Two weeks ago you received a letter from the president offering you the position, effective January 1, and you quickly sent in your acceptance.

You are looking forward to the job with anticipation. Metro College seems an ideal spot for you at this moment in your career. Located in the midwestern city of Metro (some details about Metro are cited in the previous two cases, *Metro Transit Review Commission -A* and *Metro Transit Review Commission - B*), the college is essentially an undergraduate, coeducational, private institution of 2,100 students, with a limited number of master's degree programs. Metro College has been in existence forty-five years; draws 40 percent of its students from a radius of forty miles around Metro and the remaining 60 percent chiefly from four neighboring midwestern states; offers thirty major degree programs, including an Urban Affairs program and some unusual "career-oriented" majors; and is on a very modern campus built in the past ten years by virtue of two successful

---

* *All names, dates, and places in this case have been disguised.*

fund drives by Metro industries and residents. Though its varsity sports program is limited, Metro maintains one of the country's finest small college basketball teams and numbers among its alumni three Little All-American basketball players.

Of the 2,100 students at Metro, approximately 58 percent are male; 8 percent black; 40 percent Catholic, 40 percent Protestant, and 20 percent Jewish. Approximately 70 percent of the residents of Metro are Catholic and 5 percent are black.

Following is an abbreviated organization chart showing some of the key people on the staff and faculty of Metro College:

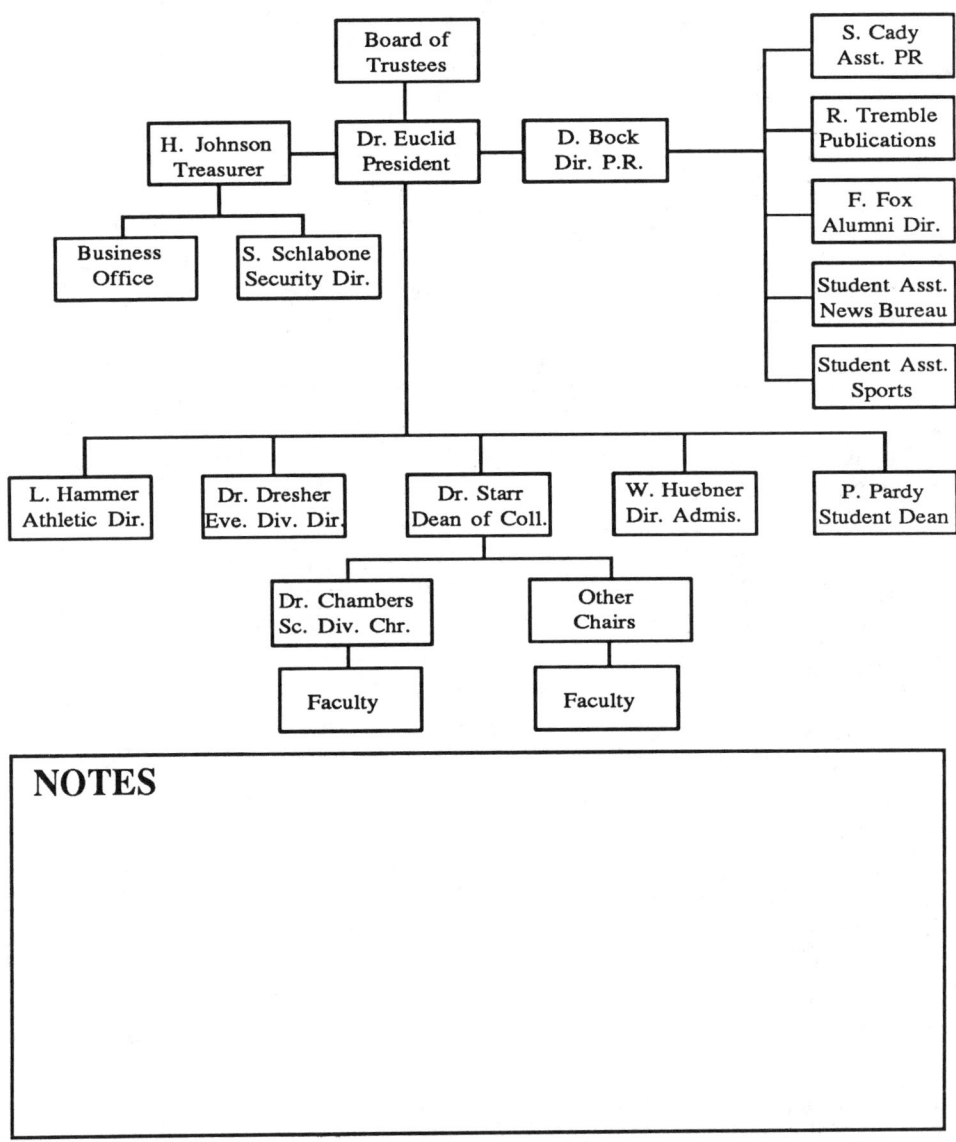

NOTES

Yesterday, Tuesday, December 10, you received an unexpected and rather shocking telephone call from President Euclid. He informed you that Don Bock had been seriously injured in a two-car crash and it was uncertain when, if ever, he would be able to return to work.

"I know you didn't expect to come to work for us until January 1," said the president, "but I'd like you to get here immediately and take over Don's work until we know more about his condition."

"Of course," you said. "I'll be there tomorrow."

"Good," said the president. "I'll get out an internal memorandum advising everyone that you will be handling Don's work for the time being. I'm very grateful."

It is now 9 AM, December 11, and you are seated at Don's desk. His secretary has set in front of you various memoranda, messages, letters, etc., which were in Bock's action file or had arrived with yesterday's mail.

Bock's secretary had also advised you that the president's weekly general staff meeting is scheduled for 10:30 - an hour and a half from now - and you're expected to attend.

You are to indicate your reactions to each of the memoranda, messages, letters, etc.; your reasons for said reactions; and what you propose to do about each item.

Memorandum

From: Harley Johnson   November 26,19--
To: Don Bock
Subject: Revised equipment budget request

As you know, we delayed decision on approval of equipment requests for the current academic year in order to ascertain the effect of actual Fall enrollment on the college budget.

Fall enrollment figures, which have now been tabulated, indicate that we will be $75,000 short of anticipated tuition income. The president has

---

NOTES

therefore decided that all equipment requests should be trimmed accordingly.

Examination of your equipment indicates that you have submitted the following requests:

Item	Number	Description	Approximate Cost
1	1	Copier	$1400
2	2	Electric typewriters	$1600

The president has suggested that you decide which one of the above two budget items you prefer. We are trying to put the budget into final form before mid-December and I would appreciate your decision by December 12.

Note: Bock had scribbled the following note to himself at the bottom of the above memorandum: "Make sure to get out a return memo to Johnson giving my decision by December 12 at the latest."

Telephone Message

From: Ted Baxter, Sunday editor of the *Courier*
Time: 10 AM, Tuesday, December 10
Message: Mr. Baxter said that the long feature you sent in last week looks very good to him and he's scheduling it for this Sunday's entertainment section. He needs identification of the people in the three pics which accompanied the story and would appreciate it if you got back to him before noon on Wednesday because he has a deadline to meet.

NOTES

Letter

23 Wills Drive
Metro, Illinois
November 28, 19--

Mr. Donald Bock
Director of Public Relations
Metro College
Metro, Illinois

Dear Mr. Bock:

I am writing this at home tonight following the staff meeting you held today, at which you informed us that you have hired a young man named Steve Cady to be Assistant Director of Public Relations.

As you know, I have been a loyal member of the staff of this college for the past 12 years and have always felt that hard work and loyalty will be rewarded by those in the position to make such reward. I must speak frankly and say that I was shocked to learn that no consideration was given to those of us on the staff when it was decided to establish a new position in the department.

I know that I have only a high-school diploma, but I am sure you are aware that I have now accumulated 68 hours toward my Metro degree and that I have been in charge of college publications for the past eight years. I had hoped that when the opportunity arose for promotion to a new position, due consideration would be given to the aformentioned facts. For the sake of the college, I hope that the active role I have taken in the past two years in the Metro Women's Liberation Movement had not been held against me when various people were being considered for the new position.

NOTES

When the opportunity arises, I hope you will allow me to present my case to you. I also hope it is not too late to alter the decision that has been announced. If I do not hear from you by Friday, December 6, I shall assume that the decision regarding young Mr. Cady is final. In such case I would like you to consider the week of December 9 my last week of service with your department.

Sincerely yours,

Ms. Rose Tremble

Note: Bock had scribbled the following note to himself at the bottom of the above letter. "Damn! Must talk to Rose at the earliest opportunity."

Letter

TIME, Inc.
23 North Wacker Dr.
Chicago, Ill.

Dec. 3, 19--

Mr. Donald Bock
Director of Public Relations
Metro College
Metro, Illinois

Dear Mr. Bock:

I'm very glad we've been able to firm up the visit to your campus of Peter Travis, one of our bureau men, and his research assistant.

NOTES

As I advised you on the phone, we're preparing a cover story on today's college scene. We're trying to cover the entire college spectrum - ranging from large urban universities to small, church-affiliated colleges. Metro will be one of the ten institutions which we intend to treat in some depth as being representative of the broad middle group of private colleges.

Travis and his assistant will be arriving on December 12 and staying at the Metro Sheraton. He'll get in touch with you shortly after arrival; you can expect him to stay in Metro for several days. We appreciate your cooperation.

Sincerely yours,

Raymond Dorris
Chief of Bureau

(Bock had scribbled the following at the bottom of the above letter: "At long last, a major media break! Make sure to give Travis the royal treatment.")

Telephone Message

From: Sam Schlabone
Time: 4:30 PM, December 10
Message: Mr. Schlabone said he's learned through his contacts that the sheriff's department, the city police, and the state police have a dozen John Doe warrants and will be making a pre-dawn drug bust on Durham Hall (men's dorm with 110 residents) at 4 AM December 12. Schlabone wants you to know that the president has been informed of the bust. Schlabone said there is no way he can head off the police. He seemed very agitated.

NOTES

Memo

From: Dr. Harvey Chambers Dec. 9, 19--
To: Donald Bock
Subject: Publicity for Dr. Reid

Dr. Reid received some exciting news today. He's been invited to deliver a paper at the annual meeting of the East Asian Studies Conference in East Lansing, Michigan, on Feb. 14. Dr. Reid's papers will describe the 10-year study he's completed on the East Asian titmouse. We in the division think this would be of real interest to readers of the Metro *Courier*. I hope you will have one of your people follow through on this .

Memorandum

From: Angus Euclid December 6, 19--
To: Don Bock
Subject: Board of Trustees Action on Contraceptive Request

As you know, The Executive Committee of Student Government met with me last month to submit a request that we dispense through the Student Health Center a full range of birth control information and birth control devices. I promised to submit this request to the Board of Trustees, and in turn the committee agreed to say nothing publicly, pending action by the Board of Trustees.

The Board is scheduled to meet here on campus Wednesday, December 18, and I shall submit the student request at that meeting. I have no way of judging at this time what the Board's decision will be, but I feel we should be prepared in advance for steps we shall take regardless of whether the decision is positive or negative.

NOTES

I would therefore appreciate hearing from you on how you would handle this rather delicate matter - in terms of what your office will do if the decision is positive and what your office will do if the decision is negative.

Please get the above to me sometime this week so we can have time to discuss your proposals and suggestions.

Note: Bock had scribbled the following note at the bottom of the above memorandum: "This is a tough one, but they're all tough. Must make sure I get to this by Friday, December 13."

Memorandum

From: Business Office   December 6, 19--
To: Donald Bock
Subject: Status of mail account

Mr. Johnson has asked us to evaluate the status of the various account numbers assigned to the major offices of the college and to report how each stands.

All of your accounts, with the exception of one, seem in good order at this point. Account #415.6, Postage, now shows a deficit. You were allocated $1,150 for this account number and you have already spent $1,250. As you know, the $1,150 has been allocated to cover your postal expenditures until June 30.

cc: Mr. Johnson

NOTES

Telephone Message

From: Main post office, Metro
Time: 2 PM, Tuesday, December 10

Message: The main post office called and said that we've put insufficient postage on the letter from the president which we're sending out to all parents. As you know, this is the special letter we're mailing to notify parents that tuition next year will be $5,200 and it contains the supplemental material demonstrating why we have to raise tuition by $775. We sent the letter out under the regular first class rate, but the post office says the letter is over that weight and requires double the normal first class rate. They're holding the 2,100 letters until they hear from us.

Telephone Message

From: Paul Spellbinder
Time: 4 PM, Tuesday, December 10

Message: Paul (editor of the college weekly) called to remind you that he's holding space on the front page of this week's issue of the *Clarion* for that story you promised him about the tuition increase. He wanted me to remind you that his deadline is 9 PM tomorrow night. If he doesn't hear from you by then he'll probably run with a story citing "informed sources."

NOTES

Memorandum

From: Dean Star
To: Don Bock

Subject: Who's Who Among Collegians

    The attached seems to be a project that would provide some good exposure for the college. It doesn't seem to fit into any of the other offices of the college, so I'd like you to handle it. Keep me informed.

cc: President Euclid
Attachment: Letter from *Who's Who Among Collegians*

                    Who's Who Among Collegians, Inc.
                            380 Madison Avenue
                             New York, NY 10022

                                            November 28, 19--

Dean
Metro College
Metro, Illinois

Dear Sir:

We are instituting this year an exciting and meaningful search for the outstanding young collegians of America and are inviting your institution to take part in this new program.

Each year, we intend to select the outstanding leaders - men and women - on American college campuses. A quota has been set for each institution

NOTES

invited to participate in this valuable new program, said quota to be based on the number of full-time students enrolled.

Each college and university taking part in the program will be asked to nominate for *Who's Who Among Collegians* leaders who have demonstrated their excellence in academic, athletic and extra-curricular affairs. Nominations will be forwarded to us for final decision and approval. Those who survive the final judging will be enrolled in that year's honor list of America's top college students. They will also have their pictures and a short biographical sketch included in our annual volume of *Who's Who Among Collegians*.

We would appreciate learning whether or not you will officially accept this invitation to take part in our nationwide selection process. We have taken the liberty of considering that your reply will be affirmative. We are including you among the list of institutions in the program and have reserved 20 places for your nominees. We would like to suggest at this time that you try to complete your selections and send us your list of nominees with pictures and short biographical sketches by December 13.

Sincerely,

John Paul Jones
President

NOTES

Case 7

METRO COLLEGE - B*

After reading the various memoranda, messages, letters, etc. which you (Steve Cady) found on Bock's desk when you reported to work at 9 AM on December 11, you decided to take immediate action in regard to some of the material. This delayed you to the extent that you were 15 minutes late for the president's general staff meeting, and it was with some embarrassment that you tried to slip into a seat at 10:45. The president, however, spotted your entrance and cut short his remarks to welcome you to the group.

"This is Steve Cady," he told the twenty members of the general staff. "We all know and are sorry about Don Bock's unfortunate accident, and I know I speak for all of you when I wish him a speedy recovery. Meanwhile, however, I think we're extremely fortunate in having with us, two weeks earlier than expected, the young man who will be serving as Don's assistant. As I told all of you in the memo I sent around yesterday, Steve will be handling Don's work until we learn more about the extent of Don's incapacity. I appreciate the fact that you've joined us at such short notice, Steve, and I know you will receive full cooperation from everyone on the staff. Welcome to Metro, Steve."

You acknowledged the president's remarks with a short nod, and the meeting proceeded. As it moved along from one subject to another, you took notes of the discussion with special care to note items and issues which seemed to fall within your jurisdiction. You had hoped to make a quick exit at the end of the meeting, but when it adjourned at noon the president made a special point of inviting you to lunch. Thus you didn't get back to your

---

* *All names, dates, and places in this case have been disguised.*

desk until 2 PM. Awaiting you were another set of messages and the morning's mail. You spread them out with the notes you had taken at the morning's meeting.

You are to indicate your reactions to each of the messages, memoranda, letters, notes from the meeting, etc.; your reasons for said reactions; and what you propose to do about each item.

Notes From Morning General Staff Meeting

President spoke briefly - seemed almost as an afterthought - about student problems today and mentioned as one of them the problem of drugs on campus...said this is a problem on all campuses and he assumes ours is not much different from other campuses...suggested we all keep this in perspective and don't over-react about occasional busts and things like that...didn't mention anything about a specific bust...reaction on the part of the group was one of mild interest, nothing more.

Hammer (director of athletics?) said the last black basketball player on the varsity team resigned yesterday and gave as his reason alleged racism on the part of Coach Norville Fletcher...big game Friday against arch rival Salem College and he expects Black Student Union to be picketing our Field House...I have lots of questions about this; must check with Hammer and Fletcher soon, get details about the situation...what about coverage by local papers and school paper?

Director of Admissions (Huebner?) reported what was taken to be encouraging news...under the newly instituted guaranteed early admissions program, the college currently has acceptance for next fall from 540 incoming students...last year's total freshman class was 760.

Harley Johnson reminded the group that budget request forms were distributed some weeks ago and that all budgets for the academic year which starts July 1 are due back in his office this coming Friday.

NOTES

Hammer announced that all teams invited to play in the annual Metro Holiday Basketball Tournament - to be held on campus January 2 and 3 - had accepted invitations...He said that Bock was supposed to have submitted to him by today the text for the citation to be given to the coach of the New York Knickerbockers, who is being inducted into the Metro Hall of Fame at the final game...It was assumed that Bock hadn't submitted the text, and it was agreed that I would write it today so that the citation could be sent to the printers in time for the presentation.

Above item reminded Euclid that the state-wide Friends of the United Nations are holding their annual meeting on campus December 27-28 and he's supposed to welcome them at 10 AM, December 27 in Lawrence Auditorium with a short five-minute address...Euclid said that he assumes that Cady will write an appropriate address for him and have it on his desk Thursday...Everyone laughed...Big joke!

Business manager said that faculty will take off for Christmas intersession right after they give exams, but we are to remind staff people working for us - secretaries, clerks, etc. - they're off from 12 noon December 24 until 8:30 AM December 26 and from 12 noon December 31 until 8:30 AM January 2.

Business manager said that the only parking lots to be kept open and clear of snow during Christmas intersession period will be lots A, B and F.

NOTES

Telephone Message

From: Chuck Wilson, Minister of Information, Black Student Union
Time: 11AM, Wednesday, December 11

He'll be in to see you at 3 PM today to talk to you about coverage for the one-day state-wide conference of Black Student Unions which our BSU group is hosting this year for the first time. Said he's particularly interested in getting coverage of the opening speech which is being given at 10 AM, December 27, in Lawrence Auditorium.

Memorandum

From: Dean Star   December 9, 19--
To: Don Bock
Subject: Who's Who Among Collegians

My secretary reminds me that I sent you a memo on December 2 with an attached letter from Who's Who Among Collegians, Inc. and asked you to handle it. If I recall correctly, they gave us some sort of deadline so I'm wondering what action you've taken or what your recommendation is. Please let me hear from you soonest.

cc: President Euclid

NOTES

Memorandum

From: Angus Euclid   December 6, 19--
To: Don Block
Subject: Letter Greater Metro Women's Association

How about taking care of this?

Attachment:

Letter from Greater Metro Women's Association

GREATER METRO WOMEN'S ASSOCIATION
8134 N. Main St.
Metro, Ill.

President
Metro College
Metro, Illinois

Dear Sir:

We are an "umbrella" association and our membership consists of a wide variety of women's organizations in the Greater Metro area. As president of the GMWA, it has been my aim this year to make GMWA a real resource to our associated members. I am therefore writing to ask the assistance and cooperation of the college in a joint venture.

Specifically, I would hope that the college could co-sponsor with GMWA a one-day course or conference dealing with the practical aspects of public relations. My thought at the moment is that this would consist of a morning session, afternoon lunch with speaker, and afternoon workshops, culminating in a final assembly devoted chiefly to questions and answers.

NOTES

I thought we might schedule the proposed one-day conference for early Spring. Of course this is predicated on your interest and cooperation. I would appreciate hearing from you or a designated representative, and I hope your reply is in the affirmative.

Sincerely yours,

Ms. Agnes Morehead,
President

P.S.: I forgot to mention this in my letter, but we have 48 organizations affiliated with us and they represent a total membership of 1,250 women. My rough guess is that we could expect between 150 to 200 women at the conference.

Memorandum

From: Charles Dresher   Dec. 9, 19--
To: Don Bock
Subject: Publicity on evening courses

I'm very glad you agreed to get out some publicity in the Metro press during the Christmas break about the following special non-credit courses we are offering for the first time this Spring. Course descriptions are cited below; you can probably use them for writing your stories. Call me if you have questions.

Sex and the Modern Woman
       Historical overview of women's sexuality. Physiological, sociological and psychological aspects. Women's role in sexual intercourse. Mating and post-mating gamemanship. Role-playing and sensitivity training as a means of overcoming inhibitions.

NOTES

Personal Investing
    The tax bite. How to buy and sell securities. Obtaining investment information. The ouija board theory. The in-and-out theory.

Memorandum

From: Paul Pardi   Dec. 6, 19--
To: John Star
Subject: Request from Gay Liberation Alliance

The attached letter from the Metro Gay Liberation Alliance seems to have been sent to me by mistake. I assume it was meant for you. By the way, do we have any policy on this sort of thing?

Attachment: Letter from Gay Liberation Alliance

Memorandum

From: Dean Star   Dec. 9, 19--
To: Don Bock
Subject: Request from Gay Liberation Alliance

    As you will note, Dean Pardi has referred to me the attached letter from the Metro Gay Liberation Alliance and I am taking the liberty of forwarding it to you. This is one of those things that don't seem to fit into anyone's niche of responsibility, but it does seem to have definite public relations implications and for this reason I am moving the letter along to you. I'm sure you will have some sound ideas on how to handle it, and by all means let me know your conclusions.

Attachment: Letter from Gay Liberation Alliance
              Memo from Paul Pardi

NOTES

Letter

Dean
Metro College
Metro, Illinois

4 Prospect Street
Metro, Illinois
Dec. 5, 19--

Dear Sir:

I am writing to you as president of the Metro Gay Liberation Alliance to request use of your mini-gym for a dance we plan to hold on Friday, Jan. 10.

We note that the college has been hospitable enough to open its doors at various times to other organizations in the city of Metro; we hope this spirit of graciousness extends to a group such as ours.

We can assure you that we are a mature and responsible organization, with a constitution. Our membership is made up of people from all walks of life, including some professional people and a couple of students on your campus newspaper.

Our organization is perfectly willing to pay any rental that the college may charge for the use of its mini-gym for one evening. We are also willing to defray the cost of any special security you may want to have on hand for the occasion. We do not feel that such security would be needed, however.

We would appreciate hearing from you at your earliest convenience. We certainly welcome the opportunity to discuss this request with you.

Sincerely yours,

Walter Diamond, president
Metro Gay Liberation Alliance

NOTES

A Visit and Telephone Call

About 2:45 PM, as you were reading, reflecting about taking action on the items on your desk, your secretary announced that Chuck Wilson of the Black Student Union was here to see you. You told her to show him in; when he entered you introduced yourself and asked him to have a seat.

"I guess you want to talk about the conference you're holding," you said. "Well..."

The inter-com buzzed. Your secretary said it was Michael Watts of the *Bulletin* and you told her to put the call through. You explained to Watts that you were Bock's new assistant and had come on the job two weeks early because of Bock's accident.

"Sorry to make life rough for you the first day on the job but we've learned you've got a hot potato on your hands and the city editor suggested I do a story about it," said Watts.

"Oh," you said, "What's that?"

"We understand that your student government has requested that the college start offering through your Student Health Service birth control information and contraceptives for all students who ask for them," said Watts. "This is the sort of story which is sure to interest our readers, so I'm checking it out with you."

Pick up the conversation at this point. When you're finished you should continue the conversation you were having with Chuck Wilson.

NOTES

Case 8

HEYWOOD HOSPITAL*

Several months ago your doctor advised you that it's imperative that you take up residence in a state with a dry climate and you therefore made inquiries through various channels to seek a public relations position in one of the Rocky Mountain states. These inquiries turned up a promising lead in Pendleton, a city of 123,000 residents.

The position for which you have applied is with Heywood Hospital, an 80-year-old, 300-bed voluntary hospital which moved to its present site thirty years ago. The other two hospitals in Pendleton -- both voluntary -- are Paxton, a 160-bed hospital built in 1935, and Borkum-Brown, a 240-bed hospital built in 1940.

Pendleton is the third largest city in the state and has had considerable growth in the last 20 years. It has a diversified industrial base with three large unionized plants of national corporations and numerous small plants employing from 50 to 200 people. The majority of the small plants are also unionized. Approximately 63 per cent of the residents are Protestant, 35 per cent Catholic and chiefly of Mexican descent, and two per cent Jewish. About two per cent of the population are blacks.

There are two television stations in Pendleton, one affiliated with NBC and one with CBS; a morning newspaper (circulation 32,000) and an evening newspaper (circulation 64,000), both owned by the same company; four AM radion stations, three of which are independent and one affiliated with CBS; and two FM stations which are independent.

Thomas White, administrator at Heywood, has sent you, at your request, a packet containing all Heywood Hospital publications. These include the following:

---

* *All names, dates, and places have been disguised.*

1. A brochure for patients, entitled "Your Hospital," produced ten years ago.

2. A mimeographed three-page list of rules and regulations for non-medical employees.

3. A mimeographed employee newsletter. In an appended note, White stated the newspetter was last published three years ago. Prior to that time, he added, it had been issued periodically, but not on a regular schedule.

4. A four-page, mimeographed Annual Report, dated last year, signed by White and directed to the Board of Trustees.

From correspondence you've had with White and from your reading of various library publications and other materials he's enclosed with his letters, you know the following about the three hospitals:

Heywood

Total of 100 doctors on active medical staff and total of 800 employees including nurses. . . . no interns or residents. . . . emergency department manned around the clock by a paid medical and nursing staff. . . 20-member Board of Trustees. . . . accredited. . . . situated in South Pendleton (considered the best section of the city) but right on the edge of a low-income area populated mainly by Mexican-Americans. . . . main building, constructed in 1952, is three stories high. . . . a $1.5 million School of Nursing building, which includes class room and living quarters for 90 nurses, completed three years ago. . . . complex on spacious plot of land sufficient for present and future parking and expansion of buildings.

Paxton

No interns or residents. . . . limited emergency room manned when needed during the day by those on medical staff who are in the hospital at the time and manned at night on a rotating call basis among the doctors. . . .

NOTES

oldest hospital in the city situated on a small plot of land in the middle of South Pendleton a mile from Heywood. . . . four stories high with limited parking facilities and no room for expansion. . . . 18-member Board of Trustees. . . . accredited. . . . a friend of yours who knows Pendleton told you that Paxton has long held the reputation of being the "elite" hospital of the city even though it is now overcrowded and in need of extensive physical rehabilitation.

Borkum-Brown

No interns or residents. . . . emergency department manned around the clock by a paid medical and nursing staff. . . . most modern hospital in Pendleton located in the middle of South Pendleton but on a spacious 20-acre plot of land across the road from Pendleton's 90-acre, two-year community college. . . . accredited. . . . main hospital unit is five stories high with a new three-story $2 million extended care facility adjoining the main building. . . . 15-member Board of Trustees.

Your friend has also told you that the three hospital administrators have cordial relationships and meet at intervals to coordinate activities of mutual interest. There is, he says, a certain amount of rivalry among the medical staffs, each considering itself superior to the other two. Room and other charges at all three hospitals are relatively similar with some slight variations. Wages for non-medical personnel are highest at Borkum-Brown, due chiefly to the fact that these employees were organized a year ago by a national union. According to your friend, the union recently started a drive to organize non-medical employees at Heywood and Paxton but has not yet sought an election at either hospital.

Along with the material sent you by White were some clippings of news stories from the Pendleton papers dealing with the Patterson Report.

According to these stories, Dr. Anthony Patterson, a nationally known hospital consultant, had made an extensive study of the Pendleton hospital situation. In a report issued two weeks ago Dr. Patterson

NOTES

recommended that Borkum-Brown, Paxton and Heywood merge within ten years into one hospital at the Borkum-Brown site by adding two large wings to Borkum-Brown's present plant. Dr. Patterson, according to the news stories, recommended that the proposed new Paxton Wing be completed in five years and the proposed new Heywood Wing be completed within ten years. None of the news stories reported who had sponsored the report, nor did they cite any reasons advanced by Dr. Patterson for recommending consolidation of the three hospitals. The first accounts of the Patterson Report were carried in main lead stories in both newspapers and these were followed several days later by editorials in both newspapers lauding the recommendations and urging their approval by the Trustee Boards of the three institutions. The editorials said that the merger would eliminate costly duplication of services, would provide superior medical service for the entire community, could lead to affiliation with a medical school, and many other economies.

The most recent clippings sent to you by White reported that the Trustee Boards of both Paxton and Borkum-Brown had endorsed the Patterson Report recommendations and that it was expected that the Heywood Board would meet soon to make its decision.

The Present

White has invited you to Pendleton for an interview. You have just had a tour of the facility, been introduced to various department heads, and are now back in White's office for a final talk. Sitting in during the interview is Charles Finney, vice president of a local bank and president of the Heywood Board of Trustees.

White - whom you judge to be about 60 - informs you that he has been administrator of Heywood for the past 25 years. You judge from his remarks, manner of speaking and general attitude that he is in almost total command of the hospital. He is definitely a no-nonsense type of person; his clean desk and crisp responses in numerous telephone conversations during your interview confirm this assessment.

NOTES

"I have always felt that the most important task of a voluntary hospital is to serve the public in the most efficient manner," he states. "In trying to achieve this goal I've tried to have Heywood provide the best medical care and service at the lowest possible cost. I understand from my fellow administrators at other hospitals in Pendleton and in other cities that a public relations department can be of value to a hospital, but I didn't think we could afford to set up such a department because it would add to the cost of patient care.

"However, Mr. Finney and some other Board members have convinced me we can no longer afford not to establish a public relations department at Heywood and that's why I've asked you here for this interview. I'm very impressed with your background and experience and I'm prepared to offer a salary commensurate with your qualifications." (He mentions the proposed salary and it meets your expectations.) "At this point, however, I'd like to find out how you would handle what seems to be some pressing immediate public relations problems and also evaluate your ideas and thoughts about future public relations programming."

White nods to Finney and he picks up the conversation.

"Mr. White," he says, "has sent you news stories about the Patterson Report, so you know that the boards of Borkum-Brown and Paxton have endorsed the recommendations and that the local newspapers have also urged approval by the three hospitals. This has placed us in a very difficult position for these reasons:

"1. As a voluntary hospital we feel we should chiefly serve the needs of our immediate community and that community is among the Mexican-Americans living near us.

"2. We have a fine location here with sufficient space for future expansion. In addition, of course, we recently completed our School of Nursing building and are quite proud of it and of the fact that it's the only school of nursing in the community.

NOTES

"3. Unknown to anybody except our board, Mr. White, and our chief administrators, our board recently approved a projected capital fund drive whose goal will be used to build a much-needed addition to our main building and a new enlarged emergency room facility. We have been planning these two additions for the past year, have architectural plans all set, and had intended to publicly announce the drive last week. We suspended this announcement when the Patterson Report came out.

"4 We have strong reason to suspect that Dr. Patterson's recommendations are exactly what John Stuart wanted them to be. Stuart, you see, is president of the non-profit Pendleton Health Planning Board and he also happens to be president of the Paxton Board of Trustees. His paid job is general manager of Pendleton Manufacturing, our largest employer. The newspaper stories have never mentioned this, but it was the Pendleton Health Planning Board that engaged Dr. Patterson to do his study and everyone connected with Pendleton hospitals knows that Paxton has been seeking merger with Borkum-Brown for years now.

"5 In the past two weeks we have been subjected to intense but conflicting pressures. Leading citizens - many of whom have been large contributors to all three hospitals - have called me and other Heywood trustees urging us to endorse the Patterson proposal of merger. However, leaders among the Mexican-American community - and I might add that this community has become increasingly militant in recent years - have strongly urged us not to merge. They predict large-scale rioting if we leave our present site.

"6 Our board has not yet taken action on the recommendations of the

NOTES

Patterson Report, but we will make our decision at a meeting schedule for next Monday. We feel this is a very difficult decision which has definite public relations ramifications and we would appreciate your advice and counsel before making this decision."

"Could I ask two questions at this point?" you ask.

"By all means do so," is the reply.

"First," you state, "what is the general sentiment of your board in regard to the consolidation proposal? Second, I noticed that the news reports about the Patterson Report did not cite reasons why Dr. Patterson proposed consolidation. What are the reasons for proposing merger, and are they in the report?"

"Regarding your first point," says Finney, "I'd say that most, but certainly not all members of our board, favor rejecting merger, but I want to assure you we have an open mind on the subject. I also want to assure you that we want your honest answer, not an answer which you think will secure the public relations position for you. So far as I'm concerned, the job is yours right now.

"As to the reasons, they are set forth in the report and I imagine they were not mentioned in the news stories because of space limitations. In any case, they are as follows: There is a definite trend throughout the country towards an organized approach to health care. Consolidation of all three hospitals would save the community money through economies gained by virtue of having one hospital complex instead of three separate hospitals. The community would avoid costly duplication of services and special expensive equipment. A single complex could provide better medical care at less cost and would more likely be able to keep up with the latest advances in the hospital field. Finally, a complex could more easily lend itself to affiliation with medical schools, bringing in interns, residents, and training programs for staff people.

"I think it's important to point out that even if the Patterson Report is accepted by all three hospital boards it will be almost a decade before

---

NOTES

Heywood is added to the Borkum-Brown complex. Regardless of what action is taken on the merger proposal, we at Heywood recognize the need to have a public relations staff person at the hospital who will develop a public relations program and be responsible for its implimentation."

"What do you want me to do at this point?" you ask.

"Well, as a first step," Finney replies, "we'd like to know what questions you have in mind and which we could answer right now. These can be about the immediate problem of the Patterson Report; about Heywood and/or the community; or perhaps about the public relations position. Either Mr. White or I will be glad to answer them. I think we have fairly thick skins, so just fire away. The only restriction I will put on you is in regard to time, so please restrict your answer to the five or six questions you consider most important and essential."

Simulation 1

Formulate and ask the five or six questions mentioned above. In addition, explain to the instructor and the class - who will serve as observers - exactly why you have asked each question.

Simulation 2

After you have posed your questions and received answers to them from Finney and White, the latter says that he would like to know what you consider to be the major short-and long-term objectives of a public relations program for Heywood Hospital. Set forth your perception of short-and long-term objectives of a public relations program for the hospital.

Simulation 3

"We have one final request," Finney now says. "As you know, the hospital board is meeting Monday and we would like you to meet with the members at that time. We've reserved a room for you at the Pendleton Inn, and we'd

NOTES

like you to spend the time between now and the Monday meeting on a memorandum and presentation to the board. Part 1 should consist of your advice and counsel as to the stand we ought to take in regard to the Patterson Report and its proposed consolidation. Include your reasons for your counsel, and frame them within a public relations context. By all means be as explicit as you feel necessary, and also explain in some detail why you suggest the action you propose we take.

"Part 2," Finney continues, "should consist of an explanation of the public relations program you would propose for the hospital with a detailing of steps you would take in carrying out said program. Include strategies, themes, programming details, media and means to be utilized, and any other points you feel are appropriate. You should be prepared, of course, to answer any questions board members may want to ask at the meeting."

You have been given two days to prepare your memorandum. Today is Monday and you are in attendance at the meeting of the Heywood Hospital board. You have spent the weekend preparing the memorandum requested by Mr. Finney, and you have brought it along with you. Your classmates are to consider themselves to be members of the hospital board; your instructor is to play the role of either Mr. Finney or Mr. White. He has introduced you to the board, explained the assignment he gave you, and he now asks you to make your presentation to the board. He leaves it up to you to explain how you want to proceed and how you want to respond to questions.

NOTES

An Excerpt For Discussion:

A Model Public Relations Performance*

By Jeanne King

While the Humana medical team was making history with the mechanical heart implant operation on William Schroeder, the Louisville medical center's public relations staff was turning in a textbook performance that could serve as a model for all media specialists.

The key elements in the Humana press operations were:

- The principal briefings were conducted by a primary source, Dr. Allan Lansing, who assisted Dr. William DeVries in the historic operation.
- Media needs had been anticipated and provided for even before the first of the hundreds of reporters and photographers arrived on the scene. There was an impressive easy-reference looseleaf briefing book that covered all the routine who's-he, how's-that-spelled and what's-that-mean questions that tend to clutter up news conferences and slow down coverage.
- A highly professional photo lab was used to cope with the urgent demand for pictures.

What could have been a media nightmare was averted at the start by Robert Irvine, director of public relations at Humana, who realized that his hospital's press room was too small.

Accordingly, a press command center was established at the Commonwealth Convention Center in downtown Louisville, about seven miles from the Humana Hospital.

The first press conference there was Saturday, November 24, at 8 PM. By the time the first of the 225 reporters, photographers and television crews checked in, there were 50 beige push-button phones spread out over about 64 feet of five huge tables, a far cry to veteran reporters who covered

---

* Reprinted by permission from the January 5, 1985 issue of *Editor & Publisher* magazine.

the Barney Clark case two years earlier when they had to fight among themselves for the dozen or so telephones that had been placed against a fifteen-foot wall in a tiny cordoned-off area of the University of Utah hospital cafeteria.

In one corner of the 30-foot-by-90-foot work area at Louisville, sofas, lounge chairs and coffee tables and lamps were put in.

Anticipating that the action could get hectic, Humana planned to section this area off with curtains so that reporters could catnap between developments without leaving the center.

Eventually the section was used by the media to conduct private interviews.

Multiple outlets were strategically placed on every table so that those with the Radio Shack TRS 100s or other equipment could have instant communication with their offices.

Every press representative registering was given an impressive looseleaf briefing book that was indexed according to biographies, background information, medical policy and guidelines, questions and answers, a glossary of medical terms, maps of the city, hotel, motel and entertainment and restaurant guides as well as handy telephone numbers and current airline schedules listing all flights to any point in the country to and from Louisville.

Any reasonable request was granted by the public relations staff within the framework of time available.

Extensive medical briefings were held twice daily by Dr. Lansing.

Whatever fears he and the Humana team might have had about coming before such a large press corps soon disappeared by midweek when the media began informally calling the briefings "The Allan Lansing Show," and "H-e-e-e-ere's Allan."

Lansing relaxed and fielded questions as if he were an old pro from some late night TV show.

At the conferences, reporters delved into the minute details of Schroeder's white blood count, his urinary output, his Bilirubin test results,

NOTES

his BUN, his cardiac output. It was more information than any reader or viewer would ever want to know.

As one editor later observed: "Too bad you all weren't getting college credit for this."

The most frequently asked question which brought groans from those who had followed the case from Day 1 was whether Schroeder would reject the artificial heart. Answer: No, there's nothing to reject since the plastic and metal heart is made of inactive synthetic materials and not living tissue.

On Sunday, November 25, the day of the surgery, the press center opened at 6 AM. George Atkins, director of public affairs, kept the press informed hourly on the progress of the implant.

At the same time, Bob Irvine was in a nearby photo lab darkroom screening negatives coming out of the operating room and selecting pictures for print and video.

Two-and-one-half hours after the 8 AM surgery began, the first photos of the operation were made available to the media.

Urns of hot coffee, tea and cold drinks, as well as danish and donuts were always on hand for the media.

On the day of and following surgery, Humana brought in a huge selection of sandwiches for those reporters unable to get out for lunch.

An hour after the six-and-one-half-hour surgery ended, Dr. Lansing, wearing a white medical jacket, walked into the command center where he was bombarded with questions.

For over an hour, he gave the media a graphic description of what took place before and after surgery, who said what to whom and what Schroeder said to doctors after surgery.

Twenty minutes later, reporters watched an 18-minute unedited videotape of the operation.

Not only were we able to distinguish the voice of Dr. DeVries and others in the operating room as Schroeder's old heart was cut out and the mechanical heart was implanted but the background music of Mendelsohn's "Midsummer Nights Dream" came through clearly.

NOTES

Dr. Robert Jarvik, inventor and designer of the artificial heart that bears his name, made himself available to the press and granted countless interviews.

Mimeographed interview request sheets were also provided by Humana and although the granting of some requests were not acted upon promptly, by the end of the first week, one-on-one interviews with Dr. DeVries were being filled.

Scheduled interviews were under way with Schroeder when he suffered a stroke last Thursday. These will be resumed once he has sufficiently recovered.

The command post for press coverage was manned by Humana public relations staff from 6 AM to 12-1 o'clock the next morning, depending on what was occurring at the moment. Atkins or Irvine and sometimes both were on hand at all times of the day and night to answer questions, which was not always the case in Utah when reporters wasted valuable time hunting down University of Utah personnel for answers.

When it became apparent early in the week that most reporters were going to have to vacate their rooms at the Hyatt Regency and Galt House, the two hotels closest to the press center, because of a previous commitment to a recreation-vehicle convention, Humana officials got on the phone and by the next morning, Louisville Mayor Harvey Sloane was in the pressroom assuring concerned reporters that adequate lodging would be found.

Two convention representatives worked alongside Humana personnel to find housing for displaced reporters who moved that week an average of three times.

"We'll put you up in our hospital beds if we have to," Irvine joked.

"The advance press preparation literally began 15 minutes after Dr. DeVries' press conference last July when he announced he was moving to Louisville," Irvine told *Editor & Publisher*.

The overall approach was not public relations, Irvine said. "The overall approach was media anticipation. I learned from Salt Lake City how many reporters had been there, how long they stayed, the types of

NOTES

information they were interested in and needed, the kind of time demands they had, and the time demands put on a hospital and from that we built our whole approach on trying to accommodate what that media interest was going to be."

Irvine spent from July to November getting ready for the media.

Towards the end, George Atkins became more directly involved working with all the key players: DeVries, Lansing and Schroeder.

"My job has been to keep the engine room going, making sure we were ready, that we had the materials we needed, that we had photographs out of the lab. George has been coordinating interviews, handling the person to person stuff," Irvine told *E&P*.

Over 40 color and 80 black and white photos were released during the week. As many as 50 to 75 sets of color surgery slides were duped during the week.

"We released as much as we could humanly possibly process," Irvine said. "Hundreds of slides and photos were duped all week. We haven't even gotten a count yet."

Anything learned from all this?

"We've got to come up with a better way of handling photography. We've got to be able to process our pictures and get them out faster. The problem we had with photos was demand. The demand far outshot anything we had ever considered.

"The other problem was that Bill Strode, our photographer, was getting so much good stuff that we were developing more than we planned on. And the more we developed, the more the demand would pick up."

NOTES

Part 2. Business and Industry

Case 9. Eager Instrumatics, Inc. - A
Case 10. Eager Instrumatics, Inc. - B
    Excerpt For Discussion: P & G Licking Its Wounds
Case 11. A.H. Robins And The Dalkon Shield
    Excerpt For Discussion: An Interview With Kal Druck
Case 12. Basic Chemicals International - A
Case 13. Basic Chemicals International - B
    Excerpt For Discussion: Some Considerations In Dealing With Public Opinion
Case 14. Empire Enterprises
    Excerpt For Discussion: An Interview With George Hammond
Case 15. Bruce Canfield Is Given The Word - A
Case 16. Bruce Canfield Is Given The Word - B
Case 17. Norton Chemicals
    Excerpt For Discussion: Inside The Amoral World of Public Relations

Case 9

EAGER INSTRUMATICS - A*

Eager Instrumatics, Inc., in September, 1984, was a relatively small but growing maker of control systems, with headquarters and plant in Fort Worth, Texas, and an employee force of 3,000. The firm had been founded by Morris Schwartz and a small executive group of twelve experienced scientists four years earlier, and within a short span of time ranged seventh in volume of sales in its field.

Though its annual sales volume represented only 5 per cent of total sales volume in the control systems field (which was dominated by three to five "giants" in the industry), Eager had built up a considerable reputation among the scientists and engineers who used Eager control equipment. Eager instrument controls, each of which ranged in price from $50,000 to $200,000, were used to control radar antenna acquisitions for space flights, petro-chemical plant processes, and calculation of scientific experiments. Purchase decisions for such equipment were generally made by line scientists or engineers who used the equipment, but recently a new line of Eager equipment had enabled the firm to move into the business accounting field where purchase decisions were made by top management personnel. Originally privately-owned, Eager had gone public in 1983 when it was found necessary to seek and find new sources of operating funds. Its stock was traded on the New York Stock Exchange.

Schwartz, 44, was a dynamic instrument control expert who had made his early reputation in the space instrument field shortly after graduation from Cal Tech, had briefly served as department head of math at Purdue, and then started his company in 1980 with an original investment of $100,000.

---

* *All names, places, and times in this case are disguised.*

Denise O'Reilly, 38, had been hired by Schwartz in 1981 as vice president of marketing. A Phi Beta Kappa who had majored in philosophy and minored in physics at Stanford, O'Reilly had been director of marketing for a major firm in the electronics field before joining Eager.

Working almost from scratch, O'Reilly had built up a ten-person marketing department by 1983 when Douglas Freeman was hired by Schwartz as director of advertising and public relations. Freeman, 35, had worked for several years as a writer for an advertising trade journal, then ad director of *Instrument Journal,* and finally, before joining Eager, as advertising and public relations manager for another instrument equipment company.

When he hired Freeman, Schwartz explained that he would report and be responsible to O'Reilly in respect to budgetary and administrative matters, but would be expected to counsel Schwartz on public relations matters. "We're so busy we don't have time for fancy organization charts, but this is where you fit in," Schwartz said, and he sketched the following chart:

**EXHIBIT 9-1
PARTIAL ORGANIZATION CHART**

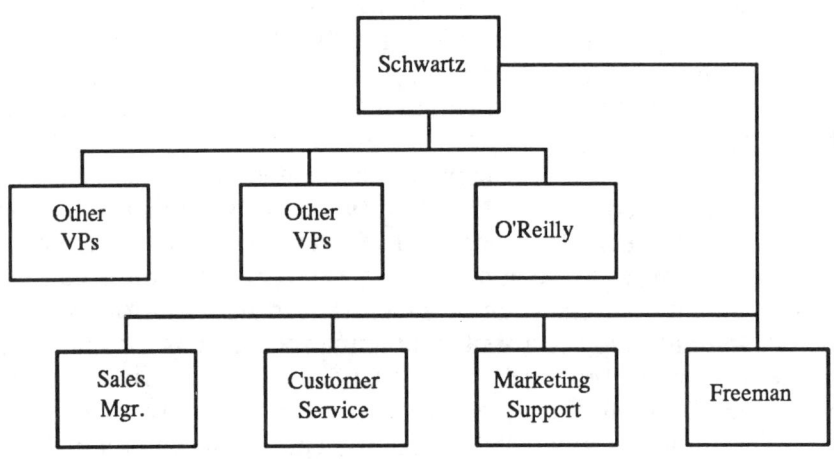

NOTES

In looking at the chart Freeman noted at once that he had a direct line relationship to both Schwartz and O'Reilly and he assumed this meant that he would be responsible to both and under their direct control. He felt it would be advantageous for him to have a direct line to the president on public relations matters. However, he was uneasy about the fact that because he was also linked to O'Reilly on a direct line he might well find himself in the middle if Schwartz and O'Reilly differed on a public relations issue or situation. He thought briefly about expressing his misgivings, but he decided he would be wiser not to say anything at the moment and see how matters worked out.

In actuality, they worked out very well. O'Reilly quickly made it known to Freeman that she expected Freeman to handle advertising and public relations without much direct supervision; O'Reilly also said she was too busy with other marketing problems to get involved in Freeman's functions. Though Schwartz was extremely busy, Freeman had no difficulty in reaching him and getting his support and cooperation when it was needed. A much more demanding person than O'Reilly, Schwartz nonetheless repected Freeman's expertise in public relations and generally deferred to Freeman's advice and counsel. By September, 1984, when discussions were initiated on the introduction of the new Gamma 4 line, Freeman was administering an active three-person department with a total budget of $750,000: $500,000 for advertising and $250,000 for public relations. Both budget items were incorporated into the general marketing department budget administered by O'Reilly.

O'Reilly and Freeman were first told about the new Gamma 4 line at a meeting with Schwartz held early in September, 1984. Schwartz told them this would be a new generation of instrument controls which would combine both scientific and business capabilities, would represent an entirely new design, and resulted from the firm's extensive research and development program. Schwartz said that initially the line would consist of at least three large instrument control systems: the Gamma 4-1, costing from $250,000 to $1 million; the Gamma 4-2, costing from $200,000 to $500,000; and the Gamma 4-3, costing from $50,000 to $200,000.

NOTES

"We can announce the line anyway we want," Schwartz told O'Reilly and Freeman. "From a production point of view, there's no reason to introduce one over the other, but we do expect to get into production on all three models by March, 1985. From that point on we'll be able to deliver the Gamma 4-1 and the Gamma 4-3 by the fourth quarter of 1985 and the Gamma 4-2 by June, 1986. You two figure out how you want to release the announcement about the line and let me know. I'll go along with any reasonable decision you make."

In the ensuing discussion between O'Reilly and Freeman the former said she favored announcing all three elements of the new line at a press conference in New York City sometime in March.

"If we announce all three at the same time we're sure to make a bigger splash," she argued. "We'd get a major news break and could really do the thing up brown. Further, we wouldn't have to hold back information or dodge questions about what's coming up next, as we'd have to do if we simply announce the line one element at a time. Finally, I know we could get Schwartz to make the announcement of all three at on major press conference, but I'm not sure we could get him to do it more than once."

"That's all true," Freeman said," but if we announce the elements separately we stand a good chance of making a big splash on the first and still getting further story breaks when we announce the other two elements of the line. Second, we won't be able to promise delivery on Gamma 4-2 for 15 months from March, 1985, and that's an awfully long spread between announcement and delivery date. Besides, if we announced the entire new line at one time customers might stop buying our present line because they would see that the new on is an improved one at a lower price."

"But that would apply any way you announced the line," O'Reilly said.

"Well, I haven't had time to think this out thoroughly, but I'd suggest we break the news about the Gamma 4-1 first with a press conference in New York City. We won't be able to show the actual hardware, but we could get mockups made; I'd put together a press kit with release matter and

NOTES

pics; and Schwartz and you could be available to make the actual announcement and handle questions. We could break the story some time in March, and after we see what kind of coverage we get, we could make plans for the other two elements in the line."

"Well," replied Reilly, "I still don't like it, but it's your baby, really, so handle it any way you want. Just keep me informed as you go along."

"Oh, by the way," O'Reilly added, "I'm not up on the prompt disclosure rules of the Security and Exchange Commission and the New York Stock Exchange, so I'd appreciate it if you'd check these out and let me know how they apply. Both of us are also members of PRSA, so that's a consideration we should keep in mind."

"I don't know much about prompt disclosure either," Freeman admitted, "but I'm sure that's not really involved here, so I wouldn't worry about it."

"Okay if you say so," O'Reilly replied. "Just remember to keep me informed."

After O'Reilly left, Freeman read through the provisions of the PRSA code and by-laws dealing with standards of professional practice, particularly as they relate to financial relations (See Appendix for the PRSA code and by-law provisions). He also scanned some material in his files dealing with regulations and guidelines of the Securities and Exchange Commission and the major stock exchanges governing prompt and accurate disclosure of information which could materially affect security values or have an influence on investment decisions.

Freeman jotted down the following rough notes summarizing pertinent excerpts from the financial disclosure material in his files:

> SEC and major market exchange guidelines require that publicly-held companies should reveal promptly and accurately information which might affect in a material way the value of securities or influence investment decisions.

> Guideline not entirely clear about what kind of specific information is material.

NOTES

Among corporate developments mentioned as calling for prompt and accurate disclosure are those involving new products, cited as either "major new products" or as "a significant new product or products."

Seems to be general agreement that information is considered material if it is considered to be essential to an investor's informed decision-making process.

SEC and the exchanges recognize there may be valid business reasons for a delayed disclosure. Example: one authority says disclosure mey be delayed where disclosure would endanger a company's goals or provide information helpful to a competitor.

However, the presumption should always be in favor of disclosure because there are only a few circumstances where disclosures might be withheld, says same authority. Quote from *The Amex Company Guide*: "The circumstances where disclosure can be withheld are limited and constitute an infrequent exception to the normal requirement of immediate prompt disclosure. Thus, in cases of doubt, the presumption must always be in favor of disclosure."

After reviewing the above notes, Freeman decided that it would probably be wise to have another talk with O'Reilly.

NOTES

Case 10

EAGER INSTRUMATICS - B*

After his second talk with O'Reilly (See *Eager Instrumatics - A*), Freeman decided to go ahead with his plans to announce the Gamma 4-1 at a press conference in New York City. He set the date for March 14 and informed Schwartz and O'Reilly. They agreed to be on hand, accompanied by a technical man, to handle the announcement and answer questions from the press. He then contracted with one of New York City's finest eating establishments for a continental breakfast, meeting room, cocktails, and lunch for a hundred people. Total cost for all food, liquor, special lighting, microphones, shipping, and other services came to $7,000. Freeman's staff put together a press kit consisting of (1) a general and a scientific press release about the Gamma 4-1, describing its special features, citing it as "the first in a new generation of Eager Instrumatics control systems," citing its cost and fourth quarter of 1985 delivery date; (2) three still shots of the Gamma 4-1 and its auxiliary equipment; (3) a general brochure about the company; and (4) a special brochure about the Gamma 4-1.

On March 7, Freeman's staff sent out press conference invitations to a hundred representatives of the daily press, wire services, news and trade magazines, and the financial community. The invitation letter read as follows:

All names, places, and times in this case are disguised

EAGER INSTRUMATICS, INC.
1410 Raymond Avenue
Fort Worth, TX

(Salutation)

7 March 1985

On Tuesday, March 14, Eager Instrumatics will announce a major new family of instrument controls which we believe will be of significant interest to your readers.

The new Eager line features a unique design concept and represents the first such announcement since the Monitor 340. Eager President Morris Schwartz and other officers of the company will be present to answer your questions.

We hope you will be able to attend our press conference. It is scheduled for 10:00 a.m. Tuesday, March 14, at La Place, 45 East 54 Street, New York. A continental breakfast will be served prior to the meeting. Cocktails and lunch will follow the conference.

An indication of your plans to attend the conference on the enclosed reply card would be appreciated.

Very truly yours,
EAGER INSTRUMATICS, INC.

(signed)

Douglas Freeman
Assistant to the President

NOTES

On March 8 Freeman left for New York City. When he arrived he contacted, both in person and by telephone calls, those on the press conference list in whom he had particular interest from a publicity point of view. Freeman was particularly interested in talking to contacts on the business desks of *Newsweek* and *Time* magazines.

He had initiated talks several months before with the Fort Worth bureau staffers of both publications, with the aim of interesting them in doing a profile of Eager Instrumatics as a young, aggressive company bucking the giants in its field. The bureau staffers had indicated that their business desks were definitely interested in the story, but neither publication had printed it yet.

Freeman's *Newsweek* contact informed him that the story, by coincidence, was running in the issue due out on the newsstands the day he called (March 9), and the *Time* man said the story was scheduled to run in the issue due out on the newsstands the day before the scheduled press conference. When Freeman called his home office March 9, he relayed the information to Schwartz, and the latter was highly pleased to learn that the company was getting such "excellent news breaks." O'Reilly, who was in on the conference-type call, also praised Freeman for his advance work, but said she was worried that the stories in the news magazines might backfire.

"Backfire?" repeated Freeman.

"Well," said O'Reilly, "how would you feel if you were with the *Wall Street Journal* and you found upon reading *Newsweek* or *Time* that they had an advance story on a press conference to which you had been invited but which hadn't yet been held?"

Freeman, aware that Schwartz was listening in, said that the *Newsweek* and *Time* stories were general profiles and not really about the Gamma 4-1. He did admit, however, that when he had talked to both publications' bureau people two weeks previously he had given them some data about the Gamma 4-1; he expected they wouldn't feature it but would rather feature the "rising young company versus the Goliaths" aspect of the story.

NOTES

"Let's cut this," Schwartz interrupted. "We're busy here, and you must be also. The important thing is that we'll be getting into *Newsweek* and *Time* and that doesn't happen to us everyday. We'll see you the night of the 13th, Doug. So long, and good job."

Approximately seventy showed up for the press conference on March 14. Fifty-five were accredited media people, and the others were company representatives, friends, and financial specialists. Following coffee and Danish pastry at 10:00 a.m., President Schwartz spoke about the company and the new model. He was followed by O'Reilly.

In the question-and-answer period, one of the trade press representatives asked O'Reilly to amplify the statement in the press release that the Gamma 4-1 was "the first in a new generation of Eager Instrumatics control systems."

"Well," said O'Reilly, "we expect several systems to evolve in the Gamma 4 series ultimately."

"Several?" said the trade press rep.

"Several, three to five," Schwartz broke in, and the matter was dropped at this point. The conference broke up on schedule for cocktails and lunch at 12:30.

Freeman, O'Reilly, and Schwartz were very pleased when they checked the evening and morning papers following the conference. The *Wall Street Journal* ran a 400-word inside page story; the *New York Times* ran a 350-word story on its first business page; the AP sent out a 125-word story; and the New York *Post* ran a 100-word story among its business pages. UPI carried nothing, *Newsweek* ran a full-page story in its business section which lead off with several paragraphs about the new David among the Goliaths, five paragraphs about the Gamma 4-1, and four paragraphs about President Schwartz, the young dynamo from out of the West.

Time carried nothing about Eager Instrumatics, and when Freeman returned to Fort Worth, the *Time* bureau woman there told him that the story had unfortunately been cut out at the last minute in favor of a late-breaking story about another company. The *Time* woman said the story itself was not completely dead, but she wasn't certain when or if it would be run.

NOTES

Both Schwartz and O'Reilly were very disappointed about the failure to get into *Time*, but they agreed that this was something out of Freeman's control. They were extremely pleased when Freeman, about a month after the press conference, showed them clippings and stories which had appeared in numerous major newspapers and in various trade publications which were important to the company. They were especially pleased with a one-page story with a picture of Schwartz which appeared in *Business Week* one week after the press conference, and with a four-column, quarter-page *New York Times* profile on Schwartz which appeared two Sundays after the press conference.

The story resulted from a ten-minute interview with a *Times* staffer which Freeman had arranged after the press conference proper. It included not only material about Schwartz as a personality but also material about the company, its newest product, and its future potential.

"You know," said Schwartz pointing to the clippings and stories, "all this looks impressive, but just what does it all mean? We spent $7,000 just for the press conference itself, and of course we spent much more when you consider travel time, hotel expenses, and the hidden time costs of those of us who spent valuable time away from the office to participate in the conference. Well, did we get our money's worth? Just how do you measure and prove what it's all been worth to Eager Instrumatics?"

Neither O'Reilly nor Freeman had a ready answer, and as Schwartz didn't press the matter they simply let it die right there. Freeman, though, wondered what he might have said to Schwartz, or whether he should have expressed his thoughts in a memo to be sent to Schwartz later.

With announcement of the Gamma 4-1 out of the way, Freeman and O'Reilly discussed plans to announce the Gamma 4-2 and the Gamma 4-3. Both agreed that the Gamma 4-3, the smallest member of the line, had the same nine-month delivery date as the Gamma 4-1 and, as it was also the smallest of the line, it wouldn't be worth a major press conference. The alternative, both agreed, was a press release, and so announcement of the Gamma 4-3 was made by mailing a press release on August 2. Although coverage was not at all comparable to that given to the first of the line, Eager

NOTES

got some very good space with the third member of the line. The two staffers then prepared to handle announcement of the middle of the line. The only firm last-minute date they had was January 5, when brochures would be in the hands of the firm's salesmen who would be making their calls with data on the Gamma 4-2 from that date on. Freeman suggested another major press conference to be held in New York City in December.

"Very few press conferences are held in December," he reasoned, "and as we've got some good solid information we could make a good splash without too much fear of competition."

O'Reilly agreed with Freeman and suggested that Freeman talk to Schwartz. However, when Freeman brought up the subject, the president rejected the suggested immediately.

"That's out," Schwartz said. "I'm tired, I've covered too much ground already this year, and I don't want to get on another plane until some time next year."

Freeman and O'Reilly then concluded that they ought to hold the press conference without Schwartz, but when they raised this suggestion the president rejected it also. Although the president gave no reason other than the one he had already stated, Freeman got the impression that Schwartz felt that if anyone was going to handle announcements at a major press conference it should be the president.

Listing the alternatives, Freeman figured that there were only two: (1) send the announcement through the mail as had been done with the Gamma 4-3, or (2) have Freeman make a trip to New York and hand-plant the story with various media people. Freeman also figured this was as good a time as any to bring up another matter he had been mulling over.

"It seems to me," he said to O'Reilly, "it would be worth it if we opened a New York office and put a person in it to cover announcements of this kind. As we grow, there's an increasing need also to have a regular New York City-based person on our public relations staff."

"We'd have to build a solid case, and I'm not so sure we have one," O'Reilly replied. "We have a need for another professional in your department and there's money in the budget for one, but setting up an office

NOTES

in New York is another matter. I'd have to be convinced it's needed, and I'd have to convince Schwartz that it's needed and would be economically justified.

"If you think you'd like to make a case for a New York City office, just let me know and I'll set up a meeting with Schwartz and you can make a personal presentation. Either that, or you can put your ideas down on paper in a memorandum."

Freeman said he'd think about it, and the two then went on with discussion of handling announcement of the Gamma 4-2.

NOTES

An Excerpt For Discussion

P & G Licking Its Wounds With PR Revamp*
by Laurie Freeman and Nancy Giges

Proctor and Gamble has revamped its communications department in order to handle a stepped-up load of promotion and publicity for its products.

The move is in keeping with the company's attempt to improve its image and, in effect, blow its own horn, a practice eschewed in the past. Until recently, P&G was satisfied with letting its products' performance speak for themselves.

But a new set of circumstances - a different management and difficulties in key categories, primarily disposable diapers and toothpaste - has encouraged a greater sensitivity to how the company is portrayed, especially in the financial media. Additionally, it's no secret that the company has stumbled in some of its attempts to stage media events, and this organization will allow better specialization.

The communications department has now been divided into two units - one to handle publicity and special-events projects for all divisions; the other, media inquiries, also for all divisions.

Previously, public relations representatives handled all promotion, publicity and media queries of the operating units of P&G assigned to them.

P&G pr director Robert Norrish, who directs both units, commented, "We used to be organized according to the divisions in the company. Now with all the growth in our publicity activity to better promote products, we felt we should get organized functionally, one group to handle nothing but publicity and the other to handle regular press inquiries."

The publicity unit is headed by associate directors Pat Hayes and Barry Smyth, two veteran P&G media-relations spokespeople. Sydney

---

* Reprinted with permission from the September 16, 1985 issue of *Advertising Age*. Copyright 1985 by Crain Communications, Inc.

McHugh, who primarily handled press inquiries on paper products, is now section manager for the trimmed-down pr department.

P&G more than a month ago informed its pr agencies, including Burson-Marsteller, Hill & Knowlton and Manning, Selvage & Lee, about the reorganization.

"P&G did this in order to better stage glitzy press events," a source close to the company said. "They want to do more events, like having people jump out of planes with Liquid Tide bottles in their hands."

During the last three years, P&G has increased its pr agency budgets for both product publicity and special projects, agency sources say.

But some do not see any change in the company's orientation. "P&G has always wanted to carry on an ongoing dialog directly with the consumer, but not through the media," said a principal in a New York-based P&G agency.

This new approach to shaping events involving the company indicates P&G aims to get back to its consumer pr roots, another agency source said.

Other sources believe P&G was forced to realign itself in order to deal with the current competitive environment.

No longer is the household-goods marketer breezing along as the undisputed leader in categories such as disposable diapers and toothpaste. This has forced the once unassailable company to adopt defensive strategies, said Hugh Zurkuhlen, P&G watcher at Salomon Bros., New York.

Additionally, P&G watchers say there used to be two untouchable companies in terms of image in the media - Coca-Cola and P&G. Everything these companies did seemed to get good publicity; even minor product introductions would be overplayed and look positive in the business press.

Now that isn't always true anymore, and "it must be hard for people in media relations at P&G to accept," a major competitor said.

In the past, when P&G routinely reported record sales and earnings each quarter, any negative publicity could be played down or even ignored.

NOTES

Now that P&G is struggling in some of its key product areas, the company has become much more sensitive to how it appears in the media.

"The people there don't know how to cope under adverse situations; they never admit anything is really wrong," the competitor said.

P&G's first attempt at staging a media event in recent memory was the introduction of advanced formula Crest in 1981. The company originally tried to limit the guest list to science writers, positioning the announcement as a scientific breakthrough, and not of interest to general-business writers.

Even after admitting business reporters to the press conference, questions concerning marketing, advertising and what effect the introduction would have on the company's financial picture went unanswered. Officials were furious when any publication even hinted that the reformulation was in any way tied to improving sales and market share.

What followed was a 3 1/2-year hiatus from press events, until a recent round with Liquid Tide detergent, new Pampers disposable diapers and the Church of Satan-P&G debacle (AA, Nov. 26, *et seq.*).

By the time the Liquid Tide press conference was held, P&G appeared to have learned some lessons. Press releases still touted product superiority, but the company injected a little pizzazz as well.

The hot, ultra-trendy New York disco Visage was the chosen location for the Liquid Tide press conference. A two-story-tall inflatable Liquid Tide bottle greeted guests at the door. Inside, a jazz band played, while reporters and editors circled laundry baskets and an exhibit showing Tide outwashing various competitors.

While sources at Burson-Marsteller, the Liquid Tide pr agency, say they and P&G considered it a success, many in the press felt there was something lacking.

Normally, press events at these discos are in the nature of a party, usually jammed with people, dancing or trying to talk even though music is loud; any product information or program is fairly incidental to the party atmosphere. This was not the case with P&G's press conference. At this event, the small group that gathered seemed out of place.

NOTES

The apparent product tie-in, that both Liquid Tide and Visage were somehow related to the modern era of space-age technology, was a little farfetched. After some introductory scenes of Liquid Tide blasting off from P&G's Cincinnati headquarters building, the presentation was a straightforward rundown of Liquid Tide's formula.

It was pretty much a stab at the high-tech press conference on a shoestring. It certainly didn't reflect the conservative nature of P&G and would have been more appropriate in a smaller room at a more sedate hotel or restaurant.

The true corporate flavor was better reflected in the Pampers press conference. Although it was clear P&G was putting a bright veneer on a negative situation, the demonstrations were P&G all over: Blue liquid was poured from beakers onto diapers to show containment and absorbency. And P&G invited members of the media to participate in the demonstrations that took place at several tables around the room.

In addition, the company was more agreeable to answering inquiries, even when the questions were not on the P&G's agenda.

However, another example of P&G's inexperience in handling adverse events was reflected in what critics characterized as its "sloppy" handling of the Church of Satan-P&G logo situation.

Pr experts say P&G let the rumor drag on too long, and in the end management did not keep its pr people informed about considerations to drop the logo from packages. Just a week before the company held a press conference to announce the removal, the pr person handling calls was asserting that to take the logo off the product - or even change it - would be tacit admission that the company was associated with the devil and the company would *never, ever* do so.

"It seemed as if they thought they could wave at a couple of mosquitoes and didn't realize they were growing into wasps," a New York-based competitor said. This pr expert noted that if P&G had called in any major pr agency and heeded its counsel, the problem would have been tackled promptly, head-on. Pr officials contrast P&g's studied response to

NOTES

that of Coca-Cola's quick reaction when the Atlanta-based soft-drink company saw it had a problem with new Coke and fixed it fast.

But many of these snafus can be attributed to a company exploring new territory, a company that is inexperienced in taking an aggressive role with the media. The pr reorganization recognizes this shortcoming and is a step to develop this expertise.#

NOTES

Case 11

A.H. ROBINS AND THE DALKON SHIELD*

November 15, 1984. 10:44 p.m. EST. It's the third commercial break during "Knot's Landing." A woman's face comes on the television screen.

"This important health warning is for women still using the Dalkon Shield," she says. "There is substantial medical opinion that continued use of the Dalkon Shield may pose a serious health hazard, and it should be removed." A telephone number flashes across the bottom of the screen, a toll-free number at which women still using this contraceptive device can reach its makers, the A.H. Robins Co. Robins, the woman says, will pay to have the shield removed.

Since this ad, and its print counterpart, ran, says Roscoe Puckett, Robins's public affairs manager, Robins has received 18,000 calls and paid for the removal of 3,730 Shields, at a cost of some $700,000.

Product recall. Reminiscent of such similar cases as Tylenol, Rely tampons, X-cars. Only there's a crucial difference here. The Dalkon Shield was taken off the market over a decade ago, amidst great controversy and publicity. Why then is Robins running this ad - part of a $4 million public information campaign undertaken by the giant pharmaceutical concern with the assistance of Burson-Marsteller - now? Why are so many women still wearing a product that a U.S. District judge recently called a "deadly depth charge"?

To get a sense of what has happened, what inspired Robins to undertake this campaign, what led Burson-Marsteller to recommend the approach that was chosen, and what the effects of the campaign have been for Robins, it is useful to start at the story's beginning.

---

* This case study, written by Christopher Policano, is reprinted with permission from the March 1985 issue of the *Public Relations Journal.*. Copyright 1985.

In the 1960s, America witnessed the much heralded "sexual revolution," a development featured on magazine covers, discussed on television talk shows, analyzed in newspapers and academic treatises, and fostered, say many observers, by the introduction of the birth control pill.

In 1968, Irwin Lerner, an inventor of medical devices, and Dr. Hugh J. Davis, then-director of birth control at Johns Hopkins University in Baltimore, MD, invented a device they called the Dalkon Shield.

The Shield was an intrauterine device designed to prevent fertilized eggs from adhering to the uterine wall. To allow women wearing the Shield to make sure it remained in place - and it could remain in place for at least two years - Davis and Lerner equipped it with a multifilamented "tail string" so that it could be easily checked.

Davis and Lerner tested the Shield for effectiveness and safety. It was Davis's contention that the IUD, and specifically the Dalkon Shield variety, was a safer, more effective form of birth control than the pill. At a 1970 Senate subcommittee hearing, he testified to that effect, claiming, in response to questions, that his interest in and support of the Shield was professional and not financial.

In 1970, Davis and Lerner, through Dalkon, the company they had set up to develop the device, sold the patent to Robins, a firm well known as the maker of Robitussin, for a quarter of a million dollars, and a year later Robins introduced the device to the American market under its label. Sales in some 79 foreign countries started a year later.

The Shield was a success. At the time it was introduced, such side effects as blood clotting, high blood pressure, liver problems, and depression were starting to cloud the pill's reputation. The Shield allowed women to avoid these potential complications. And it provided the same level of ease and convenience the pill had promised. By 1974, 4.5 million women around the world were wearing the Dalkon Shield.

But Robins's success with the Shield was short-lived. In July 1974, *Science News* reported that while "an unpublished British study [notes] a 3.6 percent pregnancy rate in second-year users" of the Dalkon Shield, " a researcher from Beth Israel Hospital in Boston, Johanna Perlmutter,

NOTES

reported a pregnancy rate of 18.5 percent." Other critics charged that Davis had neglected to mention that he'd tested the Shield in conjunction with a spermicidal foam, a backup protection that women wearing the Shield were not supposed to need. This, they said, may have accounted for the low pregnancy rate.

But more serious than the charges of ineffectiveness were the questions about safety. Complaints arose about adverse side effects, most commonly inflammation of the pelvis. And, by 1974, seven Dalkon Shield wearers had died of miscarraiges that were termed "infected spontaneous abortions." The Dalkon Shield was implicated in these deaths.

As a result of the ensuing controversy, Robins took the device off the American shelves in 1974, and stopped selling the device worldwide the following year.

The decision to discontinue the Shield was Robins's own. Because IUDs were then considered medical devices, not drugs, they did not fall under the jurisdiction of the Food and Drug Administration (FDA). Moreover, even if the FDA had been able to rule, it would have had the power only to seize, not to recall. Given the nature of the product, a device implanted in women's uteruses, seizing the Shield would have proven impossible.

As the controversy mounted and the Shield was withdrawn, Robins handled its relations with the press and public in a way that was a more common practice at the time: reactively, not proactively. It answered questions from the press and provided information about the Shield and about the company's actions. And if Robins never claimed culpability in the matter, as many of their critics charged they should, it was because, as Robins's chief executive officer said, years later, "Our company has never viewed the Dalkon Shield as posing any risk higher than those associated with other IUDs."

Still, Robins's involvement with the Shield was damaging. In August 1974, *Forbes* reported that problems with the Shield and with an appetite suppresant called Pondimin, which had not lived up to its sales expectations, had caused Robins's stock to drop from $40 to $12 a share in

NOTES

a year. And by late 1984, Robins had been named defendant in 11,000 lawsuits and reported "after taxes" expenses related to the lawsuits of close to $13 million.

One would think that in the 11 years since the Shield was withdrawn things would have quieted down. That hasn't been the case.

In 1976, the National Women's Health Network (NWHN) was formed. A Washington, DC-based nonprofit advocacy group, NWHN took as one of its chief missions "seeking all available injunctive relief, criminal penalties, condemnation, and seizure" of the Dalkon Shield. "In 1979," says Sybil Shainwald, a New York City attorney who heads NWHN and is one of Robins's most outspoken critics, "the National Women's Health Network filed a worldwide class-action suit against Robins in federal district court on Boston. But the judge couldn't do anything about it, and said, 'This is a matter for the FDA.'"

In 1983, NWHN followed up this suit with a petition to the FDA, asking, among other things, that Robins be required to "order notification that the Dalkon Shield presents an unreasonable risk of substantial harm to the public health," and "order A.H. Robins to submit a plan for total recall and to bear the costs of such a recall..." The petition also demanded that the banning of the Shield be backdated to 1972.

While the FDA claimed it didn't have the power to act on the Shield in the early seventies, it did, Shainwald says, issue a warning within 10 days of her group's 1983 petition. "But it's not enough," she says.

Shainwald and the NWHN have not been alone in their criticism. As the suits continued - 3,768 of them were still pending late last year - U.S. District Judge Miles Lord brought top Robins officials before his bench for a reprimand.

"None of you has faced up to the fact that more than 9,000 women made claims that they gave up part of their womanhood so that your company might prosper," he said. "Confession's good for the soul, gentlemen. Face up to your misdeed...Rectify this evil situation...Seek out every woman wearing a Shield and recall this deadly depth charge in their wombs, ready to explode at any moment."

NOTES

Judge Lord was later chastised himself by a federal appellate court. Quoted in the *Wall Street Journal,* the court told Lord he had "gone beyond the bounds of judicial authority in making the speech," and ordered his remarks stricken from the record. Robins said it was satisfied with the higher court's decision.

Wayne Pines worked for the FDA during the seventies and early eighties as the associate commissioner for public affairs. In April 1983, he joined Burson-Marsteller/Washington as a senior vice president. In late September of that year he got a call from Robins.

"I was asked to meet with Robins's attorney in Washington," Pines says, "and discussed the problem with them. They recognized the need to notify women and wanted to reach as many potential wearers of the Shield as quickly as possible, since there was a health factor involved."

Robins chose Burson-Marsteller as the firm to handle this project largely because of its experience with Rely tampons, a Procter & Gamble product withdrawn from drug store and supermarket shelves after it was implicated in the toxic-shock syndrome (TSS) scare in 1982. Burson-Marsteller had developed Procter & Gamble's TSS education campaign. Pines had worked on the FDA side during the incident.

Using the Procter & Gamble campaign as a model, Pines and five other Burson-Marsteller staff members put together a proposal for Robins in a week and presented it to Robins's board of directors.

"We recommended a public relations program that consisted of a commercial and print advertising campaign, a program to reach physicians, and an international program to try to reach women in the 79 countries that the Shield had been distributed in," Pines says. "No creatives were done - first we had to get the board's approval on the concept, which came through the following week."

Burson-Marsteller recommended that the action be taken immediately, rather than at the end of 1984 or in early 1985. Later on, said Pines, it would have been more difficult to make the advertising buys. The team recommended not buying radio spots. "Radio is too diffuse. There are too many radio stations," Pines said.

NOTES

Participation in the program by Young & Rubicam, Burson-Marsteller's parent company, was limited to providing legal counsel. All account work and creatives were handled by Pines's team, and the media buys were made by Robins's in-house staff, based on Burson-Marsteller's recommendations.

The print ads appeared in 177 daily newspapers across the country, 13 minority newspapers, in *USA TODAY* and the *National Enquirer*, and in such national magazines as *Newsweek, People, TV Guide*, and *Time*.. The television ad ran during such shows as "Dallas," "Miami Vice," "Wheel of Fortune," "Family Feud," "Love Boat," "The Young and the Restless," "Sale of the Century," "Facts of Life," and "Good Morning, America." The commercial also ran on "Super Stations" WGN, WOR, and WTBS as well as on the Spanish Information Network. A "Dear Doctor" letter, urging removal of the Shields, was sent out to 185,000 physicians nationwide. (A similar letter had been sent to 120,000 doctors in the U.S. as well as distributors and governmental agency personnel in 1974.)

On the day the campaign broke, Robins delivered letters to the Washington embassies of the 79 countries where the Shield had been sold, addressed to the ambassador of each. "While the Dalkon Shield has not experienced the controversy, litigation, and negative publicity in your country that it has in the United States," the letter read, "we believe your government should be aware of our action. Robins seeks the guidance and counsel of your government in determining whether or not it would be appropriate to conduct a Dalkon Shield information program in your country."

There was no press conference announcing the campaign. Says Pines, "Robins didn't feel the need for one. The ads spoke for themselves."

However, E. Claiborne Robins, the company's chief executive officer, did make a public statement, announcing the company's concern for women still wearing the product ("because current wearers will have had the device for at least a decade, and it is time, from a medical standpoint to see that all Dalkon Shields are removed") and its position on the controversy ("Our company has never viewed the Dalkon Shield as posing any risk

NOTES

higher than that associated with other IUDs"). Burson-Marsteller sent Robins's statement out as part of an 8 1/2-minute videotape to television stations across the country via PubSat, the Washington, DC satellite communications company.

How successful was the campaign? Pines is proud of the results. In the three weeks it ran, he says, the campaign reached its saturation point.

"You never get 100 percent," says Pines. "But our audience estimates indicate that we reached 93 percent of the target audience very quickly, in a concentrated period of time. In terms of scope, I had never worked on anything comparable to this."

Internationally, the results have been less dramatic. The letters to ambassadors have produced fewer responses than they hoped for, Pines says. Most countries did not respond. But, he notes, "there are programs beginning in Australia and Canada."

While the campaign did generate attention and did result in the removal of at least 3,730 remaining Shields, it did not, of course, silence all the criticism, or the cynicism about Robins's motives in launching the campaign.

Dale Larson, a partner in the Minneapolis law firm of Robins, Zelle, Larson & Kaplan, and the attorney for the plaintiffs in some of the remaining Shield-related suits, believes the campaign was a "wise act" carefully timed to blunt any negative publicity resulting from the early November settlement of 198 lawsuits against Robins. (Although the exact amount of this settlement was not disclosed, press reports indicated it was about $38 million).

"The campaign was timed to be done ahead of the settlement announcement," said Larson. "Robins knew exactly when the settlement would become public - one had a great deal to do with the other."

Robins, for its part, denies that the timing was a critical factor. "Our concern was with getting out a crucial health message to as many women as possible, and as quickly as possible," said Thomas Poe, Robins's public relations manager. "Larson's entitled to his opinion, but we have undertaken a positive program. It is important now to focus on reason, not rhetoric."

NOTES

There are still unanswered questions. Why did Robins wait 10 years to mount this public information campaign? Why were so many women still wearing the Shield despite its well-publicized, albeit alleged, hazards?

One answer certainly lies in changes that have transformed the practice of public relations over the last decade from a chiefly reactive to an increasingly proactive profession. Corporations have learned lessons from such incidents as the TSS scare, and these lessons, with growing frequency, translate into public relations initiatives.

Had these lessons been learned in 1974, Robins may well have handled the initial recall of the Shield differently. Still, by most measurements, their 1984 campaign was successful, and, for the nearly 4,000 women who may not otherwise have had their Shields removed, it made a critical difference.

Author's Postscript

On August 21, 1985, the Robins company filed for bankruptcy protection from its creditors under Chapter 11 of the U.S. Bankruptcy Code. According to the *New York Times*, the company said the claims and damage awards against it threatened its viability and it hoped that the Federal bankruptcy court in Richmond would set up a payment schedule that would ensure victims would be treated fairly while at the same time the company could survive.

"In a Chapter 11 bankruptcy filing," reported the *Times*, "a company asks a judge to postpone the payment of its pressing debts until a manageable repayment schedule can be drawn up. The judge can order a company to be liquidated to pay these debts, but normally it emerges from bankruptcy and continues to operate."

The *Times* story cited the company as stating that as of June 30 Robins and its insurers had paid $378.3 million to settle 9,230 cases. Legal expenses totalled another $107.3 million and the company said about 5,100 cases were still pending.

NOTES

An Excerpt for Discussion

An Interview With Kalman B. Druck*

Q: Let me pose a philosophical question. As you have described the situation and as I believe it has existed up until now, you have public relations people on both sides of these questions bumping heads with each other, so to speak, with their opposing arguments. Should public relations people attempt to look at their functions somewhat differently? Should they, in a sense, try to be compromisers, rather than exponents of opposite points of view?

D: Yes, I think they should. I think that in any given group of people in the management of a government agency, or a business enterprise, the voice that speaks for the public interest should be the public relations person. In other words, the engineer talks about what he needs to produce, the financial person talks about what it takes to get money to come into the enterprise, the marketer talks about marketing and promotion. I think that the public relations person should be talking about - first of all, practically - will the public accept this product or this idea or this piece of legislation? And secondly, is it in the public interest? Which gets you into the ethical problem. Now, the point that I was making before is that it's very difficult, in most cases, to define the public interest, because it depends on which public you're talking about...

    I think that the public relations voice should be the one that says, "Well, now look, here's how the issues balance out, and therefore here's what I

---

* Kalman B. Druck, a former vice president of Carl Byoir & Associates and a principal of Harshe-Rotman & Druck, was interviewed by J. Carroll Bateman in 1977 in one of the oral history interviews sponsored by the Foundation for Public Relations Research and Education. This excerpt is from a transcript of the tape made by Professor Hunter P. McCartney in 1985 under a grant provided by the Foundation. Reprinted with permission.

think we ought to be doing about it." So that point of view goes into the mix that finally results in the decision being made. But I think that where the decisions are being made without that voice, then the entity, whatever it is, is more likely to be ineffectual and to get into trouble...

Q: How much of an ethical problem is posed for the public relations practitioner who is expected to voice a point of view that he feels is not in the public interest? How do you look at this kind of problem? I don't know whether you've ever experienced it (and as a counselor, you're in a position to turn down accounts that you don't like or don't agree with), but what should be the ethical position of a public relations man who is faced with expounding a point of view with which he personally disagrees or feels is wrong?

D: Well, I think that that kind of problem has its own built-in safety factor. Since the nature of our business is to go out and try to develop public understanding and support, we go public with every idea that we are dealing with. If we're faced with a product or an idea that is not in the public interest, we are, in effect, committing suicide to espouse it because we ought to be smart enough to see that if we go out and try to persuade 1,000 newspapers to run the story about a product or an idea that's a bad one, then we're not going to be very welcome there. We're pushing the wrong thing, even if you are not terribly tuned to ethical principles - right or wrong - but you figure that you'll do what you can get away with. Even at that level, you realize in this business that, as a practical matter, if it's a bad idea you're not going to get away with it. So there's a built-in safeguard there that tends to make you ethical.

Q: You're ethical for pragmatic reasons.

D: Yes, but I don't want to imply that I think that's the controlling factor. I must say that most of the people that I know in this field are pretty decent

NOTES

people. They have a good home life. They love their children. And their impulses are pretty good impulses.

Q: Of course, under the marketplace of-ideas concept that many public relations people espouse, or used to espouse, even unpopular ideas are entitled to be voiced in this marketplace of ideas. We do know that some very prominent public relations firms or public relations individuals have undertaken causes that some people, at least, consider to be wrong...Yet, they don't seem to have an ethical problem when they do this. At least, they don't voice it to us.

D: I think that the whole consideration is whether you can live with yourself. If you can really face up to the fact that you're being paid to persuade people to do something that you know in your own heart is very wrong, I don't think that you really can be terribly effective for very long. I think that ours just happens to be the kind of a business that operates in the spotlight more than most. Therefore, our transgressions tend to be more short-lived than most. And we tend to realize that it's not a very good risk.

I think that, in the ethical field, the problem we have is that there are about four levels of ethics. We get confused because we confuse the levels. I think that there's a level of personal ethics where most of us wouldn't do anything deliberately to hurt some other person. And then you have the second level, which is business ethics, where you have a system where the buyer and the seller are bargaining and haggling, and there's a certain amount of salesmanship or covering up of the negative in order to emphasize the positive. Within certain limits, it's ethical to do it that way.

The third level is national ethics, where we've gone through a catharsis in our political system in Watergate in a lot of the revelations about the lives of some of our politicians in Washington and other parts of the country. We were taught in school about the ideas of the founding fathers, ideas espoused in the Declaration of Independence and the Constitution, which are the highest-sounding that one could imagine. And then we have

NOTES

our national ethics - where we go out and take the Panama Canal because we want it, or we get involved in other kinds of national activities that raise questions about ethics. So you have this third level of national ethics.

Then you have the fourth level, international ethics, where we have 150 different countries of the world and many different societies with different ways of looking at how people live together and deal with each other. We sure don't have the right to impose our particular ethics on others, nor they on us. But if we're to live in a world where a multinational corporation may be doing business in 65 different countries, we must have some kind of a notion of what our policies are going to be.

So you have these four levels of ethics, and I think we're in a particular period now where some of the evidences of transgressions have brought up the whole subject of how you deport yourself - what's right and what's wrong. Companies are developing creeds about how they're going to operate, and we just happened to have elected a President who was more than usually outspoken about his religious precepts, and the world is going through upheavals and revolutions in many countries around the world, with new types of governments that are taking over. I think that it's a very trying period; it's a period where I don't see any clearcut superimposition of one-world ethic on everybody. And we're constantly going to be in the marketplace of ideas, trying out new ideas and new directions. And this is an area, I think, of challenge for public relations people. It may be that we ought to take a double major in college: one in philosophy and one in public relations. I'm serious about this...

NOTES

Case 12

BASIC CHEMICALS INTERNATIONAL - A*

Basic Chemicals International was a multinational company with two major divisions: Basic Chemicals, U.S. and Basic Chemicals, International. Approximately 60 percent of its $600,000,000 in annual sales came from the United States and 40 percent from its international operations.

The 20,000 employees of BCI (about one-third serving with the international unit and two-thirds in the United States) worked in twenty-five plants and research facilities at twenty locations, twelve of these in the United States. Listed on a major exchange, the company had 75,000 shareholders.

Approximately 60 percent of the products of the company were in the chemical industry category; this included the firm's own consumer products as well as chemical product ingredients the company sold to other chemical manufacturers. The remaining 40 percent of the firm's business was divided among a variety of nonchemical fields, including beverages, drugs, paper, electronics, and textiles.

BCI corporate headquarters occupied fourteen floors of a thirty-story modern office building at 845 Third Avenue in mid-town New York City. Executive offices were located on the 28th floor and the nine-member corporate public relations staff had offices on the 10th floor.

---

*All names, places, and times in this case have been changed

The published organizational chart of the department (Exhibit 12-1) showed the members of the staff.

EXHIBIT 12 - 1

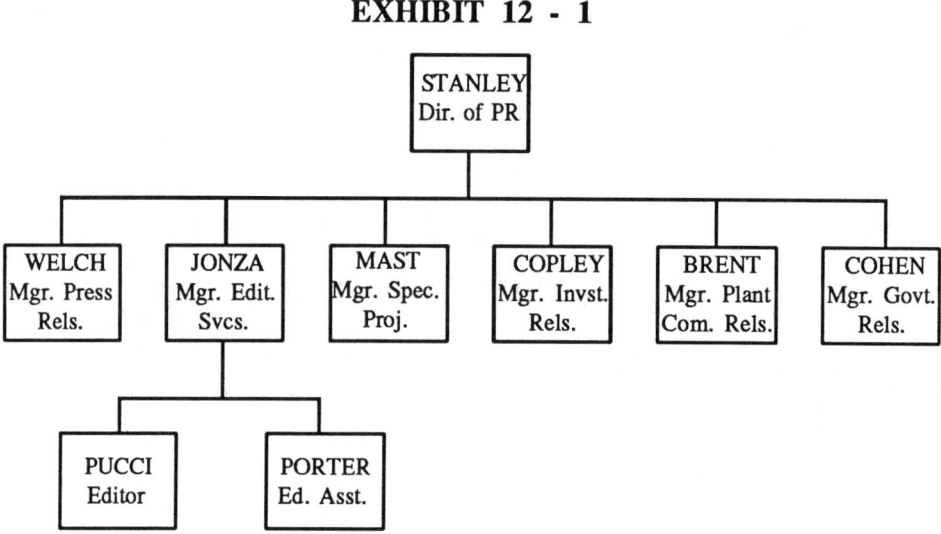

Hubert Stanley, director of public relations, was 44 years old and had been with the company in this position for six years. He was acknowledged to be an excellent writer, particularly of speeches; he had eight years experience in public relations with another major chemical company and four with a chemical trade association. His media experience was limited to two years in his late twenties as a reporter with a metropolitan newspaper.

Stuart Jonza, manager of editorial services, was 42 years old and had joined the company three years ago. He was responsible for publication of the following: monthly management newsletter, monthly employee publication, monthly headquarters office publication, the news flash bulletin board system, college recruiting brochures, and the pension plan report. He

NOTES

had five years experience as director of employee publications for a multi-plant manufacturing concern, six years experience as news service director of a major food concern, and four years experience as public information manager of a chemical firm.

George Welch, manager of press relations, was 41 years old. He joined the company last year when Mast (see following) gave up his press relations work to devote full time to other corporate public relations staff duties. He had worked eight years as a reporter for a major metropolitan newspaper and two years in a press relations capacity for a national trade association.

Peter Mast, manager of special projects, was 36 years old and had been with the company three years (he and Jonza were hired at the same time). He joined the public relations staff with responsibility for both press relations and general corporate staff work. He had served as a reporter for one year with a 60,000-circulation newspaper, as news editor of a general magazine for two years, and as a public relations counselor for four years.

Ramona Copley, manager of investor relations, was 34 years old and had joined the company last year. She had several years experience on a 125,000-circulation newspaper as a financial writer and two years experience with a press association in a major Eastern city.

Peter Brent, manager of plant community relations, was 54 years old and had joined the company five years ago. He was responsible for supervision and guidance of the company's plant public relations managers. He had fourteen years experience as a reporter for various medium-sized daily newspapers, ten years experience as editor of a plant newspaper for a heavy industrial firm, and two years experience as a salesman.

Jason Cohen, manager of government relations, was 40 years old and had joined the company four years ago. He had six years experience as city hall reporter for a metropolitan daily, ten years experience as a Washington representative for a national trade association, and three years experience as administrative assistant to a Congressman. He spent most of his time in an office the firm maintained in Washington; but he also worked in one of the offices the department had on the 10th floor.

NOTES

Ronald Pucci, editor, was 28 years old and had joined the company two years ago after four years Army service (two in public information work) and three years experience as editor of an employee publication for a large drug company.

Judy Porter, editorial assistant, was 23 years old and joined the company this year. She had an undergraduate degree in public relations from Utica College of Syracuse University and a master's degree in public relations from American University. She had worked as an editorial assistant for one year with a chemical trade journal.

In handling the above staff members, Stanley gave each manager a wide degree of latitude and a minimal amount of supervision. He operated on the theory that if one hires men and women with sufficient experience and expertise in their areas of competence, there should be no need for close supervision. As he explained to Mast one day during luncheon:

"When I hire a person to handle press relations, I expect him to do his job without need of supervision. If he doesn't measure up after a suitable period, then the time has come to consider replacing him with another man, moving him to another slot, if one is available.

"Besides, I just don't have time for supervision. Dorn (president of the company and the man to whom Stanley reported) keeps me busy enough writing speeches, advising, and suggesting action on policy matters relating to public relations."

Clapping Mast lightly on the back, Stanley added: "Anyway, the men in the department know they can always go to you if they need help or direction."

In actuality, some of the managers did and some did not. Though each manager reported directly to him, Stanley was usually too busy with his own work to spend time on supervision, held few staff meetings, and gave others in the department to understand that Mast could and should handle matters of daily routine. When inquiries relating to various public relations matters filtered into the department, they were usually relayed first to Mast. He, in turn, relayed them to the appropriate managers.

NOTES

Mast himself felt that personal relationships in the department were good. There had never been a major dispute and no one had been dismissed since Stanley took over. But he also felt that supervision of the managers was too loose; there wasn't any real direction given to the people in the department. In effect, Mast felt, each manager worked as a specialist in a specialized area of public relations activity, and there was little coordination of efforts. Starting with just two people six years ago, the department had expanded with expanding business - but at no time had anyone set down a formal set of objectives or a formal plan of action. As Stanley explained when Mast was hired:

"We've just been too damned busy doing the job for which we're paid. Besides, basic objectives really don't change: we all know full well that we're here to gain goodwill for the company and acceptance for its products. We know that we're here to assist in the marketing of company products and head off present and potential trouble for the company and its executives; and of course to provide the executives with public relations assistance."

Mast recognized that each person in the department was productively busy, but he felt that the department wasn't functioning as it could under closer supervision and concerted plan of action. It was also his belief that some of the managers - particularly Jonza and Welch - failed to demonstrate sufficient creativity and were too content to follow routine ways of handling their work. However, though he was critical in his own mind about the state of the department, Mast wasn't certain what could be done to improve matters and felt that he wasn't in any position to bring about changes.

Mast's hopes for improvement in the workings of the department were raised in January when Stanley moved his office to the 28th floor at the suggestion of the president. The action, explained Stanley at a special staff meeting called to announce the change, was made because the president wanted him to be close at hand rather than far removed on the 10th floor. The move, he said, reflected greater management acceptance of the public relations function.

NOTES

At the same time, Stanley announced that Mast would become assistant director of public relations and would take over his old corner office on the 10th floor. Stanley advised the staff that the assistant directorship represented a "proxy" when he was not available for routine matters. Stanley asked if there were any questions, and when none were forthcoming he distributed the new department organization chart shown in Exhibit 12-2.

EXHIBIT 12 - 2

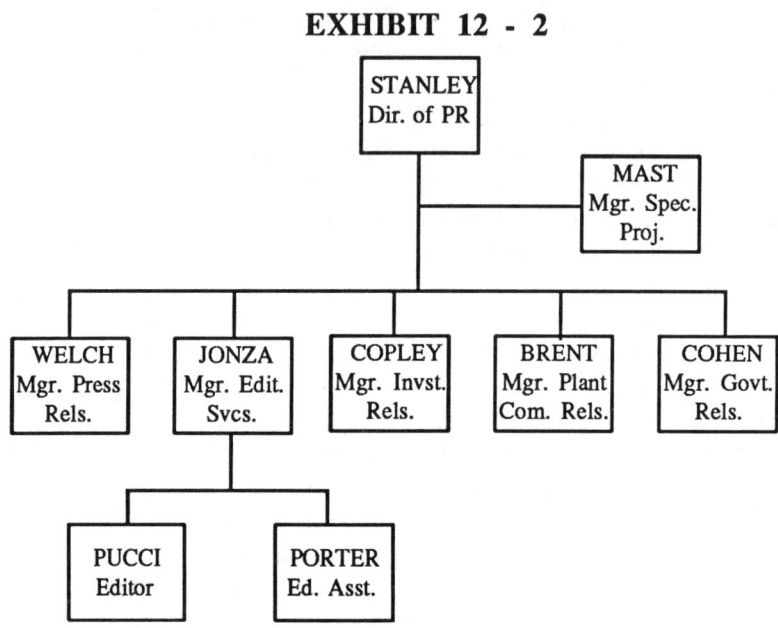

Mast, who had received a raise with announcement of the departmental change, felt the move would be beneficial to the department; he decided, however, to withhold judgment for six months. One afternoon in May, Mast reviewed the departmental set-up and concluded he had three major problems.

NOTES

THE DEPARTMENT ITSELF

Mast felt that he was more of an assistant *to* the director rather than *the* assistant director. He felt that, while personal relationships between him and the other staffers and between him and Stanley remained good, he was being used mainly as a sounding board. When other managers thought they had problems, they went first to Mast rather than to Stanley. Mast advised action but did not order it because he felt he didn't have the authority.

Mast realized that he could ask Stanley to give him line authority in the department; but at the same time, he felt that asking for this authority would clearly imply to Stanley that Mast was critical of Stanley's own failure to provide direction. Further, Mast felt that he personally had no proven record of administrative effectiveness and no real supervisory experience - though it was his opinion that he had administrative talent and ability. Finally, he recognized that he was among the youngest of the staff, even though he had about the most experience with the company. For these reasons, he hesitated to press the issue.

WELCH

Mast was definitely dissatisfied with the level of work done by the press relations manager. He also viewed the function differently. Welch, Mast knew, saw himself as a "press officer" who answered press inquiries when they were directed to him. Mast, on the other hand, believed that the press relations manager should be more aggressive in initiating placements and "selling" stories to media representatives. In the past year, Mast reflected, he had suggested at least three assignments to Welch, but somehow they had never been carried out. Most of Welch's output consisted of routine stories about promotions and financial items, but his record of direct placements of major stories in major outlets was nil. Stanley himself had acknowledged some dissatisfaction with Welch's work. Yet, when Mast had suggested that Welch needed closer supervision, the director had replied that men at the manager's level were expected to handle their

NOTES

areas without close supervision. Further, Stanley had said, such close supervision was in itself too time-consuming because it cut into the supervisor's own work. Neither Stanley nor Mast had expressed to Welch their dissatisfaction with his work. Stanley, Mast felt, would agree to any strong recommendation Mast might make regarding Welch.

JONZA

Considering Jonza's performance over the past three years, Mast recalled that Jonza had accepted the job at BCI at the same salary he was getting on his old job because he had strongly wanted to get back to New York City. He spent the first two years with BCI getting management acceptance of a full-blown publications program; Mast knew this had been a wearing experience. Constantly irksome also was the fact that Jonza had major contact with a personnel director who was not particularly cooperative and who tended to undervalue Jonza's counsel and work.

Both Stanley and Mast recognized that Jonza's workload was heavy; to assist him the department two years ago had taken on Ronald Pucci as editor and Judy Porter as editorial assistant this year. Both Stanley and Mast had a very high opinion of Pucci's work, and thought he had a great deal of promise.

Both Stanley and Mast knew that Jonza had some major personal problems; a recent ulcer operation, some undefined but rather obvious family troubles, and a financial drain due to the fact that he had on his hands an unsold house at his previous location in Iowa and a new one in the New York City area.

And both recognized his problems in a general sort of way. Stanley had mentioned to Mast that Jonza could not be counted on for creative initiative because he had lost his drive. Mast felt (and Stanley agreed) that Jonza was a very competent writer; his broad experience in employee communications also represented an unusual resource for the department.

Mast was of the opinion that Jonza needed some help to regain the promise of his earlier years, but he wasn't certain how this could be done.

NOTES

Neither Stanley nor Mast had expressed their doubts about Jonza to Jonza personally, and Mast felt that Stanley would agree to any strong recommendation Mast might make regarding Jonza.

Finally, Stanley called Mast to suggest lunch that week at the University Club, to be followed by a long talk in one of the club's private rooms. "It's been five months since we made the change in the department set-up," Stanley said. "I think an all-afternoon session, without interruptions, would be fruitful."

The two set their luncheon date for that coming Friday.

NOTES

Case 13

BASIC CHEMICALS INTERNATIONAL - B*

You are Peter Brent, manager of plant-community relations for Basic Chemicals International, and as noted in the first BCI case material you work in the public relations department of BCI in New York City. Working for you are a part-time writer and secretary. There are plant-community public relations managers at ten of the twelve major locations throughout the country where BCI has either a plant or a research facility. These men report and are directly responsible to the general managers at their plant or research facilities, and they operate under the budget of these facilities.

Your office provides the field public relations managers with advice and counsel, and with print and other public relations "hardware" which generally have a company-wide connection. The public relations managers at the field installations are not obligated to use the material you send them nor to take your advice and counsel, but you have built up a sound rapport with them and generally the material is used and the advice and counsel taken.

Once a year, usually in late June, you sponsor at a suitable location a three-day plant-community relations communications conference to which

---

* *All names, data, and places in this case have been disguised.*

the field people are invited. Attendance in the past has been excellent because the conference programs have generally been of high calibre and the discussions at the conference of real value to the participants. Your budget covers all conference expenses at the conference site, but the participants are expected to cover their travel and routine expenses through their own public relations budgets. This year's conference is scheduled for Arden House, Harriman, N.Y., from June 28-30.

Today is Monday, June 12. You have been away from your office since Wednesday, June 7, attending a national public relations seminar at Wichita State University. Your secretary has arranged on your desk various letters, memoranda, etc., which have accumulated since you left for the conference and you have started to leaf through them.

Memorandum

Thursday, June 8

From: Hubert Stanley

To: Peter Brent

Re: Query from Charles Sturbin

Sturbin, the new man handling public relations at our Syracuse installation, called me this morning. He's gotten a request from the mayor of Syracuse and the Mondale people asking permission to have Senator Mondale address people in our plant there on Wednesday, June 14. As you know, Syracuse is a nominal Republican city, but the mayor is a Democrat. We have no company-wide policy on this sort of thing, but as it's an election year, I'll be working out a policy as soon as I can get to President Dorn to discuss it with him.

NOTES

Meanwhile, I'd prefer that you handle this when you get back to your desk Monday. I told him to check with you some time Monday for guidance. I have no idea what Mike Potts (manager of the Syracuse plant) thinks about this.

By the way, I would appreciate it if our plant PR people would work directly through you rather than call me, especially at this time of the year.

cc: Peter Mast

Memo From Your Secretary

Friday, June 9

As you requested, I checked the status of our various account numbers today with the comptroller's office. We are generally on target at this time in terms of our budget allocations for the year. In fact - and I am taking into consideration our projected expenses for the coming Arden House conference - we should be about $7,000 to the good on our Community Projects account at the end of the six-month's period ending June 30.

NOTES

Memorandum

From: Peter Mast   Friday, June 9

To: Peter Brent

Re: Query from Charles Sturbin

    As you know, Hubert sent me a copy of the memorandum he sent you yesterday regarding the query from Sturbin. As I will be out of the city Monday, I thought I'd pass along my reflections and observations. They may be of some help.

    On the one hand, there's the fact that Senator Mondale is a very hot press personality these days with the Democratic primary in New York coming up on June 20. The national press is covering him like a blanket, so we're sure to be mentioned in connection with any remarks he might make in our Syracuse plant on Wednesday if we give the go-ahead. It never hurts, either, to keep on the good side of the mayor and the Democratic Party.

    On the other hand, President Dorn in the past has been a heavy contributor to Republican campaigns and will probably continue to be so in the upcoming Presidential campaign this Fall. I have always known him to be fair-minded, but I just don't know how he feels about the matter of speeches made at our plants.

    Regarding the last item in Hubert's memo, I'm sure that Hubert would not object if your plant PR people checked with me when they can't get to you. The important thing is to make sure they don't bother Hubert.

    I'm sure you will use your good judgment on Sturbin's request. By all means let me know what your decision was when I get back.

NOTES

Letter

Baxter Drug Divison
Basic Chemicals International
Joplin, Missouri

Thursday, June 8

Mr. Peter Brent
Manager, Plant-Community Relations
Basic Chemicals International
845 Third Avenue
New York, N.Y. 10017

Dear Pete:

In talking with me today one of the top editors of our influential local paper told me he's going to be attending an editors' conference in NYC from June 16-18 and he said he would sure love to be able to see "Cats" on Saturday night, June 18. I told him I'd see what I could do for him. Can you get two tickets for that night? I'm sure it would be much appreciated.

See you at Arden House. Best regards.

Cordially,

  (signed)
Ray Bolger, Manager
Plant-Community Relations

NOTES

Letter

Nutron Textiles, Basic Chemicals International
Metro, Illinois

Wed., June 7

Mr. Peter Brent
Manager, Plant-Community Relations
Basic Chemicals International
845 Third Avenue
New York, N.Y. 10017

Dear Pete:

The local CBS television station has come up with a very interesting proposition which I am relaying to you in the hopes that you may see fit to share some of the costs and benefits involved.

They are proposing that we take over sponsorship of a one-and-a-half hour segment of TV time every Saturday evening (11 p.m. to 1 a.m.) for thirty weeks running time from October through April. The segment would be called the "Nutron Movie of the Week" and for $1500 weekly we would be entitled to opening and closing "Billboards," a maximum of twelve minutes of air time for public relations messages as well as a specified but as yet undetermined number of promotional announcements during the week. Normal charges for the above would usually amount to $1800 a week, but if we sign up for thirty weeks we would get the special rate, the program name, and the use of commercial time for any public relations messages we want to put on the air.

Plant Manager Walter Craig is very interested in the station's proposal because he sees it as a fine public relations vehicle to counteract much of the negative public reaction to problems we have had with pollution, etc. He feels, however, that headquarters public relations should share some of the costs because the program would obviously resound to the credit of BCI as well as to Nutron Textiles. He is willing for us to cover $1200 of the weekly cost but would like your office to cover the remaining weekly expense.

NOTES

I hope the answer will be affirmative. I imagine that you are committed in terms of budget to the usual budget items but I thought it might be possible for you to find a way to cover this new item. It would represent, I should imagine, a trial run here which might well be wise for the corporation to duplicate elsewhere if it proves successful.

Please let me know your reaction at the earliest.

>Cordially,
>(signed)
>Charles Smith, Manager
>Plant-Community Relations

cc: Walter Craig

Letter

>Mason Textile Divison
>Basic Chemicals International
>Greensboro, N. C. 27407

Wed, June 7

Mr. Peter Brent, Manager
Plant-Community Relations
Basic Chemicals International
845 Third Avenue
New York, N.Y. 10017

Dear Pete:

Unless you can figure out a way of shaking me loose, I'm afraid I won't be able to make the Arden House conference.

NOTES

When I casually broached the upcoming conference on Monday to George Madden, divison manager, he blew his stack and said that he had been trying to hold down expenses this year because of our poor earnings picture. He said, and I quote him: "I don't want any of my staff people wasting division money attending fun and games at places like Arden House."

Unless you can do an end-around run by getting to George through someone at headquarters who carries more weight with him than I do, I don't see me attending the conference. I hope you can work something because it looks like a fine program and I'm sure the conference would be very helpful to me.

Cordially,

(signed Tony)

Anthony Ascot, Manager
Public Relations

Telephone Message

From: Sally Olcott, Walnut Plant, Los Angeles

Time: 10 a.m. June 8

Mrs. Olcott called to say that she's terribly sorry but she cannot attend the Arden House Conference because of a lack of funds. She said that through error of the account department she had been advised she still had $1500 in her conference budget account, but she was told yesterday that she has already overspent the budget. If you can cover her expenses, she'll be glad to attend because she says she finds the conference very helpful and a great way of exchanging ideas with other plant-community managers at BCI.

NOTES

Letter

Red Lion Division
Basic Chemicals International
Newark, N.J. 07111

Friday, June 9

From: David Story

To: Peter Brent

Re: Upcoming Boycott

I recall when I took over this job as manager of public relations for the Red Lion Beverages Division of BCI, you told me that you would always be available for consultation and that I would have a relatively free hand so long as things seemed to be moving smoothly.

You have been as good as your word, and I should hope that matters have worked out smoothly. I haven't had to bother you with my problems, but a really tough one has arisen and I would certainly appreciate some advice.

First, a brief summary of pertinent details. We're the largest producer, distributor and seller of soft drinks here in Newark, and sales in the city comprise about 30 percent of our total sales. Blacks, as you know, are in the majority in Newark, and it is estimated that about 60 percent of our sales are to blacks.

About three months ago a group of twelve black leaders representing the Newark Black Alliance met with Raul Walsh, our general manager, to discuss our employment policies. Stating that they represent the total black population of Newark, the leaders very politely told Walsh that they hoped Red Lion would take positive steps to increase the number of qualified blacks in responsible positions in the organization.

NOTES

That meeting and two others that followed ended cordially enough, but at the last one the visitors requested, and Walsh agreed to, another meeting in three weeks. That meeting took place yesterday and Walsh told me the details about it today. Rather upset, he told me that the black leaders this time specifically requested that Red Lion take steps in the next three weeks to hire twenty office workers (we have a total office work force of 200 with one black among them) and to upgrade into supervisory positions within six months a number, not specified, of the bottling plant work force. (There are no blacks in supervisory positions in the plant).

Walsh told me he reminded the black leaders that we operate in a free enterprise economy, but in reply they said that there hadn't been much freedom for blacks in an economy and work situation such as exists at Red Lion. They said, according to Walsh, that unless the situation changed according to their request, they would call a city-wide black boycott of all Red Lion products commencing July 1, and would maintain the boycott until the company changed its employment policies. About 40 percent of our yearly sales occur between July 1 and September 30.

Walsh is well aware of the fact that within the last year the Newark Black Alliance has made similar demands on three other Newark organizations which deal in consumer products. In one case, I understand, the company acceded to the demands within the scheduled time, but in the other two the Alliance called into being boycotts which lasted two months in one instance and three months in the other.

After informing me today about the meetings he's held with the Alliance, Walsh said the final decision is his but he would like my advice and counsel. I am meeting with him again at 4 p.m. Wednesday, June 14, and I would certainly welcome any advice you can give me.

Sincerely,
 (signed)
David Story, Manager
Public Relations

NOTES

Night Letter

CHI 195 BU NMA 22LNPD. CEDAR RAPIDS, IOWA JUNE 11
PETER BRENT BASIC CHEMICALS INT, THIRD AVE, NYC

LOCAL SUNDAY PAPER HAS A WIRE SERVICE STORY OUT OF WASHINGTON CITING INFORMED SOURCES WHICH, IF TRUE, CAN HAVE DIRE CONSEQUENCES FOR OUR CEDAR RAPIDS PLANT HERE. STORY SAYS IT HAS BEEN LEARNED THAT WILLIAM D RUCKELSHAUS, ADMINISTRATOR OF THE ENVIRONMENTAL PROTECTION AGENCY, IS EXPECTED TO ISSUE AN ORDER WEDNESDAY, JUNE 14, BANNING ALMOST ALL USES OF DDT. THIS WOULD BE THE CULMINATION OF ALMOST THREE YEARS OF ADMINISTRATIVE AND LEGAL PROCEEDINGS, SCIENTIFIC REPORTS, AND PUBLIC HEARINGS. CRUX OF THE EXPECTED DECISION, SAYS THE STORY, WILL BE A 40-PAGE STATEMENT IN WHICH RUCKELSHAUS WILL DECLARE THAT THE CONTINUED USE OF DDT IS AN UNACCEPTABLE RISK TO THE ENVIRONMENT AND MOST LIKELY DETRIMENTAL TO THE HEALTH OF MAN. STORY SAYS THAT THE ORDER WILL BE EFFECTIVE DECEMBER 31, AND THAT IT REPRESENTS A DEFEAT FOR THE MAKERS AND FORMULATORS OF DDT AND FOR THE DEPARTMENT OF AGRICULTURE. IF THE REPORT IS TRUE THIS COULD BE A DISASTER FOR OUR PLANT BECAUSE AS YOU KNOW WE ARE ONE OF THE MAJOR FORMULATORS OF DDT AND IT'S OUR MAJOR PRODUCT AT THE PLANT.

I'M SURE THE LOCAL PAPER WILL WANT TO BE FOLLOWING UP THE WIRE STORY AND WILL BE TRYING TO CONTACT US AT THE PLANT TOMORROW (MONDAY) FOR A STATEMENT REGARDING THE EFFECTS ON US OF THE DDT BAN IF THE EPA ORDER IS ISSUED WEDNESDAY. FORTUNATELY, THE PLANT CLOSED DOWN FRIDAY FOR OUR ANNUAL TWO WEEK

NOTES

VACATION. THIS MEANS, OF COURSE, THAT THE PAPER WILL NOT BE ABLE TO REACH ME AT THE PLANT. HOWEVER, IT ALSO MEANS THAT I CAN'T REACH LARRY RUTH, PLANT MANAGER TO WHOM I REPORT, BECAUSE HE HAS TAKEN OFF FOR THE UPPER MICHIGAN REGION AND LEFT NO FORWARDING ADDRESS OR TELEPHONE.

CAN YOU CHECK OUT WHETHER THE WIRE STORY HAS VALIDITY AND IF THE ORDER WILL BE MADE AS THE STORY HAS REPORTED? SECOND, IF THERE IS TO BE A BAN ON DDT DOES BCI HAVE ANY PLANS FOR OUR PLANT? THIRD, WHAT, IF ANYTHING, SHOULD I SAY TO THE MEDIA? I CAN USE ALL THE HELP YOU CAN GIVE ME, BUT DO NOT CALL ME AT HOME BECAUSE I WILL NOT BE ANSWERING THE PHONE. I WILL CALL YOU 4 PM YOUR TIME MONDAY. HOPE YOU HAVE SOME ANSWERS FOR ME.

LOREN STACY

NOTES

An Excerpt For Discussion

Some Considerations In Dealing With Public Opinion*
by Earl Newsom

I should like to assume at the outset that we are agreed on three general considerations:

First, I assume we agree that all over the world "sovereign power" seems to have passed from small groups of people to the great masses, and that, as a result, any institution which expects to prosper in the social and economic climate of today must have the confidence of large numbers of sovereign people.

Second, I assume we agree this requires that most difficult of all types of objectivity - objectivity toward ourselves. The only way we can hope to learn to deal intelligently with public opinion is to try as honestly as we can to understand human nature and why we behave as we do - as individuals and as members of groups and crowds. We must face ourselves squarely and honestly.

Third, I assume that each of us approaches this problem with a strong sense of personal obligation to strengthen and develop the processes of democracy and the conception of human dignity and individual freedom upon which our democracy rests. I assume that ours is the worthy and fruitful search for rules and techniques which will enable large groups of people in an increasingly complicated free society to deal with one another effectively on the basis of understanding.

The most prevalent and perhaps the least questioned hypothesis in the whole field of human relations is the one that says we can "educate the people" by giving them "the facts in the situation."

---

*From a lecture given at the New School for Social Research, New York City, April 12, 1950. Reprinted with permission of the author, the founder and head of the counseling firm of Earl Newsom & Company.

We hear this hypothesis variously stated. Some say, "You can overcome public apathy, misunderstanding, and prejudice by publishing the facts." Others - more cynical - say, "People will believe anything if you tell your story often enough." Most of us at one time or another assume that it is we and we alone who know "the facts" on any controversial issue and that all we need to do to make a better world is to "give the people the facts" as we see them. Thereafter, we assume, "the people" will agree with us and have confidence in us...

A Closer Look at the "Education" Hypothesis

When we start to look into the validity of the hypothesis that our objective is to educate the public by giving them the facts, we see immediately that several concepts have been merged into a single concept.

First, there is the concept that an informed opinion is essential to democracy. With that general statement not one of us, I am sure, would disagree. But there is a catch in that word "informed." What does it mean? Of course, it is impossible for anybody to be completely informed about everything - or even about anything.

Consider the average man...If there is an average man in the audience, I need not remind you how preoccupied you are with everyday problems and frustrations and hopes and ambitions. These personal matters take up most of your waking hours - and many of the hours when you should be sleeping. The time or inclination you have to spend on keeping informed on all of the thousands of things that thousands of people would like to see you informed about is very small indeed.

People will never be "informed" in that sense - and we break our heads against a wall if we are foolish enough to attempt it.

What are "The Facts?"

Let us consider another concept - what is meant by "the facts in the situation." Do we mean statistics, or interpretation of statistics? Do we mean

---

NOTES

a line of reasoning? Do we mean an idea? Do we mean our own view as to cause and effect? Do we mean a projection of our own fears as to what might - but not necessarily will - happen as a result of a set of circumstances as we may happen to view them?

Actually, we are not talking about "the facts" at all. We are talking about conclusions, at which we have arrived as a result of a great many influences to which we have been subjected and about which we may be only partly aware. These conclusions are opinions, and people instinctively recognize them as opinions.

And what are we going to do with that word "educate," another separate concept that has somehow got involved in our hypothesis?

Our belief that an informed public opinion is essential to a successful democracy depends for its fulfillment largely upon the notion of formal education available to everybody. That is the reason for our public schools...

You and I as Americans have faith in human liberty, and since one of the cornerstones on which it rests is freedom of education, we demand that there be no muddying of the definition of that phrase. Freedom of education is unfettered search for the truth. It involves the constant exposure of the human mind to all ideas - not only the ideas about which you and I might be excited at any given moment.

So when we use the word "educate" in discussing problems of public opinion, I think we are not talking about "education" at all, in the sense of an unfettered search for truth. What we really have in mind is probably something like this:

The Meaning of "Educate"

We have a point of view about what is going on in the world in which we live. That point of view depends, in part, upon whether we are a Republican, a Democrat, a union leader, an officer of an industrial corporation, a government official, a schoolteacher, a farmer, a Catholic, a Jew, a Protestant, or a Negro.

NOTES

It depends upon how much money we have, the amount and kind of formal education we have had, our ambitions, our conception of our own importance, our manner of life, the prestige of our job, our personality traits, our opportunities - and countless other influences (in an infinite and unpredictable variety of combinations) that affect our behavior.

Whatever that point of view is, it is very precious and important to us. It is shared by "our kind" of people.

We are confident that we and "our kind" of people have the right point of view. All others have the wrong one. If only everybody could see things as we see them, everything would be fine! There would be no more strikes, no more wars, no more crises.

But what people see is not detached and pure truth but advocacy of a viewpoint. We are one advocate among many.

The Value of a Free Press

At this point it is clear that we are wrong when we think and say it is the duty of the press to help us. We are not here concerned with a passionate search for truth but with passionate advocacy of a viewpoint which is for some reason very dear and important to us. When we do things, we can legitimately help by reporting to the press as best we can; but whether it is news, how important news it is, and its significance as news is the job for the editor. When we think we can, or ought to try to, persuade the press to slant its coverage of the news to fit more nearly our point of view, we are selling part of our heritage - our precious freedom to seek truth - for a very small mess of pottage indeed. The duty of a free press is to report what happens as objective reporters are able to see it - to comment on the significance of the news in terms considered significant by editors who wear no man's collar.

On the other hand, any good American is entirely free to get on a soap box and say what is on his mind. If he has the money, he can buy an advertisement and say what he wants and sign his name. If he has lots of money, he can buy lots of advertisements; he can buy time on the radio; he

NOTES

can write letters and broadcast them through the mail until his money runs out. He can print booklets and pamphlets. He can have movies made, and if they are interesting, thousands of civic and social groups all over the land will look at them even though they may be slanted to his own special point of view.

Is not this, then, what we have in mind when we talk about "educating public opinion by getting the facts of the situation to the people?" Don't we really mean the use of modern mass communication to "sell" our ideas to large groups of people - to get the people to change their minds and agree with our opinions?

In this state of mind, we cast about for ways of expressing ourselves and of making what we say effective. We may be the head of a corporation, or a labor union, or a university, or a civic enterprise, or a political party. We are the leader of a group, the group has problems, and the group point of view insists upon being heard. We feel obliged, somehow, to deal with public opinion.

We remember how government and industry - with the help of publishers and the advertising profession - banded together during wartime and "sold" the American public on buying War Bonds, on saving scrap, on conserving gasoline and rubber and electricity. In the memory of the success of those "educational" campaigns, we get together with those who share our point of view and our sense of responsibility. We decide to set up an association of many businesses, many labor unions, or many colleges - and pool resources to pay for what we decide to call an "educational" campaign, using all types of mass communications to "give the people the facts" as we see them, to "sell" our convictions, our opinions, to the American people.

How often it fails to work! How often we fail to do what we set out to do! Editorials and public opinion polls may even indicate to us that our program caused us to lose the confidence and friendliness of the majority of people.

Well, what can we do - properly, practically, and with any hope of success? In all of this confusion, are there no rules, no general principles

NOTES

we can follow? Is there nothing whatever to rely upon? Is it all just a matter of flying by the seat of our pants through the strong winds of conflicting opinions?

It is not as bad as that. With the help of the rapidly increasing number of students of public opinion, light is being thrown on the scene. There are signposts to guide us.

There Is a Need for Opinions

And there is a market for ideas, for opinions, for points of view - even as there is always a market for products. The needs of people are served as certainly by ideas as they are by the goods they consume. People thirst for them. Man is not solely an economic being - not simply a consumer. He is something more than a biological machine for using up the material things of life. People will "buy" ideas.

What, then, is this market? Is it a wide-open one in which people will buy anything - depending on which barker talks the loudest?

If that were so - if it were true that the opinions of others could be made to conform to our own by the sheer weight of our propaganda - then the group in our economy with the most money to spend would have pretty much its own way in our democracy.

Fortunately, that is not true. In fact, the people quite often follow the leadership of those who have little money to spend in advertising and publicizing and promoting their ideas and opinions.

What kind of ideas are people, then, ready to adopt - to "buy" - and under what conditions? For what sort of opinions, what sort of points of view about what, do people seem always to be shopping - consciously or unconsciously?

Curiously, the sponsor of an idea, or a point of view, or an opinion, tends to get so absorbed in his notion that he never asks this first simple question about it: "Does it clearly help toward the solution of a problem which worries those I am addressing?" In fact, we often condemn people to

NOTES

whom we would like to sell a point of view when, having no personal need for what we have to sell, they turn their backs on us.

Here, then, is our first signpost:

The Identification Principle

People will ignore an idea, an opinion, a point of view unless they see clearly that it affects their personal fears or desires, hopes or aspirations.

This we may call the "Identification Principle."

The longer we look at this first signpost - *the principle that people will interest themselves only in those matters which consciously or subconsciously touch the sensitive nerve of their fears and desires, their hopes and ambitions* - the more familiar it becomes. The strange fact is that we so reluctantly apply this test in the market place for ideas. We are continually trying to sell gramophone ideas in a television market...

And the personal interests of people are in the things of today and tomorrow - not yesterday. Their desires and fears, their hopes and ambitions are for the present and future - not the past. They ignore opinion about past accomplishments of free enterprise, for example - or any other economic theory - except when they clearly see such ideas in terms of solving their present and pressing problems or reducing their fears of what might happen to them in the foreseeable future.

First of all, then, *it seems to be true that the size of the audience for your idea will be limited to those who feel - or can be made to feel - that they have a personal stake in it.* If your idea has to do with race discrimination or dust bowls or free enterprise, the chances are that you will catch the attention of those who are immediately involved - or who come to feel they are involved by what you are doing or saying about race discrimination or dust bowls or free enterprise.

And that brings us to a second signpost:

NOTES

The Action Principle

People do not buy ideas separate from action - either action taken or about to be taken by the sponsor of the idea, or action which people themselves can conveniently take to prove the merit of the idea.

This may be briefly termed the "Action Principle."

As in the case of any product we are asked to buy, we want evidence that it is more than a blueprint. Most people aren't interested in abstract notions. Their application to personal problems, their work-ability, is too remote to be easily grasped. People want action. They like action. Action is news; it is interesting. Carrying out an idea, putting it to work, showing that it is workable, is action.

When we are asked to "buy" an idea that seems to us divorced from any action going on to make it workable in the solution of our problems, we tend to label it as somebody's propaganda. "Somebody" is ganging up on us to sell us a bill of goods. We resist.

Most of all, we scoff at sponsors of an idea who seem to us not to be using it themselves. It is still true that leaders must practice what they preach.

And yet, how often have we heard noble sentiments from people who, while they undoubtedly believe in the truth they proclaim, do not apply it to their own actions and policies? There is a touch of sanctity about our ideas and opinions. We think of them as related to eternal principles - something set apart from everyday life.

But people do not buy ideas set apart from their everyday life. Successful information campaigns - programs often involving news, advertising, movies, radio and direct-mail - are really reports of action taken to carry out an idea that may affect importantly some of our important personal interests. If the idea touches the interests of many people, the action taken to advance it is news...

And that brings us to a third signpost:

NOTES

The Principle of Familiarity and Trust

We the people buy ideas only *from those we trust*; we are influenced by, or adopt, only those opinions or points of view put forward by individuals or corporations or institutions *in whom we have confidence.*

This can be stated as the "Principle of Familiarity and Trust."

We suspect ideas from alien or unfamiliar sources. While we do not always see what is wrong with the opinion or point of view, we have a feeling that there is a catch in it somewhere - that we are being fooled.

If we are wise we will not be critical of this human tendency to regard only the opinions of those whom we trust - and to make those opinions and points of view our own. How else are we going to get along in a very complicated world? It is impossible for us to know everything about all of the things on which we are supposed to pass judgment in a democracy. We must take our cue from those whose judgment we respect.

And the fact is that most of us do have opinions about everything we are supposed to have opinions about - however much or little we may know about them.

We adopt these emotional attitudes as the result of a great many influences, but one of the strongest among them is the opinion of those in whose judgment we have confidence. It may be the expressed opinion of our favorite newspaper or radio commenator, or of a leader of our political party, or a respected teacher, or our doctor, or our minister, or a trusted friend. Or it may be a compromise decision we arrived at ourselves after listening to discussion among several people whose opinions we trust.

This tendency to give our attention to those we trust is one of the shortcuts to intelligent living without which we would fall into complete confusion.

It is, of course, a complete misconception of the idea of democracy to think of it as a giant communal society in which every member casts his vote on every decision made everywhere. We leave decisions on details to those to whom we directly or indirectly delegate those powers - to the leaders who rise up to serve our needs.

NOTES

The essential quality of democracy is our freedom to cast aside leaders in whom we are dissatisfied or in whom we have lost confidence - leaders in government, in business, education, medicine, entertainment, philanthropy, and every other aspect of modern life. For we are constantly expressing our approval or disapproval. Our every act is the voicing of a preference. We "vote" when we pick our grocery store, our gas station, our doctor, our college, the movie we go to, the radio program to which we listen, the charities to which we send our checks.

It is possible, for example, that there would have been no labor unions if management had itself attacked the social and economic problems created for employees by a mass-production economy. In fact, there is no better example of how people will eventually create institutions and develop leadership to meet their problems when they are not recognized by existing institutions and leadership. And today, wage-rate employees will, in general, attend to the opinions of their union leaders and distrust the opinions of management when there is conflict between the two. They respect the points of view, the opinions, the ideas of those they trust, those who in their opinion will work for their benefit.

As we examine this third signpost - the signpost which warns us that the audience we reach and influence with our opinions can never be much larger than the number of people who have confidence in us - we see more clearly that the first goal of any large industrial company in dealing with public opinion today must be to gain the confidence of large numbers of people so that it can be heard...

In closing, I would like to stress not the signposts which we have examined here together, but the great need to seek out and find the principles which we need if we are to deal intelligently with the problem of communication and mutual understanding in a great free society. The field in which we work is new and largely unexplored. The best work has been done by philosophers, psychologists, psychiatrists, and social scientists. But the most significant work in the years ahead should be done by those who see in the field we now call "public relations" a challenge to test and try in a spirit of relentless honesty...

NOTES

Case 14

EMPIRE ENTERPRISES*

A little more than a year after the events described in *Basic Chemicals-B**, Peter Mast was offered and accepted a position as vice president of media relations at Empire Enterprises, a large conglomerate headquartered in St. Louis, Missouri. At the suggestion of Charles Scully, his superior at Empire, Mast prepared and mailed out to the public relations and advertising trade press and to the heads of public relations at the 62 companies that comprised the Empire family of firms a release announcing his new job and describing his prior experience in public relations.

The corporation which Mast joined had started out 80 years ago as a small oil company. It began to branch out in the early sixties and by 1986 it had become one of the nation's largest corporations. As a result, in 1985 total revenues of Empire Enterprises amounted to $14.5 billion; total employment reached 180,000; and the number of wholly owned firms operating under the Empire banner reached a record 62.

In apprising Mast of these facts a few weeks after Mast joined the firm Scully, senior vice president of public relations at Empire, expressed a concern felt by him and the board of directors at Empire.

"Our acquisitions, mergers, and buyouts," Scully said, "have made us one of the largest corporations in the world, but our surveys of public opinion show that most Americans know virtually nothing about us. Obviously we have a public relations problem." Scully directed Mast's attention to a chart he took from a folder on his desk. It was headed "Empire Enterprises Public Relations Staff."

"You'll note that we have a total of 15 professionals on the corporate public relations staff here at headquarters," said Scully, and he then pointed

---

* *All names, dates, and places in this case have been disguised.*

to the bottom half of the chart, "but if you look down here you will see that there are more than 94 other public relations professionals working in the total corporate structure of Empire Enterprises. Every time we've absorbed another company we've absorbed the staff who work for that company. This past year, for example, when we bought Ocra Foods we absorbed Ocra's 15-member public relations staff, and when we merged Shore Ship Containers into Empire their four-member public relations staff joined us.

"Many years ago we made a conscious decision to maintain a lean public relations staff here at corporate headquarters. We're responsible for the public relations activities of the total corporation on a national level and for the advice and counsel we provide top management here in St. Louis. The other 94 professionals are responsible for public relations activities and counseling within their own firms. They operate under the budgets of these firms and report to the management of these firms.

"This arrangement worked well when Empire was not as large as it is today, but we recognize that one of its major defects is an identification failure."

"You mean, non-identification with Empire?" Mast cut in.

"Exactly. There are other faults, such as a wide disparity of quality among the 94 professionals out there, but our board of directors is mainly concerned about the fact that the Ocras and the Containers in our corporate family fail to identify with Empire Enterprises, and this is where you come in."

"Just what do you have in mind?" Mast asked.

"Well, I'm not sure myself," said Scully. "At the last quarterly board meeting one of the board members said we ought to do something to identify all companies and divisions within Empire Enterprises as being members of the Empire family. No formal vote was taken on this idea, but the chairman of the board said he would discuss the matter with me, and he subsequently did last week. He said it was clear from discussion at the meeting that the board is in favor of having all entities within Empire identify publicly with Empire Enterprises, in their advertising, their publications, and their releases to the media. The chairman did not specify

NOTES

how we should bring this about, but he did say that he expects a progress report from me by the next board meeting, which is two months from today."

Mast nodded that he understood, but said nothing.

"I've decided we must start somewhere," Scully continued. "We have only two months leeway and that doesn't give us enough lead time to do anything substantive about advertising and publications. I've therefore decided that we ought to start with media releases and media conferences, and of course that's your area of responsibility. You can handle this anyway you want to, but I expect to have a report from you six weeks from now. Okay?"

"That doesn't leave me much time," Mast said, "but of course I'll get right on it."

In the next few days Mast reflected on his options, and he concluded he didn't have many. In the month since he had assumed his new position he had spent most of his time reading through files, getting to know people at corporate headquarters, and in general sizing up the nature of his job and role in the organization. He had visited with the head of public relations at Chicago Products when he was in Chicago on a trip to introduce himself to key media people in that city, but this was the only personal contact he had had with public relations people in the Empire family. Mast knew that he could arrang to take a trip around the country to meet with some of the public relations professionals in the 62 firms that made up Empire Enterprises, but he felt he didn't have nor could spare the time for personal visits. Mast concluded therefore that his only option was to draft and send out a letter to the head public relations person of each of the 62 firms. His letter, which was mailed one week after his meeting with Scully, read as follows:

NOTES

Empire Enterprises
1114 Mathews Avenue
St. Louis Missouri 63101

Office of Vice President
  of Media Relations   (date)

To: Executive Head, Public Relations
     All Subsidiaries

When I notified you via a press release announcing my appointment as vice president of media relations I intended to follow it up as quickly as possible with a personal visit. Recognizing that there are 62 public relations departments among the firms that comprise the Empire Enterprises family, I realized that commitment would take some time to fulfill but I hoped to achieve it within a reasonable time period.

Unfortunately, a matter of serious import to all of us has developed which requires immediate action and I am therefore forced to use this impersonal communication to deal with it.

Recent public opinion surveys have shown that most Americans have little knowledge of Empire Enterprises, despite the fact that we are one of the world's largest corporations. At the last meeting of our board of directors concern was expressed that many of the firms within Empire's family fail to identify with the parent corporation. We at corporate public relations were subsequently directed to ensure that all entities within the Empire family identify publicly with Empire in their releases to the media.

NOTES

As a start in seeking to reach this objective, I am writing to direct that all releases from your office sent to major and especially national media incorporate appropriate phraseology identifying your firm with Empire Enterprises. In most instances this can be achieved by means of a phrase such as "a wholly owned subsidiary of Empire Enterprises" or "a division of Empire Enterprises of St. Louis, Missouri" or "a member of the Empire Enterprises family of firms."

I expect we can see immediate implementation of this directive, and of course feel free to call me if you have any questions relative to it. I appreciate your cooperation.

>Sincerely,
>(signed)
>Peter Mast, Vice President
>of Media Relations

Mast considered sending a copy of the letter to Scully and also noting at the bottom of the letter that such a copy was being sent to Scully, but after some deliberation he decided not to do either.

For the next four weeks Mast carefully scanned as many major and national publications as he could get his hands on. These included the *Los Angeles Times*; *New York Times*; *Chicago Tribune*; the Dallas, Fort Worth, and Houston newspapers; *Boston Globe*; *Washington Post*; *Wall Street Journal*; *USA TODAY*; *US News and World Report*; *Time*; and *Newsweek*.

A total of 46 stories relating to firms in the Empire family appeared in the publications scanned by Mast. These stories ranged from small (two inches deep) to large (one or several columns) ones. Five stories carried a phrase which identified the firm as being a part of Empire Enterprises, and of these five three related to one firm.

As he absorbed this information Mast glanced at his calendar and realized his report to Scully was due in one week.

NOTES

An Excerpt for Discussion

An Interview With George Hammond*

Q: Now let me ask you something - going back a little. Where did Byoir staff people come from - mostly newspapermen?

H: We never hired anybody without some form of journalistic experience. As you can imagine, we are not exactly popular because we generally believe that while you can study public relations, as such, the work is essentially communications, and it is so much more likely that your communications are going to be clear and effective and acceptable if you have that experience on a press association or under a good city editor. It hurts to have to say this to a graduate of a public relations course, but it becomes easier when you explain to him what his problem is. Suppose he comes to us without that experience and we make an exception? Even though he understands the theory of public relations probably better than someone else, he loses when the opportunity for advancement opens up because it almost invariably goes to the person who is producing, and that requires facility in newswriting plus the objectivity that you get from journalism that you don't get from any other field...

The whole business is communication, and the ability to write clearly and persuasively and quickly is something that you learn in journalism and you don't learn anywhere else. Novelists have all day to write the chapter, and they fuss over it. Of course, there have been some great journalists who do that, but as a generality the kudos go to the journalist who can write

---

* George Hammond, a former president and chairman of Carl Byoir & Associates, was interviewed by L.L.L. Golden in 1975 in one of the oral history interviews sponsored by the Foundation for Public Relations Research and Education. This excerpt is from a transcript of the tape made by Professor Hunter P. McCartney in 1985 under a grant provided by the Foundation. Reprinted with permission.

under pressure, can write it once and have it come out just exactly the way he wants it to come out, so that people can understand it.

If you sit down with the chairman of the board, and he's got a serious problem with a director or some customer or agency, he may need help with a letter, or he may need help with a presentation that he's going to make. The fact that you have that particular talent is of great value. It has been to us time and time again.

Q: Later on I want to talk to you about the future of the business, but we must discuss whether or not in the future the communication function will remain the main function and the policy function will go to the lawyers... When it comes to policy and the taking of positions - they ask their Washington lawyers. Now it doesn't mean nobody asks you and your competitors, but whether there is or is not that trend - do you want to deal with it now or later?

H: I think we should while it's on your mind. I would take exception to what you describe as the reliance upon the Washington lawyers being a trend - even strongly enough to be a trend. I don't see it happening more than once or twice in cases that become quite well known and somewhat dramatized. But for every case of that kind, you can find 100 companies where the complaint is that the company pays not nearly enough attention to the experience and judgment of its non-legal Washington people. Now this is the trend, as I have observed it, and I don't notice that the lawyers are dependent upon that kind of activity that you would call counsel. Their trade is in case work, testimony, and litigation.

I would say that the best counsel that the company leaders get they are getting right this minute from their public relations people. And they are getting it usually in the very simple act of the public relations man explaining to them what's likely to happen if they do what they sound as if they want to do. I know this is a great over-simplification, but to serve in this way is the greatest contribution we can make.

NOTES

Q: Are you hinging everything on the press reaction?

H: No, on the public opinion reaction. I do not forget that this country is a republic, and it is run by the opinion of the voters who decide what's going to happen. So I am not in any sense embarrassed when people start to talk to me with some critical note that I seem to be over-stating the case for publicity. That's all there is, really. It reflects on how our citizens learn about the things on which they base their opinions. Some books, yes, and personal experience, too - but on issues and controversies they absorb what someone, for his own interest, puts forward in some news framework...

Byoir used to say, "I'll make it simple for you. Let's talk. Now, do you want to talk about your baby or do you want to talk about my baby? And if you want to talk about your baby, I'll wait until you take a deep breath and then I'll tell you about my baby." So his thrust, and he drove it into us for 25 years, is "Forget the company's point of view. That isn't going to get you anywhere. What does the company do that people out there are interested in and that benefits them? If you can't show that what your client is doing is in the people's interest, then don't waste your time and effort."

That is the under pinning of the public relations business as Carl taught it to us: You have to work very hard to find out what it is about your business that somebody else feels good about and strongly enough about to help you to defend yourself. If you can't do that, then you have a very uphill fight, and the fact that you may have some good lobbyists works for awhile. But that just isn't the way ultimately the issues will be disposed of. And that's the reason why an awful lot of things that industry doesn't like have been put off and put off, and yet ultimately they get legislated, and industry is very unhappy about it...

Q: Let me ask you, George, how do you educate a businessman in the public relations function if he doesn't understand it. How do you get businessmen to understand the function of public relations?...Is it because they don't like the two words? Is it because of the low opinion that

NOTES

academics have of public relations men? Is it because academics don't understand the function and therefore they think a dirty trick is a public relations thing?

H: Perhaps we haven't touched on one thing that is always involved in this discussion: the omnipresent fear of thought control. And here is one of the great paradoxes of our lives. When any one of us who is passionate about these things (as I am and you are) begins to explain to people how you go out and you <u>create</u> public opinion, resistance builds up and the cry is "manipulation."

This is where they misunderstood Eddie Bernays. A lot of my friends are terribly mad at Eddie for having used the phrase "the engineering of consent," but that's what 98 percent of all public relations people are doing every day if they're any good at it.

What I'm talking about is the paradox that hundreds of thousands of psychologists, philosophy majors, and language majors in colleges all over the United States are working day and night to improve the communications process. They have fascinating models of how people communicate with each other, and if you read the *Public Opinion Quarterly* you will find learned pieces about how you tell a story so that it can more likely be absorbed this way than that way. This goes on and on and on, yet nobody is supposed to use this learning because if you used it intentionally then you would be "manipulating," you see.

So this is a funny situation. On the one hand we are all spending thousands of dollars to learn how to do this, and then if anybody admitted that he did it with a deliberate intent and with scientific knowledge of predictable success, this undertaking would be regarded as reprehensible. So what do you do?

NOTES

Case 15

BRUCE CANFIELD IS GIVEN THE WORD - A*

While working in his office one Friday the writer of this case had an unexpected visit from Bruce Canfield who was on a three-week vacation with his family and had stopped by for a brief chat. While bringing the case writer up to date on his professional career in public relations, Canfield told the case writer he was still working in Detroit and very happy in his work.

The case writer recalled that Canfield was thirty years old and upon graduation from college had joined the New York City public relations staff of the Tremount Corporation. Tremount, the case writer knew, had its corporate headquarters in Detroit and, in terms of corporate size, ranked 24th on the Fortune 500 list. The case writer was intrigued by Canfield's story of his public relations job experiences and he asked Canfield if he would mind recalling it on tape. When Canfield agreed to do so, the case writer set up a tape recorder and then later transcribed Canfield's remarks. They are reproduced below.

You may not remember this, but thanks to you I got that first job in New York City because you put me in touch with Tom Markson who had also graduated from our college with a public relations degree and who was in charge of the New York office of Tremount. It was a lucky break for me because Markson had an opening on his staff - there were four professionals on the staff at that time - and he was willing to take a chance on me because you recommended me. Of course, I had to make a trip to corporate headquarters in Detroit, but they went along with Markson's recommendation and I was hired at $16,000. Not being married at the time, I figured I could make out on that salary and of course I knew I was

---

* *Dates, places, and names in this case are disguised.*

fortunate enough to get started in a position which would bring me into contact with the top media people in the country.

The job was great because it was right where the action was and because Markson proved to be a real friend rather than just a boss. Although, as you well know, I'm not the most polished writer in the world, I was also fortunate because I wasn't supposed to do much writing but instead was expected to work with media people making publicity contacts and placements. I was really good at that sort of thing. The company must have been satisfied because they kept raising my salary and within three years I was making $22,000. In the meantime I began going steady with this girl from Tarrytown who had a job in a hospital as a lab technician. We got married and moved into a rent-controlled apartment in Bronxville.

As I said, I was doing fine on the job in New York, but I wasn't surprised when I was told the company was going to shift me to the headquarters public relations staff in Detroit because this was fairly standard operating procedure for them. My wife and I enjoyed New York and all that, but we weren't unhappy when the move came and I was transferred. They made me public relations manager of one of the company's product groups, gave me a $3,000 raise, and of course covered all our moving expenses. Within the next three years I became manager of stockholder relations, my salary went up to $30,000, and I bought a new house for $70,000 in the country where there was plenty of fresh air and room for our little Jonathan.

That stockholder relations job was not very exciting, but it was all part of the learning experience even though there were moments when I felt I was under-utilized. I imagine I felt this way because there were twenty-five professionals on the corporate public relations staff and we probably had more people in public relations than we really needed. In a way, that was a fortunate thing because just about that time the economy went into a tailspin and so did the company's sales and stock. There were layoffs throughout the entire company, and of course that included public relations.

One day the vice president of public relations called a meeting of the entire staff and told us that anywhere from 20 percent to 30 percent of the

NOTES

staff would be cut. He said they would be evaluating everyone's performance and looking for ways to cut costs because we were top-heavy with people. Sure enough, some staffers were transferred to other positions, some were simply let go, and some given early retirement. When I looked around one day I figured out that, with the exception of three of us, the entire staff consisted of veterans with years of experience and special expertise, and I got very nervous.

In a way, I guess it was some consolation to know that the company considered us good enough to keep us on board. The other two were a very talented black fellow who was going to law school and a very bright, terrific writer, a woman. The three of us - all the same age - were the only young people left. They had let others go who had a lot more experience than we had, and we used to get together for lunch every once in a while to figure out what was going to happen to us. The Equal Opportunity Commission was putting lots of pressure on the company, on all companies of course, and I said to the other two: "I look around this table and see a black guy and a woman and I'm blond-haired and blue-eyed, and I know who's going where." We all laughed; we were very close friends, but none of us really knew what was going to happen.

Well, one day Charlie Perry, the manager of corporate relations and my boss, told me they had cut all the people they wanted to cut and that I shouldn't worry because there was really nothing to worry about. However, I knew that my job was a premier job and what with all the consolidation of duties I figured they might want to get a writer on the job who could write annual reports and that sort of thing and who could also work with security analysts. I was not especially skilled at that sort of thing, and I recognized that there were guys around who were just more talented than I was in that direction. So, it didn't come as much of a surprise to me when Perry suggested we go out to dinner so we could have a little talk. What I mean is, the idea of having "a little talk" didn't come as a surprise, but the dinner did because up to this time we had gone out to lunch occasionally but never to dinner. This is going to be it, I thought, and I wasn't wrong.

NOTES

Perry said the company had been under a good deal of pressure on two fronts: in the financial community and in media relations.

"You've done a good job in stockholder relations," he said, "but you're especially strong in media relations and as it so happens that's where we can best use you. We've got other people, as you know, who have had stronger backgrounds in finance than you do, but you are a standout on media, and particularly electronic media centered in New York. What we'd like you to do is to go to New York and run the office there because we really haven't had top performance at that end ever since we brought Tom Markson here to Detroit a few years ago. We'd also want you to work closely with Jeff Peters, manager of the whole northeast region of the company and considered one of our top management people."

"What about Paul Thiel?" I asked, referring to the man who then headed the New York public relations operation.

"We want to bring him here to Detroit," Perry said, and I saw by this that Perry had his game plan all set up. It's like a game of dominoes where one goes here, another there, and every move has to fit. I knew that if I balked, then I would be creating some problems.

"Well," I said, "I have mixed reactions. I like it here and so does my family. The New York move seems like a challenge, but on the other hand I would be going back where I started six years ago."

I didn't say it, but it seemed to me that Perry was blowing up the move to make it sound real good for me. Instead, I asked: "What's the alternative, Charlie?"

"I'll be very frank with you," Perry said. "We've cut all the people we want to cut and we have a bunch of talented people we want to do something with and for, and this is what we're offering you. We can use you best in New York and would like you there as soon as possible. Don't worry about selling your house, the company will buy it if you can't find a buyer. We'd like you to go to New York, find a place to live, go next week. Take whatever money you need from the expense account, fly down with you wife, rent a car, do whatever you have to do, and come back and let us know where you're going to live and how soon you can get there."

NOTES

It was clear to me there was no alternative in the company's plans, and so we ended the evening with me saying that I would be a good corporate soldier and would be delighted to go to New York to find a place to live. That was the easy part of it; the toughest part was at home. My wife was very good about it. She said, "It's your career, it's a decision you're going to have to make. I love it here, but if we have to move, we'll move."

I looked at four-year-old Jonathan and I thought, it's great for him out here in the country and it would be terrible to take him to New York. I also knew what I would become. My whole personality changes there, and I become very aggressive. When I go to New York on occasion it takes me a day to get back to normal. My wife doesn't even like me when I get back from New York.

Anyway, we talked about all these things for a long time that night, but we went to bed agreeing that we would go to New York to look for a place to live, and we made preparations for the trip. One of the things I had to do before going was to call the program chairman of the Public Relations Society of America chapter in Detroit and tell him that I couldn't handle the program I was responsible for a couple of months from that time. Frank Danforth, the program chairman, had a job as public relations manager at Mavis Metals which had its headquarters in Detroit and was 48th on the Fortune 500 list. I called him and told him I wouldn't be able to handle the chapter's program.

"I'm being shoved off to the New York operation," I said to Danforth. "I'm not especially happy about it, but that's the Peter Principle, or maybe you'd call it the Domino Theory. In any case, I don't expect to be around here long, so I didn't want to hang you up on the PRSA program at the last minute."

I guess I was overwrought and tired, and I think he sensed that something was wrong. He asked me a few questions that didn't quite register with me at the time.

"What do you do over there at Tremount?" he asked, and I told him. Then he asked: "How many years have you been with Tremount?" and other things like that. You see, we knew each other casually from PRSA

NOTES

meetings we had attended, but that was about the extent of it. Anyway, these were leading questions to gather information, but that didn't register on me at the time as I answered them. He finally suggested that we get together about the PRSA program so he could pick up where I left off, and we made a luncheon date for the next day. So I met him the next day and gave him my file - there wasn't much in it because I hadn't done much on the program - and he asked me more questions about my job at Tremount, what I thought about the strengths and weaknesses of the job, the extent of the job, my responsibilities, experience, and that sort of thing.

"Frank," I finally said, "I'm wide-awake now so let's lay our cards on the table. You're interviewing me and I realize that now, so what have you got?"

Danforth laughed. "We don't need any financial public relations people, but we do have a job here," he said, "and it's something you may not be interested in because it's an area in which you haven't had much experience."

Danforth then went into details about the position which was within a three-person group in the public relations department and which was concerned with gathering, coordinating, and dispensing information about energy and the environment as each of these related to Mavis Metals. He said that Mavis was a heavy energy user and was also heavy into the environmental area, but people weren't aware of what the company was doing and so they had formed this group to make sure that everything done was coordinated through one agency. Danforth also said that I would be particularly involved in the areas of nonfillable beverage containers, litter, solid-waste management, and federal agencies concerned with these aspects of the industry.

When I told Danforth that I thought the job was very interesting, he said I should think about it. He asked me what I was going to do about the situation at Tremount, and I told him I was going to take my wife and family to New York to find out what it was going to take to live there because I knew there would be severe financial ramifications to consider.

"Well," he said, "you go find out about this thing. I want you to

NOTES

know that we are interviewing other people for this job but you go ahead and find out the things you must find out."

The next day I took my family to New York, leaving Jonathan with the in-laws in Tarrytown while my wife and I checked out various areas in the New York suburbs. We checked in New Jersey, Westchester, and even up in Rockland and Putnam counties. As you know, that could mean a daily round-trip commute of 2 1/2 to 3 hours, but we wanted to check all possibilities. We spent four days doing this checking and although it was a chore we also found time to visit old friends, dine out, and see some plays. I didn't go near the New York office because I didn't want to. I knew the office people, and I could always get into the personnel thing later. What I was concerned about was living and financial matters.

By Thursday I had these matters pretty well firmed up in my own mind and I figured that taking everything into consideration if I made the move to New York I ought to get about 27 percent more than I was making in Detroit just to come out even with my present salary of $30,000. So I added another 5 percent because Perry had given me to understand this would be a good move for me, and so I figured that a boost of 32 percent would just about do it. I had done my research, and knowing that the company doesn't move fast I decided to call Perry and thus give him enough time to think about it and discuss it with whomever he had to discuss it. I therefore called him and told him what I thought and about the 32 percent.

"Well, Bruce," he said, " I don't think that will happen but let me check it out and see what the reaction is upstairs."

His answer was predictable because this was standard operating procedure. You know what I mean: "Yes, Bruce, you deserve 32 percent. I can't give it to you but let me check it out."

The one surprise was that he phoned me at my in-laws about four hours later.

"I've checked it out here, Bruce," he told me, "and they're prepared to make you an offer of 18 percent."

"Gee, Charlie," I said, "we're still pretty far apart, but I'm not very

NOTES

good at negotiating. You know I'm a candid individual, so I'll tell you frankly that I'm not very happy with that and I really can't hack it with just 18 percent.

"However, I don't want to argue with you, so I'll tell you this: I have all the documentation with me about comparative living costs and that sort of thing, cost estimates signed by people, and showing what I need to raise my child in New York and have a reasonable standard of living for my family. I'd appreciate it if you would think about it over the weekend, talk to the other people involved, and see if you can come closer. In fact, I'd like you to meet that 32 percent figure."

"Okay," said Perry, "but I don't know what they're going to do."

"Fine," I said. "I'll see you on Monday."

"Monday?" he said. "Aren't you coming back tonight or early tomorrow?"

"No," I said, "I'm coming back on Sunday. I still have some money left in my pocket, Charlie, so I'm going to spend the rest of the week here and I'll see you on Monday."

Perry didn't reply, but I now knew just where I stood. I now knew where they were coming from, which was at about 18 percent, and that they would probably come up to maybe 21 percent or maybe 22 percent. Meanwhile on Friday my wife and I went to speak to a builder who had been recommended to us, and when we got back to my in-laws' house I was told that Mavis had called twice and left the message that I should get back to them. The person who had called was John Friendly, assistant to Danforth at Mavis whom I had met several times and knew to be a pretty savvy guy.

"Bruce," he said when I called, "we want this job filled and we want to make you an offer, a firm offer. If you feel you can't take it, we have another candidate who we think can handle the work. We can offer you $29,000."

NOTES

Case 16

BRUCE CANFIELD IS GIVEN THE WORD - B*

When John Friendly told me that Mavis was making me a firm offer of $29,000 I knew that if I accepted the move to New York with Tremount, I would be abe to get at least 18 percent more than the $30,000 I was then making with Tremount in Detroit. I also judged that Tremount might well go as high as a 21 or 22 percent increase. Up to this point in my conversations with the Mavis people the subject of salary had not come up. So when Friendly said their firm offer was $29,000 I said: "John, that's less money than I'm making now," and when he asked how much I was then making I bumped it up a little and said: "I'm making $32,800."

"That's not what the job pays," Friendly replied, "but I'm going to put you on hold and talk to Danforth."

"Fine," I said while I held the line. He got back to me shortly.

"I talked to Danforth and he said we can go as high as $31,000, but that's it," he said.

"John," I said, "I'll tell you this right now; I'm not going to try to hold you up, and I'm not going to try to hold Tremount up. As far as I'm concerned the job sounds like a real challenge. I really don't want to go to New York, and I'm not going to go back and play your job against Tremount. I'm telling you I'll take the job, and I accept it right now on one condition: that I pass a physical if you'll set it up for Monday."

"Fine," Friendly said. "I'll set it up. Call on Monday and we'll tell you where to go and what time we've set for the physical."

I ran into Charlie Perry when I got into the office Monday, and I said that I would be out of the office that afternoon and would talk to him Tuesday. He asked what I had found out, and I gave him all the documents, showing the higher cost of living in New York.

---

* *Dates, places, and names in this case are disguised.*

"That's very convincing, very convincing," he said.

"I certainly hope so, I hope it's 32 percent worth of convincing," I said. Of course I knew I had the other job, but even if he had matched my 32 percent I would have left the company. However, as was his habit he suggested that we get together and talk about it, and we agreed that we ought to do so on Thursday because he was tied up until then.

I took the Mavis physical on Monday afternoon and they informed me on Tuesday that I had passed it. On Wednesday there was a big staff meeting of the entire Tremount public relations staff, but I deliberately did not go. Instead I typed out my resignation from the company, saying briefly that I had had a great experience, had learned a great deal, and was sad to leave after six years but had found an opportunity with another company in Detroit which I couldn't pass up. That's all I said. I didn't name the company, but I said I would be leaving two weeks from Friday. I gave the note to Charlie Perry's secretary shortly after the staff meeting started and said to her: "You'd better take this in to him, Sandy; it's not very good news and it makes me kind of sad, but you'd better take it in to him."

I waited in the outer office and in a few minutes Perry came out.

"Bruce, you handled this very well," he said, and he repeated: "Yes, very well. Do you mind telling me who you're going with?"

"Not at all, Charlie," I said, "I'm going with Mavis."

"That's fine for you, I'm sure," he said. "We really do need you in New York, but we appreciate the fact that you didn't try to play us off against them."

And that was that. We parted on friendly terms, and two weeks later I started my new job at Mavis.

NOTES

Case 17

NORTON CHEMICALS*

Norton Chemicals is located in Sands Point, your native town which is 30 miles from Megalopolis, a city of 200,000 close to the Atlantic seaboard. A few days ago, after a luncheon meeting of the Megalopolis Chamber of Commerce devoted to the labor shortage problem in the area, a nodding acquaintance approached you and asked if you would be interested in a public relations job with Norton Chemicals. This acquaintance, who is in the management hierarchy of N.C., said the company is thinking of reactivating the public relations function and if you were interested he would arrange a meeting for you with Dr. Franz Blucher, the president. Because the opportunity with Norton promised th be a career advancement over your present job, you expressed interest and the meeting was arranged for this afternoon.

In the intervening three days, you did some research on NC. Combining this with what you , as a native of Sands Point, know of the company, this is your knowledge of NC:

Norton Chemicals is a wholly owned subsidiary of a world-renowned chemical-drug firm headquatered in Amsterdam, Holland. About ten years ago it built its present plant on a 200-acre site in Sands Point, a small town of approximately 20,000 residents located about fifteen miles from the Atlantic Ocean. The plant itself is made up of about twenty buildings in a sort of industrial park on the banks of the Sands Point River which empties into Upper Bay which in turn empties into the ocean. The area itself is basically a bedroom community for Megalopolis and also a favorite fishing, sailing, boating, and swimming resort complex made up of the town of Sands Point and the ocean front towns of Dover, South Berlin, New Berlin, Poindexter, and Exeter. The total year-round population of the

---

* *All dates, names, and places in this case have been disguised.*

entire area is about 35,000, but in the summer months this swells to 50,000 people who rent summer homes and fill the motels and hotels on the bay and oceanfront. The weekly Sands Point *Courier* is the area's only newspaper; the Megalopolis *Daily Press* has a major bureau in Sands Point and sells about 18,000 papers daily in the Sands Point area. There are no radio or TV stations in Sands Point, but Megalopolis has eight AM, two FM, and two TV stations, all of which carry clearly to Sands Point.

NC is by far the largest industry in Sands Point County, and in fact is the only major industry in the county. It pays the largest share of the county and city taxes, employs 1,500 people, and has an annual payroll of $25 million. The firm manufactures industrial chemicals which are shipped to the American plants of the parent company for processing into chemical products which are sold under the label of the parent company. Most of these products are sold in bulk to other major American firms, but some are distributed and sold through stores to the ultimate consumer and are known at the average consumer by the brand name of the parent company. Sales last year were at an all-time high.

Having toured the grounds of Norton Chemicals several years ago, you know that the complex is very clean, beautifully landscaped, and free of the noxious smoke and odors which the public often identifies with chemical company plants. The complex is set back about a quarter of a mile from Route 40, and the buildings are not visible from the main highway.

You know that company executives make a conscious effort to identify with the Sands Point community and town. Some of them serve on various community boards, and the company annually makes the largest single contribution to the United Way and American Red Cross drives.

You also recall that when the company first came into the area there was a bitter one-year zoning battle before the land on which NC now stands was rezoned from residential to residential-commercial. Thomas Greeley, longtime editor of the Sands Point *Courier*, was one of those who fought the change and his weekly column over the years has been critical of the company. Originally critical of the company on zoning grounds, he has continued his criticism in regard to pollution. He also cast one of the two

NOTES

dissenting votes when the Exeter Town Board voted 3-2 to permit the firm's pipeline to cross the dunes at Exeter in order to get out into the ocean (see later data about the pipeline).

Pay scales for unskilled, semi and skilled workers at NC are comparable with those paid at other, smaller firms in the area but are slightly below those paid nationally by other large chemical companies. In part, this is why workers went out on a three-month strike over two years ago. Represented in bargaining by the Chemical Workers of America, an AFL union, employees went back to work after gaining a package which brought them a ten percent increase spread over a two-year period. Your understanding is that this brought the wages to a level above that in Sands Point, but still slightly below the national level for chemical firms and below that of firms of comparable size in Megalopolis. In sixty days negotiations on a new contract are scheduled to open. There will be ninety days after that to the expiration date of the existing contract.

Four years ago NC was the major polluter of the Sands Point River, followed closely by municipalities along the river. This pollution was so extensive that it killed all life in the river and most of the life in the bay. It also discolored the river and led to repeated vocal complaints by residents at town board meetings and by written complaints in letters to the editor in the *Courier* and the Megalopolis *Daily Press*. Both papers assailed the pollution in occasional editorials, bearing down very hard on the fact that pollution was ruining the reputation of the area as a resort community.

However, about four years ago after extensive tests and discussions with area and state officials concerned with the pollution problem, the company built a fifteen-mile pipeline which ran from the NC complex across land, under the bay and 3,000 feet out into the ocean. Tied in with treatment beds at the plant and built at a cost of $12 million, this pipeline feeds all NC waste directly into the ocean and completely ended pollution of the river by the company. Frequent tests and constant monitoring of the pipeline terminus at the ocean end of the pipeline are made by the company to make sure that the pipeline discharge is not injurious to ocean life. Despite this fact, each summer residents and officials of the ocean front

NOTES

towns voiced their concern about the pipeline and the possible disastrous consequences that could result to summer tourism if anything went amiss. Letters to the editor in both the *Courier* and the *Daily Press* have continued to appear each summer complaining that NC is not only polluting the Sands Point River but also the ocean front towns bordering the Atlantic. The stridency and number of complaints were particularly evident in recent years when the national press carried stories about oil slicks ruining beaches everywhere, though of course these had no relation to NC and the Sands Point area.

Your contact at NC, at the suggestion of Dr. Blucher, provided you with one further source of information about the company. This is in the form of a forty-page report detailing the results of a public opinion study conducted two months ago in the area for NC by a nationally known research firm. A scientifically drawn random probability sample of 200 persons in the Sands Point area were personally interviewed.

Though no publicity was issued by NC at the time of the survey (this being in accordance with their policy of not issuing press releases), the fact that the survey was being taken became known. In one of his weekly columns at the time, Editor Greeley questioned the validity of the poll by declaring it was ridiculous to assume that 200 people could reflect the true opinions of 35,000 people.

Here are some of the highlights of the findings:

1. A total of 34 percent think the major cause of water pollution in the Sands Point-Seaside area is Norton Chemicals. Another 34 percent cited municipalities as the major cause.

2. Asked to what extent, if any, NC is now polluting the Sands Point River, 6 percent said "Very much"; 6 percent said "much"; 12 percent "somewhat"; 20 percent "little"; 31 percent "not at all" and 25 percent said "don't know."

NOTES

3. Asked to rate working conditions at NC, 39 percent said "good"; 11 percent "fair"; zero percent "poor"; and 50 percent "don't know."

4. Asked to compare wages at NC with other industries in the area, 20 percent said they're "high"; 6 percent "low"; 26 percent "average"; and 48 percent "don't know."

5. A total of 70 percent indicated they know that NC gets rid of its industrial waste through the pipeline. The remaining 30 percent were uninformed about the subject.

6. Asked to rate NC's efforts to control water pollution, 44 percent said they're "good"; 24 percent "fair"; 8 percent "poor"; and 25 percent "don't know."

7. Asked to what extent, if any, NC is polluting the air, 0 percent said "very much"; 0 percent "much"; 10 percent "somewhat"; 23 percent "little"; 41 percent "not at all"; and 26 percent "don't know."

8. Asked to criticize the company, 70 percent had no criticism; 12 percent (the largest single group citing a criticism) mentioned pollution.

9. Asked to praise the company, 35 percent had no praise to offer. Of the 65 percent citing praise, 48 percent (the largest single group citing praise) said the company "provides jobs, boosts the economy, and pays taxes."

10. Asked if NC is a liability or asset to the area, 2 percent said "it's a liability"; 86 percent said "it's an asset"; 8 percent said "both"; and 4 percent had no opinion.

NOTES

11. Asked to name the daily or weekly they read regularly, 70 percent said "the Megalopolis *Daily Press*" and 18 percent said "the Sands Point *Courier*."

Having digested the above-mentioned survey results and completed your three-day research about the company, you met this afternoon with Dr. Blucher. You judged him to be about 60 years old, courteous, well in command of himself.

During your hour-long meeting and in response to your questions, Dr. Blucher told you that NC issues no press releases locally. An annual report for NC is issued by the parent company each year, and in addition two pages of the parent company's quarterly external-internal publication are devoted to NC news. The only publication at the Sands Point complex is a one-page mimeographed daily news digest which is prepared and distributed in the plant each day by the personnel department. Dr. Blucher said that press and public inquiries having a public relations connotation are answered either by him, the assistant to the president, or the director of personnel.

In addition to asking you questions about your job as an assistant public relations director of a manufacturing concern for the past four years, Dr. Blucher solicited your views on the national economy, public relations in general, and employee, community and media relations. In concluding the interview he said he found your ideas both interesting and thoughtful.

AUTHOR'S NOTE

Two alternatives are present as the conclusion to the Norton Chemicals case. The instructor will decide whether to follow Alternative A which presents an ending designed to elicit oral response from students or Alternative B which presents an ending designed to elicit written response from students.

NOTES

ALTERNATIVE A CASE ENDING

"I'm favorably impressed with your experience, credentials and with your ideas," Dr. Blucher said. "I know that I will be putting you on the spot in asking for answers in such a short period of time, but I'm doing this deliberately to gain an idea of how you react and think under pressure. I would therefore appreciate it if you would give me your answers and reactions to the following five questions:

1. What do you consider to be the major public relations problems of Norton Chemicals?

2. If you were to set up a public relations program for the company, what would be the major short and long-term objectives for your program?

3. How would you go about achieving these objectives? That is, what specific steps would you take in carrying out a public relations program for Norton Chemicals? I'd like to know your ideas about strategies, themes, and steps, means, or media to be taken and utilized in carrying out the details of the programming.

4. What would you do about the forty-page report submitted by the nationally-known research firm? Would you publicly disseminate the findings? If no, why wouldn't you do so? If yes, what would you do and *exactly* how would you go about such dissemination?

5. If we were to give you the position as director of public relations for Norton Chemicals, what five major questions would you ask at this point about the position or the company? Furthermore, I'd like to know *why* you are asking each question?

NOTES

ALTERNATIVE B CASE ENDING

"I'm favorably impressed with your experience, credentials and with your ideas," Dr. Blucher said. "You verbalize very well, but I'd like the opportunity to judge your written response and analysis of the public relations problems that face us at Norton Chemicals. I'd therefore appreciate it very much if you would send us a long memorandum setting forth your answers to the following five questions:

1. What do you consider to be the major public relations problems of Norton Chemicals?

2. If you were to set up a public relations program for the company, what would be the major short and long-term objectives for your program?

3. How would you go about achieving these objectives? That is, what specific steps would you take in carrying out a public relations program for Norton Chemicals? I'd like to know your ideas about strategies, themes, and steps, means, or media to be taken and utilized in carrying out the details of the programming.

4. What would you do about the forty-page report submitted by the nationally-known research firm? Would you publicly disseminate the findings? If no, why wouldn't you do so? If yes, what would you do and *exactly* how would you go about such dissemination?

5. If we were to give you the position as director of public relations for Norton Chemicals, what five major questions would you ask at this point about the position or the company? Furthermore, I'd like to know *why* you are asking each question?

"I appreciate the interview and the opportunity," you respond. "When would you want the memorandum?"

"Yesterday, of course," replied Dr. Blucher with a smile. "However, I guess one week from today would be a reasonable target date."

NOTES

An Excerpt For Discussion

Inside The Amoral World Of Public Relations*

By Marvin N. Olasky

Alan Harrington's *Life in the Crystal Palace* (1959) is one of the finest books on public relations ever written. After working in a major corporate public relations department for four years, Harrington concluded that the PR man's job is "to select and distort the facts in such a way that clients will appear before the public in a good light. This could, severely, be called the art, science, skill, dodge or trade of lying." But he noted that there was not much concern about lying among his former colleagues, because it appears that the word hardly had any meaning within their solipsistic world views: "A reputable PR practitioner never deliberately lies. Rather he sees before him a world of mobile and malleable truths. A ball of wax is a ball of wax.... In the world of public relations, fact can be shaped with no damage to anyone's conscience."

A quarter-century after Harrington, restraint in the shaping of facts is held in ever lower regard at some large public relations departments of industry and government. I know this from my five years in the public relations department of one of the ten largest U.S. corporations, from interviews with fifty out of the sixty middle- and upper-level practitioners in that department, and from conversations with individuals in other large public relations offices. My assurances of anonymity (which were trusted due to the years of familiarity with interviewees) allowed many shields to come down. Many of those interviewed wanted the shields to come down, some saying that current practices should be exposed; others suggesting that students need to understand what "the real world" is like.

---

* This article by Professor Marvin N. Olasky of the Department of Journalism at the University of Texas at Austin, appeared in the Winter, 1985, issue of *Business and Society Review*. The response of Albert Abend and Professor Olasky's rejoinder appeared in the Summer, 1985, issue of the *Review*. Reprinted with permission.

For instance, one expert in "media relations" said that students should know "the real satisfaction in laying it on one of the prestige papers. *The New York Times* is always looking for an executive they can call innovative, even though he's just talking bull, so you can give them some clues and they'll 'discover' a story about an executive and his concept of social responsibility tailored for public consumption, how he wants to set up a youth basketball league or something, and they'll print it and you can look good. They rarely check back on whether the jerk's actually done anything." Another experienced PR man explained the art of learning to assess what he could get away with in talking to reporters: "You end up trying out lines on reporters, ready to retreat if they challenge us, but they accept them most of the time."

ISSUE ANALYSIS

One of the growing areas in corporate public relations is "issue analysis," defined in this way by one corporate manager: "We decide which position we want to push, then we hire some 'objective' experts to write the papers which will become the official basis for our decision. For instance, the new industrial policy debate wasn't shaping up in our favor. It was important to refocus attention away from electronics, so for a couple of thousand dollars each for the right professors we could buy the ____name and get not only a lot more attention, but credit for making a thorough appraisal of the subject." A formerly independent analyst now given a plush office explained, "I used to have to do research to arrive at conclusions. Now I know what is true before I begin - it's what the chairman said is necessary to keep the economy from falling apart - and all I have to do is manufacture the data to fit his thesis. It makes life much easier, and I don't think anything much is lost, because the conclusions I used to come to weren't all that helpful anyway."

One aspect of high-powered issue analysis is that even devices designed to show openness became further indications of closure. As one manager explained, "We put out a magazine designed to show that the

NOTES

company comes to grips with a range of opinion. But we only hire writers we can use to structure the debate to the particular 'middle road' - we always go for the supposedly moderate position - that we've already chosen to embrace. Looking back, it's very impressive to see how we've structured the debate on some key issues so we can appear to be giving in to the position we wanted all along." All the world is a John le Carre novel to this mode of thought, with "legends" constantly in the making and counterplots urged as the only defense against plotting; as one issues manager explained, "Someone puts out polls, you put out counterpolls. Someone hires academics, you hire other academics."

ADMISSION OF FEAR

Public relations leaders are also pushing for growth in corporate contributions areas, often as a ways of building ties with governmental powers. In an age of journalistic searchlights, subtlety is important. One public relations manager explained: "I like to get our executives on the same charitable boards with the regulators, so they can build relationships in a third-party atmosphere. It's worth a donation of $10,000 for us to have a neutral, innocuous place to meet." Knowing how and when to maximize contributions benefits is a mark of true professionalism, according to an introspective executive: "There are some naive people who actually think our contributions are contributions. They're not. They're public admissions of our fears - fear of a politician, fear of an executive at another company, fear of the public-interest groups, fear of kids on the streets outside our building, fear of anyone who can upset the order we've built."

The above quotations are not meant to indicate that the public relations managers interviewed are not friendly, honest persons on an individual level. Many of them are. But their thinking, when it comes to public relations practice, is almost invariably manipulative; that is what they believe professional public relations to be all about. Consequently, there was pleasure in the "professionalism" of a successful manipulation. A typical manager spoke glowingly of "the fun of misdirection. You set up a plan and

NOTES

watch them think they're chasing leads which you've let them develop just to throw them off the scent. It is one enormous pleasure to sit in your air-conditioned office on a hot day and know that one of those guys is sweat-soaked with his shirt hanging out, just yearning for a popsicle truck to come by."

MALLEABILITY OF TRUTH

Among some practitioners, there was overt talk of what Harrington described as "the malleability of truth." One upper-level manager asked, "Does the word 'lie' actually mean anything anymore? In one sense, everyone lies, but in another sense, no one does, because no one knows what's true - it's whatever makes you look good. Everybody does it. You know everyone's doing it. Like you know all those girls getting married aren't virgins, but you don't tell them to leave the white dresses home, do you? You just leve and let live." Another executive argued that "there is no such thing as truth. You judge actions depending on whether they're done by someone above you or someone below you. There's no right or wrong. If someone above did something, it's not to be viewed in the same way as stuff done by someone below. And don't give me any bull about principles. The job of a public relations professional is to make sure the plan works." A middle manager argued, "They're not paying us to tell them why they can't do X - our job is to tell them how they can. And what's wrong with that? Who knows what's really true, anyway? Their guess is as good as mine."

Other public relations managers took on the cover of latter-day Pharisees. One insisted, "I don't lie. I've never lied. There's a fine line sometimes, but I've never had data in front of me and read off the wrong numbers to a reporter. I won't do anything like that. Now, I am a company man, I admit that freely, here's where I draw my paycheck and my policy is to return value for that good pay. But I've never said that black is white - a shade of gray, sure, and I don't talk about my work to my family or to anyone outside here. But I'm not ashamed of it. I don't lie." Another

NOTES

practitioner, when pushed, arrived at her bottom line of blaming the management: "You have to build up trust. You have to let them know you'll support them in whatever they do. You'll lie for them, you'll cheat for them, you'll cover up for them - or else they won't trust you. Total loyalty. They get it elsewhere. They demand it from you."

It is important to note that a few practitioners were bothered by their practice. Information that could be the difference between life and death was suppressed regretfully. As one executive observed concerning the successful minimization of public concern about a toxic chemical's effects years earlier, "We didn't have to lie outright. We manipulated the reporters but good. We gave them misdirection information and soon they moved the spotlight anyway. It was an excellent job of professional public relations work. But it still bothers me." Another manager told the story of how a sharp reporter did "get the goods" on the effects of one carcinogenic chemical, and the company in turn "got the goods" on an incident from the reporter's past, thus keeping the story from appearing. "We survived that episode. But we were wrong to do it that way." Usage of the word "wrong" in that moral sense was uncommon.

MIXED FEELINGS

It should also be noted that those who were most aggressive not only in defending their own practice but also in justifying and praising that of others still were unable to avoid having mixed feelings about their work. For instance, one practitioner's key task was the development of "standby statements," which are prepared lists of questions reporters are likely to ask, along with approved answers. He expressed considerable satisfaction concerning the technical feat of packing so little information into a message that appeared to be forthright. Yet this practitioner, relaxing after final approval of a particularly difficult standy statement, one dealing with use of a toxic substance, talked about, "how we went through so many drafts before we finally got it the way we liked it. The first answer doesn't even deal with the key question it starts out supposedly answering, did you

NOTES

notice that? Most reporters, when you give them an answer like that, will just say 'thank you' and think they've gotten some information out of you. Then the job is fun. But I sometimes wonder about what we're covering up today.... Sometimes I even hope a reporter will call, and he'll be bright, and he'll ask all the right questions and I'll have to give out some of this information. I even wrote one standby in an especially scammy and slimy way in the hope that a reporter would see through the answers. But no one did. No one asked the right questions."

IRONIC TWISTS

There are some ironic twists brought out in this series of interviews, and it would be easy to wax sarcastic about them. When one "disinformation manager," as he labeled himself, complained that he could not trust his car mechanic to give him an accurate account, even he could see a double whammy of untruthfulness at work. There were also organizational ironies. One public relations executive observed the regnant repercussions on inside communications of a continued policy of manipulating those on the outside: "The chairman must rely on us to some extent to explain situations. But we're used to setting up legends for people outside, and now on the inside we see how one person distorts the situation to please his boss, who distorts it again to please me, and on it goes up the line.... But the laugh is on everyone. The donkey below me learns that the lie he created to please is now decreed to be the truth he must live by, and it's nonsense, but that's what he has to do to make money from now on." One of that executive's subordinates, who has not had the best of years because several of his complicated plans had fallen through, complained that he had been treated unfairly: "It's terrible that these performance ratings are all subjective," he said. "Shouldn't there be some objectivity? I'd like us to find a way to get at the true picture."

The view of the world revealed during most of the fifty interviews only makes sense, for something beyond self-preservation or perverse pleasure, if those outside the organization - reporters, ideological

NOTES

opponents, etc. - are viewed as implacable enemies. It cannot be denied that some reporters are so intently searching for a good story that they will adopt any means to develop it; some will not quail at overdeveloping it if the facts turn out to be only a washed-out, sunlit imitation of Pulitzer Prize material. One practitioner argued that, "if you want to write about lying, write that we are in a race against other liars, and the only thing that keeps us going is a balance of terror." Yet, even if such sentiments were true, the development of a balance of terror between journalists and PR men places a terrible burden on an economic system based on contract rather than force, and thus in the end based on trust itself. If the situation is as bleak as some practitioners argue, they are contributing to the process of destroying American society to save it.

In any case, many PR men and women tended to care less about the dangers of social chaos than about their own relativistic social convenience. "To talk of lying is to live in the past," one manager said. "I doubt if the word will even be in our everyday vocabularies in a couple of decades. There are no lies anymore, just interests waiting to be served." That attitude, if unopposed, will make such an outcome inevitable. The subjectivist definition of truth extends far beyond corporate walls, and an examination of its corporate dominance should not give aid and comfort to those who are opposed to corporations, period. Some within public relations who understand the deepest nature of the field's philosophical problems still believe that they should be covered up. But facts are facts, and current public relations practice will not be reconstructed unless it is first understood.

NOTES

LETTERS

PR Debate

TO THE EDITOR:

How sad that Marvin N. Olasky ("Inside the Amoral World of Public Relations," *Business and Society Review*, Winter, 1985) labored for five years in a corporate public relations department without having learned much about the profession of public relations - none of which has to do with fibbing to reporters or giving them the runaround. Olasky failed even to learn that reporters and public relations practitioners do not serve the same function in our society's marketplace of views and opinions.

Reporters are paid to locate, validate, and assemble bits of information in ways that will be meaningful to specific audiences of readers, viewers or listeners. Although reporters may bring their own perceptions to a story, in large measure they are supposed to report what they learn without interjecting their own opinions into their work.

Public relations practitioners, whether employed by a public relations agency or by a corporation, are paid *in part* to help their clients arrive at intelligent, defensible points of view on subjects that are vital to the clients' interests. Then they try to assure that these points of view are expressed and considered where they may have an impact on the resolutions of the issues at hand.

That complex social, cultural, political or business issues in a free society may encompass any number of divergent points of view should not come as a surprise. Indeed, one may express or support a point of view without its being a lie. Moreover, journalists *know* that PR practitioners will represent a particular point of view and thus are not impartial sources (as if *any* source of information on an issue is impartial). This does not mean, however, that typical practitioners of public relations provide reporters with false or misleading information.

NOTES

Where Olasky operates in the belief that there is only one self-evident "truth" for any given issue, many thinking people ascribe to the thought that there are many views of the world, and one of the public relations tasks is to help clients test their views against the views of others, to see which will have more merit in varying courts of public opinion.

Please let this much be clear: Executives in the public relations business do not simply articulate a client's point of view, as Olasky seems to believe; rather, they help the client *form* a view, and they work to change this view over time as new evidence and circumstances warrant.

To be of serious professional counsel to clients, public relations executives make it their business - quite literally - to learn and understand their clients' markets, operations, competitive opportunities, and challenges from top to bottom. To this end, often they examine and digest massive amounts of detailed information on a whole variety of subjects that are important to their clients. They then analyze and measure the wants and needs of their clients against those of others, to help clients understand the perceptions of "reality" others may hold on a given issue.

Only then, after clients understand where their interests and realities converge or clash with those of others, is an adequate, reasonable and defensible "position" staked out with the client, and a public relations program planned and executed.

There is so very much in Olasky's ill-conceived article to criticize, as any basic college text on public relations practice will confirm. (His definition of "issues analysis" is, for instance, laughable. What Olasky describes is not issues analysis - which is a method of tracking the movement and intensity of issues involving a client's interests as they develop over time - but issues management, or, more correctly, the lack of it by his former employer.)

I would suggest that once Olasky discovered he was working for a company that provided the media with "disinformation," he should have resigned on moral grounds - and that it should not have taken him five years to do so. He would have not been the first human being to have resigned a job rather than surrender his moral integrity. For my money, in fact, the

NOTES

personal ethics of any truly professional PR practitioner would have made resignation a *moral imperative* for Olasky.

Can public relations be practiced unethically? Of course it can; there are rogue elephants in every profession. But large numbers of public relations practitioners pledge themselves to a written code of professional conduct, "to conduct [them]selves professionally, with truth, accuracy, fairness and responsibility to the public. . . in accord with the public interest," with adherence to "truth and accuracy and to generally accepted standards of good taste," and so as to "not intentionally communicate false or misleading information."

The code, adopted by the Public Relations Society of America in 1950 and updated a number of times since, mandates that PR practitioners are "*obligated to use care to avoid communication of false or misleading information* (the emphasis is mine)," and to "not engage in any practice which tends to corrupt the integrity of channels of communication or the processes of government."

Indeed, PRSA members "shall, as soon as possible, sever relations with any organization or individual if such relationship requires conduct contrary to the articles of this Code."

Those of your readers who wish to learn something about "the real world" of public relations should not depend on Olasky. Instead, they should read the seminal works on the subject by such esteemed practitioners as Edward Bernays, Scott Cutlip, and Philip Lesly. Seminars on various disciplines on the PR profession are also presented nationally by New York University in conjunction with the Public Relations Society of America.

It is a fine thing that Olasky has done in leaving the public relations profession, as in five years he apparently did not learn to understand its most basic functions - none of which involve lying. It is most unfortunate, however, that he himself may now be shaping erroneous public opinions through notorious stories such as the one you have published, and through the personal biases he may pass on to his journalism students.

Albert Abend
Hartford, Connecticut

NOTES

Marvin Olasky *responds:*

I heartily agree that readers who want to learn about public relations should read seminal works by Bernays and others. If readers want an introduction to those works, they may examine the articles I published on Bernays in recent issues of *Public Relations Quarterly* and *Public Relations Review.*

What I like about Bernays is his honesty about the field. For instance, he titled one of his articles "Manipulating Public Opinion," using the word "manipulation" positively. In his 1928 book *Propaganda,* Bernays argued that public relations counselors were needed precisely to engage in "the conscious and intelligent manipulation of the organized habits and opinions of the masses."

Bernays praised propaganda and manipulation because he believed a system of behind-the-scenes control by PR men was the only one possible in a large-scale society that chooses to avoid outright authoritarian control: "We are dominated by the relatively small number of persons who understand the mental processes and social patterns of the masses. It is they who pull the wires which control the public mind.... Such organization and focusing are necessary to orderly life."

Bernays had the gumption to define "public relations counselor" as "propaganda specialist." Many PR men and women, then and now, are not so honest. But we could have a much better debate about the substance of modern public relations if practitioners stopped making Goody-two-shoes statements and frankly acknowledged that much of the current craft, at least in its "macro" applications, is based on manipulation. Some argue that such practice is essential in today's world, and we can have good discussions about that, but only if we start facing facts.

If we hide behind the PRSA Code of Ethics, however, we will never have a useful debate. The most-used public relations textbook, co-authored by Scott Cutlip, notes that during the 1970s only four cases of code violation were tried by PRSA "judicial panels," and only one penalty was incurred: suspension of membership for "flagrant account piracy." Readers

NOTES

on PRSA's code enforcement proceedings could conclude that only one of about 10,000 PRSA members did anything wrong during that decade, and his sin was taking business from a fellow PRSA member, or they could conclude the code is a farce.

I like many public relations men and women personally. I enjoyed working with many intelligent practitioners who truly thought, like Bernays, that they were saving a democratic society from chaos. Individual practitioners are not the problem, except insofar as many have departed from a free-enterprise belief structure and adopted an ideology of manipulation. My goal in all the writing I do about public relations is to point out the troublesome nature of that ideology. So let's forget about ad hominem attacks and PR for PR. Let's have a debate about the ideology.

NOTES

Part 3. Counseling

Case 18. A Letter From Peter Gantor
Case 19. A Talk On Measuring Publicity Effectiveness
   Excerpt For Discussion: Protesting Preferential Treatment
Case 20. A Search For Public Relations Counsel - A
Case 21. A Search For Public Relations Counsel - B
Case 22. A Search For Public Relations Counsel - C
Case 23   Ruder & Finn Conference On
         Professional Responsibility - A
Case 24. Ruder & Finn Conference On
         Professional Responsibility - B
   Excerpt For Discussion: S. Africa: A Thorny Ethics Problem

Case 18

A LETTER FROM PETER GANTOR*

One October morning Terry Gras, vice president of public relations for a large national organization and a former officer of the Public Relations Society of America, received the following letter from Peter Gantor. Gras recalled him immediately as a very sincere young man who had been a member of the Pinacle Group's public relations department several years ago and had left to take a better-paying position with a Chicago firm. After reading the letter Gras decided to think about it for a day or so and then respond to it.

Brentwood and LaBella
Fernwood Towers
Los Angeles, California 90038
(213) 859-6240

Date

Terry Gras
Vice President, Public Relations
The Pinacle Group
Farmington, CT 06032

Dear Terry:

Greetings. It's been some time since we last communicated. Let me quickly bring you up to date.

---

* Dates, places, and names in this case are disguised.

As you can see from the letterhead, I'm now working for an advertising agency in Los Angeles. I'm a senior advertising copywriter and an all-purpose PR person. In fact, I'm here to establish a PR arm for the agency. It's a great opportunity, quite a challenge and one hell of a tough job. That brings me to the major reason for this letter. I need the opinion of someone in the profession I respect.

Building the PR credentials of this agency means selling public relations to clients who have thus far avoided it like the plague. It also means educating agency management (the president and the creative director). It's a difficult and frustrating task. Both individuals agree they want a PR arm for its profitability, but both also admit to knowing little or nothing about the profession. (Profession is my word, not theirs.)

The president goes a little further. He openly states he doesn't like PR and doesn't trust those involved with it. His reasons are simple: he doesn't understand it, can't explain it, doesn't know how - or if - it can work, can't justify it to the client and so on. He tells me this to my face and that I can't count on him for support in front of the client (he says he'll openly shoot me down because, after all, he knows more about what the individuals will readily accept than I do), then follows up by saying he wants to see more PR activity.

The creative director, in the presence of the president, agrees with the president (to protect his own). In private, he tells me to work around the president. Then follows up by stating PR people are ineffectual pessimists unwilling to face reality. Maybe he's right (in my case). That's one of the things I would like your opinion on. But before you can develop one, you need to know a little more.

My creative director claims that he is a realist.

The first thing you should know is the creative director's distinction between a realist and a pessimist. Though, I'm not sure I'm sure. The best

NOTES

way to explain is to provide a brief example:

An insurance company (mobile homeowners' insurance) wants to sell 500 mobile homes that it has repossessed. A realist finds an interesting slant for nationwide publicity. A slant based on those 500 repos (i.e. - "Insurance company turns mobile home dealer to liquidate 500 repossessed units in Texas."). A pessimist, on the other hand, recommends *not* designing the campaign around the announcement that this company has 500 repos it wants to unload, because of the public reacting in a negative manner. Rather, there are other vehicles and other publicity approaches that do not highlight the repo thing.

Frankly, I told my creative director that I could not, in good conscience as a public relations professional, recommend touting in publicity my client's wish to sell 500 repossessed mobile homes. This, for several reasons:

a) Obviously, it's egg on the client's face.

b) It's detrimental to the company's professional image. Insurance companies make their profit from investments. These homes represent over $2 million in bad investments. (This company also has a guaranty corporation. They insure the mortgages at the time of sale. This so that: the bank will give the mortgage in the first place, so the home will be sold, so that (hopefully) the insurance company will write the homeowner's policy.)

c) It could result in a bad company image. Insurance companies are not on the list of most respected corporations (consumer view) to begin with. Some people think they run a kind of legalized protection racket. They raised their rates indiscriminately. And, when you have a claim, they no longer know you. So, we haven't got the best consumer

NOTES

attitudes to start with. Now, we're going to publicize nationally that we threw 500 people out of their homes. Why? Because they couldn't pay their rent? Or because they didn't pay their insurance? Does this insurance company somehow get a lien on your home when they insure it? Granted there's no connection between insurance and repossession. But I can foresee all kinds of fears and misconceptions developing in the public's mind as a result of this type of publicity. I feel that the questions I presented above are just a few of the possible reactions.

My creative director's reaction to my reasons (above) was: "Hell, that kind of thinking went out 15 years ago." He went on to say that I should've faced reality. The people were evicted for a reason: they couldn't pay the rent. The reality is that a lot of people lost their jobs. Repo is not a bad word: it's the real business world. Further, he says, it's an interesting story: What happened to the people that they lost their jobs, where'd they go, what are they doing now? So, he says, the insurance company would not be thought of badly for evicting people from their homes (that, he says, is an old conservative view). Rather, it's a hell of a story that the papers will use and the homes will get sold.

I said that we shouldn't stir up a hornet's nest when there was no reason to - when the homes could be sold using other techniques. He responded by saying my basic way of thinking was wrong, that 90% of all PR people he ever knew found ways to avoid doing things because of the problems that might result, rather than going ahead and accomplishing the short term goal efficiently.

I told you it was frustrating. To me, it is. I can't help but wonder if he's right. My better judgment tells me no. But I do wonder if I was over reacting public sensitivities.

I'd like your opinion. I know you'll hit me with the truth - squarely. No

NOTES

sweet answer just to make me feel better. If I'm wrong, I need to know that so I can adjust my thinking, philosophies and approach. If I'm thinking soundly, I need to know that. too.

Am I wrong to assume that as a public relations practitioner I should be keenly aware of the negative ramifications of any program or policy? That I should actually try to anticipate the problems and formulate means of avoiding and/or handling them? The key, I think, is <u>look</u>. I look very hard for any possible cause of negative public reaction before I design a campaign. Then, I design a campaign to overcome or avoid their flare-up before the fact.

You see, I was told that if I can't stop looking for and finding problems or potential problems, I should get out of the PR profession. I had always thought that <u>was</u> my profession - isolating and anticipating areas for negative public reaction and endeavoring to achieve public acceptance. Maybe my head is on backwards. I know what my convictions tell me, but I'm not beyond realizing that I may have formed the wrong convictions.

Anyway, whatever the case, I want to get a seasoned professional's opinion. If not to confirm my convictions, than to alter my course. If I'm wrong, I want to correct it. If I'm right, I don't want to turn myself into a Hollywood publicity agent at the beckoning of my boss.

I've taken enough of your time. And thank you for fighting your way through this letter. I'm looking forward to hearing from you and trust all goes well.

Sincerely,

(signed)

Peter Gantor

NOTES

Case 19

A TALK ON MEASURING PUBLICITY EFFECTIVENESS

In any one year the American Management Association holds scores of special one to three-day seminars, conferences, and briefing sessions for those interested in the science of management and in various management techniques. Participants at these AMA-sponsored affairs are generally specialists in the area discussed.
One such occasion, held on May 8 at the St. Regis-Sheraton Hotel in New York City, was a three-day briefing session concerned with the "Measurement and Evaluation of Public Relations Activities." Carl Ruff, chairman of the board of the New York public relations counseling firm of Ruff, Kiek and McAuliffee, delivered a prepared talk describing the manner in which his firm evaluates the dollar return on a client's public relations investment.
The Ruff organization prepared a two-page release which was distributed to a limited group of specialized public relations and media-related publications, including *Editor & Publisher*, *Advertising Age*, *Public Relations News*, *Printer's Ink*, the *Public Relations Journal*, etc.

On the following pages are a slightly condensed version of Ruff's talk (Exhibit 19-1); the two-page press release (Exhibit 19-2); and a full-page article which appeared in *Editor & Publisher* in its May 13 issue (Exhibit 19-3).

EXHIBIT 19-1

May 8

MEASUREMENT OF PUBLICITY EFFECTIVENESS BY INQUIRY ANALYSIS

a talk by
Carl Ruff, Chairman of the Board
Ruff, Kiek and McAuliffe, Inc., N.Y.

...Today, with the mass of messages bombarding us daily, most of our public relations communications have questionable impact in terms of generating measurable activity. And in order for publicity to be a hard-nosed, viable marketing tool, it must generate activity that can be evaluated in terms of the return on the dollar spent for it.

I'm willing to include psychological shifts - attitude changes - in my definition of the term "activity." However, few corporations have the interest - or the budget - to permit frequent measurement of public opinion. And, as we all know from bitter experience, a corporation which on any given day enjoyed a generally sympathetic public attitude, can plummet in one week to low public regard after a negative news story.

Nevertheless, the practice of public relations today and tomorrow must, I believe, be goal-oriented/activity-oriented. We're living in a day of space-age technological changes. Results, not verbiage, is the name of the game...

...I submit that we practitioners must anticipate managements' demands and soon come to grips with measurement and evaluation methods, whether we work for government, business, or non-profit institutions.

In Tom Hopkinson's survey, reported in the Winter issue of *The Public Relations Quarterly,* the most popular comment of the 500 corporations on *Fortune's* list queried was on the need for greater

NOTES

professionalism of public relations counselors. The respondents all placed emphasis on the need for research and measurement of results...

...Public relations practitioners have long made bald claims about the greater dollar-for-dollar power of editorial material over advertising. It's obvious that newspaper and magazine readers, radio listeners and TV watchers spend more time on and pay greater attention to editorial material than they do to advertising copy. But as we all know, PR does not have absolute control over its choice of media - or of the precise wording of the message. If we're good we get our client's story told where we want it told. But we can't guarantee this in advance. Nor can we always control the changes made in our lovingly written copy by a harried rewrite desk or a cynical copy editor.

So in evaluating the effectiveness of public relations against advertising I, for one, had no way of proving that editorial material generated by public relations would yield greater numerical response or motivate stronger activity than did advertising copy.

This problem has always fascinated and challenged - and frustrated - me. I can recall a number of case histories of having pulled what we considered a public relations coup, but because it defied accurate measurement, we were frustrated and tongue-tied.

There was a *Life* cover story on a retailer client - Ohrbach's - with the store's slogan printed on the cover, "Fashion Stylist for Ohrbach's Low-Cost High Fashions" - and an illustrated seven-page text story. But we had no way of measuring whether it brought more customers to the firm's stores than Doyle Dane Bernbach's full-page institutional ads in the New York and Los Angeles newspapers.

There was the occasion when *Business Week* ran as editorial material, on a two-page spread, a series of Dreyfus & Co.'s newspaper advertisements. They were newsworthy and deserved the editorial space. But I had no way of measuring the impact of this against the ads that competitive investment firms ran in the same issue.

How much greater impact is there in two pages of editorial space with third-person endorsement than in one page of self-serving advertising copy?

NOTES

How do you go about evaluating and measuring this?

I must confess that my first breakthrough to a measurement method was the result of chance - not planning - and it's far from foolproof. Last year I discovered at a sales meeting of one of our clients, Herman Miller Inc. - they're manufacturers of furniture systems for offices, schools and institutions, as well as for the home - that a clerk was keeping track of inquiries received for products and systems.

Now, product publicity is the one public relations task that lends itself most easily to measurement and evaluation. It's also the area that rates Number One in answer to the question asked of 500 managements: "In what general public relations areas has your organization obtained best results from counselors?" Product publicity rates 57% and financial public relations 44% - according to Tom Hopkinson's study.

My first objective in asking for a copy of Herman Miller's records was to make a comparative analysis of the pulling power of the publications we had assumed would be important to us.

When I received the sheets, I discovered that they broke down inquiries and marked those received from advertising and those from publicity. I was therefore able to doublecheck the pulling power of the publications by advertising as well as by publicity.

But - of great fascination to me - I was able, finally, to see how publicity stacked up against advertising in producing inquiries.

Once I determined the publicity-to-advertising ratio I had a basis, at long last, for arriving at a figure for the dollar return on the public relations money spent by the client. This was a simple matter of isolating product inquiries, determining their sources, checking the comparative in-depth readership of specific publications carrying articles and their space-rate charges, and applying the ratio.

Let me tell you some of the background so you can better evaluate the findings. When we were assigned the task of publicizing Herman Miller, we were asked to concentrate on telling the story of Action Office. This is a revolutionary new concept of office equipment which includes contemporary versions of the old stand-up, roll-top desks with file bins

NOTES

with fingertip reach, slanted tops and beautifully designed tambour tops, all designed by George Nelson. It included wall-hung and free-standing open files for information retrieval, small mobile Action conference tables and many other newsworthy departures. The Action Office system was all predicated on behavioral scientists' findings of *real* needs of office workers.

We were instructed to concentrate on telling the story of Action Office in *Fortune, Business Week, Time* and *Newsweek.*

Incidentally, the breakdown of the inquiries by publications proved that some of these magazines which the client - and we - had considered to be the prime targets were actually of little importance in producing queries. And magazines which one management group had not considered important turned out to be among those producing the greatest number of queries from specifiers of the client's products.

The advertising - which was first rate - ran from stunning four-color, full-page photographs with punchy copy placed in *Fortune, Scientific American, Interiors* and the architectural magazines, to a ten-insertion, two-column-by-14-inch series in *The Wall Street Journal.*

The publicity ran from a two-paragraph inclusion in a *Wall Street Journal* roundup to two-thirds of a page with pictures in *Fortune*, three pages with pictures in *Business Week,* a double-page spread in *Saturday Evening Post* and important coverage in the architectural and interior design publications as well as in the major newspapers...

...Publicity out-pulled advertising on Action Office by a ratio of 7 to 1.

On a magazine-to-magazine basis, our study revealed some fascinating details. In one architectural publication, publicity outpulled advertising 80 to 1; in another, 2.5 to 1. On the other hand, in *Fortune*, advertising outpulled publicity 2.5 to 1.

Once I had this average 7 to 1 ratio, I commissioned an advertising agency space buyer to make an analysis of the publicity at space rates, page for page, column for column, as if the publicity were ads.

I ruled out mentions, tie-ins, installation photos with minuscule credits and incidental publicity on the other activities of the firm or its

NOTES

designers - Charles Eames, George Nelson and Alexander Girard. It included only pinpointed, query-producing product publicity.

Heretofore I had always disdained making a space-rate tabulation of publicity for my clients. To my mind it was as meaningless as *weighing* a batch of publicity clips. I know some firms do this but it's never been my dish of tea. Now I felt justified because the total publicity space rates multiplied by seven would represent what the client would have had to spend in advertising in order to have obtained these queries.

The final figure, a qualitative analysis of public relations effectiveness by inquiry count, revealed that, for a moderate fee, the client had obtained $1,400,000 of query-pulling, product-selling and attitude-reinforcing exposure over a period of 15 months.

The total of the publicity measured by space rates was $197,000. Multiplied by 7 you get $1,378,900 - without art and production charges.

Now, I want to be the first to admit that these results were achievable only because of a perfect parlay: a good product, a good news story, a cooperative client, time to organize a saturation campaign, and professional competence. This combination doesn't happen very often. When it comes your way you can swing.

Nor do these measurable inquiry results negate the importance of non-measurable institutional editorial credits. This spring, one of the most influential magazines in the country ran an article on the furniture industry. In general it lambasted the industry. Herman Miller was virtually the only firm to receive kudos. How does one meaure scientifically, precisely, the value of this without spending a ridiculous amount of money? You don't. You accept it and hope management realizes its worth.

I might say, in closing, that this year, in Herman Miller's year-end public relations review, we have continued our analysis of the dollar return on the client's public relations investment. We're comparing returns on media advertising in relation to *its* costs *and productivity* to that of the total public relations budget and *its* productivity. This year we found that the public relations results on one new product system alone produced twelve

NOTES

times the inquiries brought in by a $50,000 advertising campaign and at a fraction of the cost of that campaign.

During the next fiscal year we are trying to find ways of tagging queries so we can trace them throug the distributive system down to sales, and measure end results. The client has a complicated distribution system that includes both dealers and its own showrooms and sales personnel, hence this will not be easy.

We know already of one Action Office sale - interestingly enough, to an advertising agency - which is directly traceable to a magazine publicity story read by the client. It brought him to our showroom ready to specify Action Office for an entire floor. This one sale more than paid for the entire year's public relations budget...

EXHIBIT 19-2

FROM: RUFF, KIEK AND McAULIFFE, INC.
      342 Madison Avenue
      New York, N.Y. 10017
      TN 7-8230

FOR IMMEDIATE RELEASE
(Full text available on request)

"DOLLAR VALUE OF PUBLICITY CAN BE MEASURED,"
AMA MEETING ON PUBLIC RELATIONS IS TOLD

"In order for publicity to be a hard-nosed, viable marketing tool it must generate activity that can be evaluated in terms of return on the dollar spent for it," Carl Ruff, New York public relations counselor, today (May 8th) told registrants at the three-day American Management Association briefing session, "Measurement and Evaluation of Public Relations Activities," at the St. Regis-Sheraton Hotel in New York City.

NOTES

"Product publicity is the one public relations task that lends itself most easily to measurement and evaluation," according to Ruff, chairman of Ruff, Kiek and McAuliffe, 342 Madison Avenue, New York City.

He told his audience that his firm had worked out a method which, while not foolproof, was enabling it to measure the value of product publicity.

To evaluate the dollar return on one client's public relations investment, Ruff, Kiek and McAuliffe analyzed inquiries received from media product advertising in relation to its cost and productivity and compared them to the public relations budget and its inquiry-producing record.

In the case of this client, the firm discovered that publicity outpulled advertising for one product system by a ratio of seven to one. To have obtained, through advertising, the number of inquiries which publicity generated over a period of 15 months would have cost the client $1,400,000, Ruff reported.

These results, Ruff admitted, were achievable only because of a perfect parlay: a good product, a good news story, a cooperative client,* time to organize a saturation campaign. "This combination doesn't happen very often," he said. "When it comes your way you can swing."

Measurable inquiry results, however, do not negate the importance of institutional editorial credits which can be measured only by spending a ridiculous amount of money, he said.

Ruff stated that his firm was trying to tag inquiries produced by publicity so that they could be traced through the distributive system of its clients down to sales. He cited one sale which had more than paid for the entire year's public relations budget.

*Herman Miller Inc., Zeeland, Michigan, manufacturer of furniture and product systems for offices, government, colleges, institutions and residences.

NOTES

EXHIBIT 19-3

In its issue of May 13 *Editor & Publisher* ran a story of the talk on page 20. The story, which incorporated material from the press release and from the talk itself, took up a full page and ran as follows:

PR Firm Evaluates Publicity and Ads

In order for publicity to be a hard-nosed marketing tool, it must generate activity that can be evaluated in terms of return on the dollar spent for it, Carl Ruff, New York public relations counselor, said at an American Management Association briefing session on public relations activities May 8 in New York City.

Product publicity is the one public relations task that lends itself most easily to measurement and evaluations, said Ruff, who is chairman of Ruff, Kiek and McAuliffe.

He said his firm had worked out a method which, while not foolproof, was enabling it to measure the value of product publicity.

7 to 1 Ratio

To evaluate the dollar return on one client's public relations investment, Ruff, Kiek and McAuliffe analyzed inquiries received from media product advertising in relation to its costs and productivity and compared them to the public relations budget and its inquiry-producing record.

In the case of this client (a Michigan furniture manufacturer), the firm discovered that publicity outpulled advertising for one product system by a ratio of seven to one. To have obtained, through advertising, the number of inquiries which publicity generated over a period of 15 months would have cost the client $1,400,000, Ruff reported.

These results, Ruff admitted, were achievable only because of an ideal parlay: a good product, a good news story, a cooperative client, time to organize a saturation campaign, and professional competence.

NOTES

Measurable inquiry results, however, do not negate the importance of institutional editorial credits which can be measured only by spending a ridiculous amount of money, he said.

Ruff stated that his firm was trying to tag inquiries produced by publicity so that they could be traced through the distributive systems of its clients down to sales. He cited one sale which had more than paid for the entire year's public relations budget.

Subject to Copy Changes

"Public relations practitioners," Ruff declared, "have long made bald claims about the greater dollar-for-dollar power of editorial material over advertising. It's obvious that newspaper and magazine readers, radio listeners and tv watchers spend more time on and pay greater attention to editorial material than they do to advertising copy.

"But as we all know, PR does not have absolute control over its choice of media - or of the precise wording of the message. If we're good we get our client's story told where we want it told. But we can't guarantee this in advance. Nor can we always control the changes made in our lovingly written copy by a harried rewrite desk or a cynical copy editor.

"So in evaluating the effectiveness of public relations against advertising I, for one, had no way of proving that editorial material generated by public relations would yield greater numerical response or motivate stronger activity than did advertising copy.

"Now, product publicity is the one public relations task that lends itself most easily to measurement and evaluation. It's also the area that rates Number One in answer to the questions asked of 500 managements: 'In what general public relations areas has your organization obtained best results from counselors?' Product publicity rates 57% and financial public relations 44% - according to Tom Hopkinson's study.

"My first objective in asking for a copy of the client's records was to make a comparative analysis of the pulling power of the publications we had assumed would be important to us.

NOTES

"When I received the sheets, I discovered that they broke down inquiries and marked those received from advertising and from publicity. I was therefore able to double-check the pulling power of the publications by advertising as well as by publicity.

"But - of great fascination to me - I was able, finally, to see how publicity stacked up against advertising in producing inquiries.

"Once I determined the publicity-to-advertising ratio, I had a basis, at long last, for arriving at a figure for the dollar return. This was a simple matter of isolating product queries, determining their sources, checking the comparative in-depth readership of specific publications carrying articles and their space-rate charges, and applying the ratio."

Ruff explained that his firm's assignment from Herman Miller Inc., of Zeeland, Michigan, was to concentrate on telling the story of "Action Office," a new concept of office equipment.

"We were instructed to concentrate on telling this story in *Fortune, Business Week, Time,* and *Newsweek ,*" Ruff related.

Where Publicity Ran

"The advertising ran from stunning four-color, full-page photographs with punchy copy placed in *Fortune, Scientific American, Interiors,* and the architectural magazines, to a 10-insertion, two-column-by-14-inch series in the *Wall Street Journal.*

"The publicity ran from a two-paragraph inclusion in a *Wall Street Journal* roundup to two-thirds of a page with picture in *Fortune*, three pages with pictures in *Business Week*, a double-page spread in *Saturday Evening Post* and important coverage in the architectural and interior design publications - as well as in the major newspapers.

"On a magazine-to-magazine basis," Ruff said, "publicity outpulled advertising as much as 80 to 1 in one architectural publication, while *Fortune* advertising outpulled publicity 2.5 to 1. On the whole the ratio of inquiries of advertising to publicity was 7 to 1. (sic)

NOTES

"Once I had this average 7 to 1 ratio," Ruff said, "I commissioned an advertising agency space buyer to make an analysis of the publicity at space rates, page for page, column for column, as if the publicity were ads.

$197,000 Worth of Space

"Heretofore I had always disdained making a space-rate tabulation of publicity for my clients. To my mind it was as meaningless as *weighing* a batch of publicity clips... Now I felt justified because the total publicity space rates multiplied by seven would represent what the client would have had to spend in advertising in order to have obtained these queries.

"The final figure, a qualitative analysis of public relations effectiveness by inquiry count, revealed that, for a moderate fee, the client had obtained $1,400,000 of query-pulling, product-selling and attitude-reinforcing exposure over a period of 15 months.

"The total of the publicity measured by space rates was $197,000. Multiplied by 7 you get $1,378,900 - without art and production charges."

Source: Reprinted with permission of *Editor & Publisher*.

NOTES

An Excerpt For Discussion

Protesting Preferential Treatment*

By M.L. Stein

Angered over losing a celebrity interview to its bigger rival - the *Los Angeles Times* - the *Los Angeles Herald Examiner* last week slapped an unusual boycott against a public relations firm it accused of reneging on the interview.

The action also kicked up a controversy over the preferential treatment given to the *Times* on certain entertainment stories by public relations agencies and publicity executives for film and television studios.

The issue arose after the Los Angeles public relations firm, Clein and Feldman, arranged a Dec. 16 interview with actress Geraldine Page for *Herald* reporter Sean Mitchell.

Subsequently, the agency cancelled the interview because the *Times* "demanded an exclusive interview with her," according to David Gritten, editor of the *Herald's* Style section.

Gritten promptly issued a staff memo that virtually killed Clein and Feldman as a *Herald* source. The agency has major clients in the entertainment industry, including the American Ballet Theater, Universal Studios and other movie companies.

"We simply will not deal with people like this," the memo said. "I have today informed one of the company's partners, Bruce Feldman, that we will have no dealings with them for the next six months at least.

"I intend to pursue the matter elsewhere and through different channels, but until you all hear otherwise, you should not talk to Clein and Feldman employees on any matter.

---

*Reprinted by permission from the December 21, 1985 Issue of *Editor & Publisher* magazine.

"Any inquiries that this company has about pitching story ideas, reviewing plays or movies, or indeed any other matter, should briefly and politely be curtailed, with the request that they be referred to me...We have to make some kind of positive stand about PR companies who rush to appease the whims of the *Times* - and behave with a gross lack of professionalism, courtesy and integrity in the process."

Gritten was backed by managing editor John Lindsay, who said the newspaper has fought the *Times'* demands for exclusivity through various public relations firms "at least five times this year."

"I've told the Style staff not to deal with them (Clein and Feldman)," he said.

In an interview with *E&P,* Gritten declined to reveal what other steps he will take in the matter.

He said, however, that the cancellation of the interview with Page, who is starring simultaneously in a Broadway play and a new movie, was the last straw in terms of being preempted by the *Times*.

"We have been aware that from time to time the *Times* will ask for an exclusive, but this is the first time I have experienced an interview being set up and then cancelled because a better offer came along," Gritten said. "If he (Feldman) breaks commitments in such an insulting way he must expect repercussions."

Feldman didn't see it that way, although he acknowledged that his agency had called off the Page interview with Mitchell in favor of Clarke Taylor, a New York freelancer, who writes regularly for the *Los Angeles Times*.

The public relations executive claimed his New York office had been unaware of the Los Angeles commitment to the *Herald Examiner's* Mitchell. Clein and Feldman represent Island Pictures, which is distributing the Page film, entitled "Trip to Bountiful."

But Feldman insisted the *Herald's* quarrel is with the *Times*, not him.

"I am infuriated that they (the *Herald*) would make an example of a public relations agency when their feud is with the *Los Angeles Times* and

NOTES

that they don't understand I have no leverage in this situation," he said bitterly.

"If they are going to embargo, why don't they embargo the tv networks and the studios? Is it because they fear a loss of advertising? Our job is to effectively promote cultural events. We can't do this without an outlet in the *Times*. That the *Times* has enormous power is undeniable."

Feldman's view was generally shared by entertainment publicists contacted by *E&P*. They agreed to comment only if they were unidentified.

Said one: "*The Los Angeles Times* only asks to be first for interviews. They've never asked me for an exclusive. But first for them means being first on God's planet. They have a major fear of losing out to the *New York Times*."

A PR executive for a major film studio said the *Times'* policy of demanding first refusal rights "angers me enormously. It makes me feel that I am being dictated to in carrying out a PR campaign. It's presumptuous to tell a publicist his business. It impinges on my job - what I do for a living."

The official added that the *Times'* insistence on being first "fills me with a sense of outrage," that he claimed is felt by a number of his colleagues in the entertainment PR business.

Another studio executive took a broader view.

"It's a situation (the insistence on first rights) you run into all the time," he commented. "But you have to remember they're the biggest game in town. The *Times* should have first crack at entertainment features, but if the publicity people want to end this policy they can do it. But there's timidity. They don't want to go up against the *Los Angeles Times*."

The spokesman said he respects the *Times'* "status in the marketplace and the marketplace should prevail." But PR reps should also be able to go to other media with top names, he stated.

"David (Gritten) knows the *Times* will get first crack, but this is a case where there was reneging on a commitment," the PR executive observed.

However, he empathized with Feldman, adding:

NOTES

"The publicist finds himself in a bind. Nobody has codified what we're supposed to do in this situation. We're caught in a vise."

Connie Koennen, editor of the daily *Times'* Calendar section, which assigned the Page interview, conceded that the section goes hard after first rights.

"We have a policy of not following anyone," she explained. "Not the *Herald*, not the *New York Times*, not *Variety*, not the (Orange County) *Register*, not the *Valley News* (*Daily News* of Los Angeles). The fact is that the *Times* is huge, weighty and powerful. Publicists are importuning us all the time to interview their clients. We consider ourselves a national newspaper and we're simply being competitive."

Calendar's rule is to either get interviews first or on a "day and date" basis with the competition, according to Koennen.

Koennen, who described the *Herald* as a "marvelous paper with too few readers," absolved the *Times* of any responsibility for the Geraldine Page flap.

"It's a problem between Bruce Feldman and the *Herald*, but the *Herald* doesn't seem to be thinking of its readers," she said.

Her boss, *Times'* associate editor Jean Sharley Taylor, confirmed the paper is highly competitive in entertainment coverage, particularly because Calendar is locked up the day before publication.

"However," she said, "I have never told a staffer to get a story by acing out the *Herald*. Of course we want to be first, but not at the expense of our colleagues. We don't want to trample on a sister paper."

Taylor said *Times'* theater critic Dan Sullivan docs not demand exclusivity.

"He believes in taking his chances and trying to do it better," Taylor said.

She attributed the Geraldine Page interview incident to a "judgment call by a publicist."

Orange County Register entertainment editor P.C. Smith said the practice of "star" interviews being given first to the *Times* is an old story to him.

NOTES

"We are realists," he said, "but at times it can be very frustrating to follow stories you really want."

Recently, Smith recalled, the *Times* published a locally exclusive interview with actor Mickey Rourke.

"We'd love to have had it, but we didn't pursue it," he said. "We are aware that some interviews just aren't offered to us. We don't phone PR people in some cases because we know they won't respond."

The only reason the *Register* was able to run a recent interview with actress Shirley MacLaine was because the publicist for her book publisher made her available, he said.

"If we had gone through normal channels (studio or agency PR reps) we would have never gotten her," he said.

Daily News managing editor Ali Sar said his newspaper has had similar problems in competing with the *Times* for entertainment features, but has tried to get around them.

"We're getting about everything we want to get," Sar said. "If the *Times* gets it first then maybe we're not doing something right."

Aljean Harmetz, who covers the Los Angeles entertainment scene for the *New York Times*, said she agrees with the *Los Angeles Times'* "us first" concept.

"I don't see any deep, dark, terrible thing when a newspaper asks for something first," she said. "It's the job of any good reporter to get a beat - to be a day ahead."

Whether she asks for exclusives, she continued, depends on the circumstances. If the story is "marginal" in terms of interest, "the only thing that makes it worthwhile is to get it exclusively," she said.

Generally, Harmetz said, the *New York Times* and the *Los Angeles Times* "are given first chance to do most things."

"That, of course, comes from the power of the two (newspapers)," she added.

Bob Thomas, Associated Press veteran Hollywood correspondent, who had an interview with Geraldine Page on the day she was scheduled to

NOTES

meet the *Herald's* Mitchell, said, "I guess I'm not in competition with the *Los Angeles Times*."

But he termed the boycott "a very bad situation."

"Personal enterprise rather than the enforcement of power should be the deciding factor in obtaining an interview," he stated.

"This harks back to the days when Louella Parsons and Hedda Hopper were fighting for exclusives and threatening the studios if they didn't get them," Thomas said.

NOTES

Case 20

A SEARCH FOR PUBLIC RELATIONS COUNSEL - A*

About four years after Monarch Laundries went public, Merton Sachs, 64-year-old head of the firm (which had been founded by his father forty years before) told Vincent Puleo that the board of directors had approved Puleo's recommendation that the firm engage public relations counsel.

"Your memorandum, the Auger study, and Professor Levin's report convinced the board," Sachs told his 32-year-old executive assistant. "Let's get on with it, Vinnie, before they change their minds."

Puleo nodded in agreement. The board seldom overrode a Sachs recommendation, but both Puleo and Sachs knew that the $100,000 first-year figure they had budgeted for public relations counsel was a bit high for some of the older board members who had little understanding or knowledge of public relations. He had been wise, Puleo reflected, in authorizing the Auger study and the Levin report; he had little doubt that these had been important factors in the board's decision.

Puleo also reflected that he was fortunate to have a boss like Merton Sachs. Though Sachs was twice as old as Puleo, he had high regard for the younger man's capabilities and person. An increasingly major share of the management of the firm had been turned over to the younger man. The two made a good team. Merton Sachs was wise in the ways of the linen service field, and wise enough to know that a bright young man can often teach an older one new tricks. Puleo was bright but not brash, and smart enough to know that a wise old man can often teach a young man much about patience and restraint.

---

* All names, dates, and places in this case have been disguised.

The Auger study, designed to explore the hospital linen service market, was completed in November by the nationally known Auger Marketing Research Corporation, at a cost of $20,000. It involved depth interviews with one hundred carefully selected hospital administrators and board of trustee members in the Northeast regarding their hospital-owned linen services, and their judgement about the relative merits of four leading linen service firms (including Monarch). The report by Professor Austin Levin, one of the nation's leading marketing authorities, had cost the firm $10,000 and reflected Levin's opinion that the Monarch "systems" approach represented a new dimension in the field of hospital linen services. In fact, Levin had predicted that if Monarch did not achieve "spectacular success" in moving into the national hospital linen service market, it would only be because Monarch had not marketed itself properly.

At the time of the study and the report, the linen service industry was divided into numerous small and medium-sized fiefdoms. Most firms restricted their operations to the city in which they had their plant, though a few venturesome firms operated on a regional basis with plants in several cities. Monarch, with sales of $20 million and 600 employees, operated out of its main plant headquarters in Albany, New York, with additional plants in Springfield and Worcester, Massachusetts. Most of its customers were large industrial and business concerns, but in recent years it had moved into the hospital linen service field.

After making detailed studies, Sachs and Puleo were convinced that the potential national market for hospital linen services, particularly utilizing their "systems" approach, was greater than existing linen services business. They had in turn convinced their board of this potential market, but they hesitated to set up new plants and "go national" before firmly establishing new customers outside their present orbit of operations. The only steps the two had completed were a commissioned 22-minute, slide-sound presentation explaining Monarch's "systems" approach to school food services; preliminary discussions with a young woman (age 30) whom they considered hiring as the firm's public relations director; a budget of

NOTES

$100,000 as the top figure for outside public relations counsel; and board approval to contract for said counsel.

HACKISS RECOMMENDS THREE FIRMS

Prior to getting the board's approval, Puleo had had preliminary discussions with a six-person public relations firm in Albany. He had rejected it, however, because he felt the firm lacked sufficient know-how and would be too "provincial" for the task. He had also had discussions with a New York advertising agency with accounts in an allied field, but had rejected it also. He sensed that the firm was primarily advertising oriented rather than public relations oriented. With Sach's approval, Puleo contacted an old college friend, Peter Hackiss, now director of public relations for a large New York City medical supply concern. Hackiss visited one afternoon with Sachs and Puleo, read through the Auger study and Levin report, viewed the slide-sound film presentation, and suggested three counseling firms: Rice Associates; Dresher-Placebo Associates; and Hammer and Rogerstein. The first two firms, said Hackiss, were among the fifteen largest counseling firms in the country, and the third was among the ten largest. Hackiss said that all three had excellent reputations, well-known national clients, and were just about the right size for Monarch. (The latter point was made in response to Puleo's concern about size. As he explained it: "We're probably small peanuts, and we don't want to get 'lost' among the many large accounts handled by the giants in the public relations field.")

Hackiss's contact at Rice Associates was Jack Costa, 36-year-old account executive who had gone to the same school as Puleo and Hackiss and whom Puleo knew by name but had never met. Costa and Hackiss had been friends for many years. Costa, Hackiss knew, had been with a Chicago public relations counseling firm for ten years and had joined Rice Associates a year earlier.

Hackiss's contact at Dresher-Placebo Associates was Glen Dresher, 54-year-old veteran counselor who was known nationally in the profession

NOTES

for his years of active work in the Public Relations Society of America. Hackiss and Dresher had been friends for many years.

The Hammer and Rogerstein contact was Bernard Apfel, 47-year-old executive vice-president of an aggressive, marketing-oriented firm and also a long-time friend of Hackiss.

With agreement of Sachs and Puleo, Hackiss telephoned Costa, Dresher, and Apfel and explained to each that his good friend Vincent Puleo was seeking public relations counsel for Monarch. Each was apprised of the fact that Puleo wanted to come to New York City for initial talks. They were told that Puleo would be having such talks with three counseling firms, though none of the three was told the others' names. Hackiss very briefly outlined the nature of Monarch's work, said the firm had budgeted up to $100,000 for counseling, and asked if the counselor was interested. All three replied affirmatively, and Hackiss set up appointments: the morning of March 6 (10 AM) for Rice Associates; the afternoon of March 6 (2 PM) for Dresher-Placebo Associates; and the morning of March 7 (10 AM) for Hammer and Rogerstein.

In setting the appointment with Hackiss, Glenn Dresher asked Hackiss if Monarch had done anything in the way of public relations. Hackiss mentioned the Auger study and the Levin report. Dresher said he had worked several times with the Auger firm, had a high regard for them, and knew Levin's reputation as well. He asked Hackiss for copies of the two reports before the meeting, and Hackiss in turn relayed the request to Puleo. The latter thought this was a good idea, but decided to show the slide-sound film at each of the three meetings, as a briefing for the Monarch "systems" approach. He then sent similar letters to Jack Costa, Glenn Dresher, and Bernard Apfel confirming the appointment date and asking to have available a carousel slide projector, a stereo tape unit, and a screen (Exhibit 20-1).

On March 1 Puleo got a telephone call from Jack Costa acknowledging receipt of Puleo's letter and confirming the date. Costa said his firm would have available the projection material Puleo had requested, and suggested lunch together after their discussion, which Puleo accepted.

NOTES

On March 2 Puleo received confirming letters from Glenn Dresher and Bernard Apfel (Exhibits 20-2 and 20-3). In discussing the coming meetings with Sachs, Puleo voiced the thought that it might be a good idea if Sachs went with him to New York.

"Our two judgments about the people I'm going to meet would be much better than just my judgment alone," Puleo pointed out. "This is going to be an important decision for the firm, so if you can free yourself I think it would be worthwhile if you went along with me." Sachs was in agreement, and Puleo notified the three contacts that he would be accompanied by Sachs.

RICE ASSOCIATES

Promptly at 10 AM on March 6, Puleo, accompanied by Sachs, announced himself at the offices of Rice Associates and asked for Jack Costa. Costa came out into the outer reception room and introduced himself to Puleo, who in turn introduced Sachs. They went into a small room attached to Roger Rice's office, outfitted like a den with leather chairs, guns and trophies, where similar introductions were made with Rice and another staff member named Stanley Joffrey. The latter was referred to by Rice as a vice president of the firm.

"We've cleared our entire morning for you, Mr. Sachs," said Rice, "so why don't the two of you tell us about your problems while we listen."

Sachs deferred to Puleo, who sketched in the linen services industry, the Monarch firm, and its "systems" approach. Questions, when forthcoming, came from Rice, with both Costa and Joffrey maintaining a respectable silence. After about a half hour Puleo broke off and suggested the slide-sound presentation.

"Jack, go out and make sure the equipment is set," Rice told Costa, and after Costa left the room, Rice quickly sketched the nature of Rice Associates and its clients. When Costa returned to say that the equipment was set, Rice suggested that he make sure a carafe of water and glasses were available. Assured by Costa that they were available, Rice ushered the

NOTES

group into the firm's conference room and the film was run. After another hour's give-and-take, during which time Rice addressed his remarks mainly to Sachs, Rice suggested lunch. The private club to which he took them was nearby, so the group walked over: Rice walking with Sachs and the other three behind.

At the conclusion of lunch Puleo said he'd like to have a written proposal from Rice Associates by March 24, and Rice said this would be done. Sachs and Puleo then went to their meeting with Dresher.

On the way over in a taxi, they discussed the morning session and found they were in general agreement. Rice, they felt, impressed them as a successful corporation executive who was somewhat pompous and overbearing with his associates. Though Puleo didn't mention it to Sachs, he also felt that Rice had treated Jack Costa like some third-rung clerk. They were both of the opinion that Rice didn't have too clear a conception of their "systems" approach and that some of his questions indicated he had not really studied the material Puleo had sent to Costa.

Though Joffrey hadn't said much during the morning's discussion, the two considered him to be a New York "sharpie," as Puleo put it.

DRESHER-PLACEBO ASSOCIATES

Though Sachs and Puleo arrived at Dresher-Placebo Associates sharply at 2 PM, they had to wait fifteen minutes before Glenn Dresher came out to meet them. Following introductions, he brought them into his corner office and introduced Everett Bushinger, executive vice president, and Ralph Nolan. The latter was not identified by title.

Dresher's office was smartly done in the best decorator style; it was large, comfortable, very well furnished. Puleo noticed three PRSA Silver Anvil awards and Dresher explained the accounts for which they had been won.

Dresher handled most of the discussion for the three men, addressed his remarks to both Sachs and Puleo, and quickly demonstrated to them an intimate understanding of their firm and its problems. He complimented

Puleo for the material sent on ahead and praised the slide-sound presentation when it was run in the firm's conference room.

Following the presentation of the film, Dresher took about a half hour to outline the way his firm operated. He cited some "case studies" the firm had handled and indicated that Nolan would probably handle the Monarch account under the close and direct supervision of himself and Bushinger. Puleo had the somewhat uncomfortable feeling that Dresher considered the matter closed and the account his.

"Is this it?" Puleo asked finally. "What about a written presentation and plan?"

"We don't operate that way," Dresher replied. "A certain chemistry works in relationships like ours. As we get to know you better, to know your problems and your people better, we'll develop definite plans and set objectives. We know we can do a real job for you. You know we're good, or you wouldn't be here. All you need to do now is to agree you want us to work for you; we'll draw up a simple contract letter and get to work."

After a few minutes further discussion, Puleo pointing out that he and Sachs were considering several counseling firms, it was agreed that Puleo would let Dresher know Monarch's decision by March 27, and the meeting ended.

At dinner with Sachs that evening, Puleo admitted that he had been very impressed with Glenn Dresher, and Sachs agreed. Both felt that Dresher exuded a great deal of confidence in his firm's ability to do the job for Monarch, seemed to have a sound grasp of Monarch's approach, and had an impressive list of clients, which included one in a field closely related to theirs.

"As for a plan, or rather nonplan, maybe that's the way things are done in public relations," Sachs mused aloud. "In a way, you know, that's the sort of approach we've been taking with our systems approach. We can't seem to get it down on paper the way we want it, so we more or less ask prospective clients to take us on faith. We tell our clients that we're good, take us and we'll show you, and that's what Dresher says to us."

NOTES

HAMMER AND ROGERSTEIN

Sachs and Puleo were on time the next morning for their 10 AM appointment. Bernard Apfel met them at once in the outer reception room and brought them into his office to introduce them to Bill Francher, a vice president.

The office and the pace at Hammer and Rogerstein, both Sachs and Puleo noted, differed considerably from the firms they had visited the previous day. Whereas Rice's and Dresher's offices were as large, spacious and decorous as Sach's own office back in Albany, Apfel's was as small, cluttered, and busy as Puleo's. When the group went down the hall to the conference room, Sachs and Puleo also noted much hustle and bustle in the halls.

The conference room was in use.

"Wasn't I supposed to have the conference room?" Apfel asked one of those present, and when advised otherwise, he laughed at his own error and brought the group back into his own office. After hasty improvisation, the equipment was set up and the slide-sound presentation was viewed. Apfel complimented Puleo on the film; then he and Francher asked questions concerning Monarch. Francher, in particular, had an excellent grasp of Monarch's problems and its "systems" approach. When Apfel had to answer his telephone - which rang several times during the morning - Francher carried the conversation along. Everyone by this time was on a first-name basis. At one point Apfel excused himself to "go out and give my secretary some instructions about the calls I got."

When Apfel returned, he discussed the nature of his firm and showed some brochures the organization had produced. He cited some of the work the firm had done for major clients whose names were household words.

Before leaving, Puleo told Apfel that he would like to have the Hammer and Rogerstein proposal by March 24. Apfel said they'd be pleased to work with this deadline.

Puleo and Sachs discussed their impressions of Hammer and Rogerstein on their way out to the airport. Both liked Apfel's friendly,

NOTES

sincere approach, had been very favorably impressed with Francher's astuteness regarding Monarch. Though the hustle and bustle of the office routine had at times interfered with their discussions, they felt that the firm was on the move at all times. They were favorably impressed with the Hammer and Rogerstein work they had seen. At the same time, they worried that the firm was so large and so busy Monarch might not get the attention they felt it needed. In parting, they agreed to hold back final judgment until the March 24 deadline had been met.

The first of the three firms to be heard from was Dresher-Placebo Associates on March 10. Puleo, at the New York Hilton with his wife for a weekend of play-going, received Dresher's telephone call transferred from Albany. Dresher asked if a decision had been made; Puleo replied that he was still awaiting letters and proposals from the other two firms. Dresher said he would be getting a letter off to Puleo early the next week. Puleo got the impression that Dresher was much interested in the Monarch account, and said he'd be glad to hear from Dresher the following week.

THE RICE PROPOSAL

On March 16 Sachs received a one-page letter from Rice (Exhibit 20-4) which Sachs in turn passed along to Puleo. The letter was accompanied by a fifteen-page brochure describing the structure and operations of the Rice organization, a short flyer describing the Rice approach to financial public relations, and a ten-page proposal outlining "A Sales Promotion Plan for Monarch Laundries."

The Rice proposal described the firm's program as a joint effort of Rice Associates and Monarch which would include sales aids, advertising, publicity, and public relations. The program recommended the following order of priorities:

1. Sales development within the areas served by the Albany and Massachusetts plants

```
NOTES




```

2. Establishment nationally of an understanding of the Monarch system among hospital administrators

3. Careful consideration given to the introduction of this system in the Albany and Massachusetts plants

4. Future geographic expansion and necessary investment to be guided by the results of the Sales Promotion Program

Thirteen steps were then detailed under the heading "Method of Operation." These included an evaluation based on personal observations of sales problems and the company posture; selection of an effective name for the Monarch system and development of a striking insignia; preparation of a selling brochure; assistance in automating and strengthening the slide presentation; preparation of a sales letter to be sent with the brochure to selected hospital administrators served by the Monarch plants; preparation of a letter to be sent to 30 groups considering co-ops; a series of ads to be prepared and placed in *Hospital* magazine; a meeting with the American Hospital Association to arrange to make the brochure available to its members; preparation initially of at least two articles for placement in national professional journals and use of reprints for follow-up to inquiries; the supplying of a booth for the August convention of the American Hospital Association; setting up of a National Advisory Council; scheduling of Rice representatives for appearance before hospital groups; preparation of an annual report, semi-annual report, and dividend enclosures.

Under the heading of "Budget," Rice Associates stated they would carry out the program for a total of $75,000 for the year. Of this total, $60,000 would cover the cost of all services including counsel and supervision by the principals of the firm and the actual time spent on the program by Rice staffers. Out-of-pocket expenses were estimated at $15,000 and these expenses would be fully itemized and billed at net cost.

NOTES

THE DRESHER LETTER

On March 17 Puleo received a four-page letter from Dresher (Exhibit 20-5) underscoring Dresher's reasons why his firm could execute an effective program for Monarch and suggesting that they proceed on the basis of a $5,000 per month fee, plus expenses.

On March 18 Puleo received a brief note from Apfel saying it would take a bit longer for his organization to send along its informal proposal (Exhibit 20-6). On March 22 Sachs received a brief note from Apfel thanking him for visiting Hammer and Rogerstein and noting that the proposal would be going to Puleo in a few days. (Exhibit 20-7).

In a discussion with Sachs on March 24 - the date Puleo had named for submission of proposals - Puleo mentioned that he was perturbed by Hammer and Rogerstein's delay.

"If this is an indication of how they operate, I don't like it," Puleo said. However, the two agreed to wait a few days for the Hammer and Rogerstein proposal to come in. On Tuesday, March 28, Puleo received a call from Bill Francher who was very apologetic about not getting off the prospectus and who said he had just returned from London and would get the proposal to Puleo by Monday, April 3, and possibly by Friday, March 31.

THE HAMMER AND ROGERSTEIN PROPOSAL

The proposal, in the form of a detailed, single-spaced, eight-page letter, was dated March 31 and arrived on April 3. It was addressed to Puleo, signed by Bill Francher, and started as follows:

Dear Vinnie:

The more I think about Monarch's problem, the less complicated it gets. Perhaps I'm over-simplifying, but here is how the equation looks to me:

NOTES

1. The care, feeding, and financing of hospital linen services is a constant source of irritation, frustration, and expense to hospital administrators, their staffs, and their boards.

2. Monarch offers proven solutions to these problems.

3. But not enough of the right people know about Monarch or its service.

4. Because they don't know, they're trying to handle the problem in a variety of ways. The most serious of these in terms of Monarch's future is the movement towards cooperative linen services. This movement is taking hold very rapidly.

5. Unless Monarch can find some way to break this momentum by interposing its own story, a good part of the market will be lost. Monarch must present administrators, staff people, and board members with what Austin Levin terms "the fifth alternative." And it must do this fairly quickly.

(At this point the proposal outlined target audiences; stated that the Monarch story has to be developed, dramatically and precisely, on paper; observed that Monarch has to establish itself as the authority with the answers in a creditable manner widely circulated; and concluded that the public relations effort must have continuity and follow-through.

(Detailing the "tools" to achieve the above-mentioned goals, the proposal described nine "projects" for telling the Monarch story and four main ways of reaching the financial community. The projects were: a basic position paper; a research job of listing target audiences, market by market; preparation, through personal interviews, of successful Monarch case histories and placement of articles about such satisfied clients; development of by-lined articles by Monarch executives; design and carrying out of an interview survey to identify viewpoints and problem areas among specific audiences and reporting of the results through appropriate publications; sponsorship of seminars as a wedge for market-by-market promotion; a concerted effort to get prospective customers to visit hospitals served by Monarch and also to visit Monarch's refurbished plant; development of important speaking dates and appearances; use of reprints for a very low-pressure direct mail campaign.

(In conclusion the letter made the points cited below.)

That's how the mission looks to us, Vinnie. Both the hospital-directed work and the financial relations program could mesh wonderfully together and the total effort could be exciting and meaningful. We'd love to do it for you.

Our professional fee is $48,000 annually. This covers the "people" side of the budget in New York, which would be a center of the whole activity.

The "things" part of the budget - like publications, photography, travel, telephone calls, etc - we can only estimate at this point. If you budgeted $30,000-$40,000 for the year, I'm pretty sure we'd be well covered (and, with the exception of truly petty cash items, disbursements from this fund are only made with your prior approval).

Finally, it would be great if we could set aside a kind of "war chest" of $8,000-$10,000 so that we could have on-the-spot support for your market-by-market program (both hospital and financial) from our regional offices. We can turn the regional office people on as we need specific support - and turn them off again when a promotion is

NOTES

wound up. They can handle things like seminar arrangements, advance publicity, newspaper, radio and TV interviews and so forth.

So the total cost should be in the neighborhood of $86,000-$98,000 for the year. We would want a firm six month agreement, cancellable either way thereafter by 60 days notice.

Bernard and I are delighted that you gave us the opportunity to think about this. I believe we could make a real contribution. If, as you deliberate on your final choice, you'd like to meet the account team that would be doing your work here in New York, we'd be delighted. So much depends on the chemistry between the particular people involved. I'll be off to London again on Tuesday, but Bernard will be calling you around mid-week to see if there's anything else you need in the way of information, people or back-up.

All good wishes,
(signed Bill)

William Francher

P.S. Since time is so short, I'm taking the liberty of sending a copy of this letter directly to Merton. Some additional copies of our Visual Report and our current client list are enclosed.

On April 3 Puleo wrote to all three counseling firms acknowledging receipts of their letters. The following day, he met with Sachs to discuss a decision on retaining one of them as counsel for Monarch.

In discussing Rice Associates, Puleo and Sachs were in agreement that they felt neither Roger Rice nor Stanley Joffrey was their "type" of person and seemed too "conservative" in their approach and programming. Puleo said he thought the Rice proposal was adequate, but not particularly outstanding. Sachs, who said he had merely glanced through it, agreed with Puleo's estimation.

NOTES

Both Puleo and Sachs agreed that Dresher was their kind of man and would do a hard and effective sell for them. At the same time, they were bothered by the fact that he hadn't really set down a program on paper. As Sachs phrased it: "Faith is important, as I said the other day, but $60,000 worth of faith is a helluva lot of faith."

Both Sachs and Puleo agreed that Francher's proposal was realistic, imaginative and to the point. It had impressed them, but they were bothered by the fact that it had come in late, and they saw this delay as a possible symptom of the treatment they might get from Hammer and Rogerstein.

"So," Sachs finally said, "what do we do now?"

EXHIBIT 20-1
MONARCH LAUNDRIES

February 27, 19--
(Address)
(Salutation)

I'm writing a note to confirm the meeting Peter Hackiss set up for us on (date) at (time) in your offices.

I'll have a short slide-sound presentation which should help give you a better idea of our story. I'll need a carousel slide projector, a stereo tape unit, and a screen. I'll carry the slides, tape and sound synchronizer with me.

I'm enclosing two studies and our most recent Annual Report to give you some background about us. Your reading of this material prior to our meeting should make the meeting more productive for both of us. Of course, I expect that the enclosed information will be kept in the strictest confidence.

NOTES

I'm very much looking forward to our meeting next week.

Sincerely,

Vincent A. Puleo
Assistant to the President

EXHIBIT 20-2

DRESHER-PLACEBO ASSOCIATES
Public Relations
(Address)

Glenn B. Dresher
President
(PRSA Accredited)

Mr. Vincent Puleo March 1, 19--
Monarch Laundries
210 Lawton Street
Albany, New York 12207

Dear Mr. Puleo:

I am looking forward to our meeting on Monday. We have a carousel slide projector, a stereo tape unit, and a screen on hand.

Meanwhile, we'll do our homework with the material you sent us.

Cordially,
Glenn Dresher
(signed)

NOTES

EXHIBIT 20-3

HAMMER & ROGERSTEIN
Incorporated
(Address)

Office of Executive Vice President

March 1, 19--

Mr. Vincent Puleo
Monarch Laundries
210 Lawton Street
Albany, New York 12207

Dear Mr. Puleo:

We are looking forward to meeting you on Tuesday, March 7 at 10:00AM in our offices, and we appreciate the material you sent us in advance of the meeting. It should help us in being better prepared, and will certainly save all of us considerable time.

We have available the projection equipment you requested, and it will be set up for you.

Looking forward to the pleasure of meeting you.

    Sincerely,

    Bernard Apfel
    (Signed and typed)

cc: Jack Hackiss

NOTES

EXHIBIT 20-4

RICE ASSOCIATES
(Address)

March 15, 19--

Mr. Merton Sachs, President
Monarch Laundries
210 Lawton Street
Albany, New York 12207

Dear Mr. Sachs:

We've spent an intriguing few days putting together the attached suggestions for you. Intriguing because we feel, as you do, that there is a great opportunity here and because the task is just difficult enough to be challenging.

Although we have had neither the opportunity nor the time to explore in depth the reaction of hospital officials, a quick probe with some of our friends has shown a real need for your services. We have no doubt, on the basis of your success in the areas where you are now operating, that your System could prove to be the answer.

Please be assured that we are confident we can provide you with the material you need to carry out your sales campaign and can bring you national publicity - at the beginning and, of course, to an even greater extent as your program progresses.

We have attached two copies of our recommendations, along with a copy of our firm's brochure and a flyer on our corporate and financial department. Please feel free to call me with any questions or for expansion of any of our suggestions. We are anxious to work with you.

Cordially,
(signed and typed)
Roger Rice

NOTES

EXHIBIT 20-5

DRESHER-PLACEBO ASSOCIATES
Public Relations
(Address)

Glenn B. Dresher
President
(PRSA Accredited)

March 16, 19--

Mr. Vincent Puleo
Assistant to the President
Monarch Laundries
210 Lawton Street
Albany, New York 12207

Dear Vincent:

There are several reasons why I feel we can be most helpful to you in the development of the most efficient and productive public relations program.

You have obviously gone "first class" in the manner in which you sought out top professional people to help you in the management and understanding of your opportunities. We like to think that we are also in the top professional ranks. We are one of the most dynamic agencies in the field, and are proud of the fact that we have been retained for many years by such clients as (name) and (name) and that we have recently been selected above all other agencies by such sophisticated people as (five well-known names listed).

In addition, many of our executives devote themselves to the

NOTES

betterment of our profession through leadership in the activities of the Public Relations Society of America (Two examples listed).

We would bring to your program a team of people with deep dedication to the highest standards of professional practice.

Another asset is our extensive specialization which means that we put at your disposal some of the country's most competent people in the areas of publicity, research, marketing, financial relations and government relations; and we provide the most comprehensive coverage of the entire country through our own large offices in New York, Chicago, and Dallas.

Third, we have extensive experience in test marketing and market expansion programs, currently working with such successful companies as (six national consumer product firms listed).

Fourth, we have considerable direct experience in the hospital field. One example is that we represent the (client named). Another is that, as Public Relations Chairman of the Westchester County Hospital Association, I have been intimately connected with hospital activities for a decade and have also been a speaker before meetings of the National Hospital Public Relations Association.

Fifth, we are heavily management-oriented. We serve as confidential consultants to the top executives of a great many successful corporations and trade associations. Since we enjoy a high degree of their confidence, we have a considerable insight into management processes and problems, and have been able to be of help and assistance in many significant ways - a reservoir

NOTES

of experience that would , I am sure, be useful to you in the expansion of your business.

Sixth, we have evolved a comprehensive concept of what public relations is and how it would be most efficiently applied to business situations. We proceed on the basis of sound research and comprehensive planning.

The Auger Study is a real contribution to an understanding of your situation, and provides an excellent basis for meaningful programming. As it happens, we are involved in many situations with the Auger organization - such as (four organizations listed). We work well together and we have devoted much combined time to working productively together.

From a public relations point of view, it is significant that there is widespread lack of awareness of your better method of linen service that you provide (attributes listed). These factors all lend themselves to public relations techniques that will dramatically and convincingly capture the interest of your important "publics," and persuade them to talk business with you.

Vincent, we are extremely interested in helping you realize what is obviously a great potential for Monarch Laundries. This is a time of great turmoil and change in the nation's hospitals, and the revolutionary impact on individual hospitals poses a situation in which effective public relations can be highly profitable.

I believe that your program should "sell," first, your concept of service, then the specifics of the service itself, and, finally, but of equal importance, the quality and integrity of the Company and its top management people. These are all areas in which we have had experience and success and we are "raring to go."

NOTES

I suggest that we proceed on the basis of a $5,000 per month fee, plus expenses. This fee will cover planning, supervision, and full staffing of your account, and I give you my personal assurance that we will do everything possible to provide the best program that experience and talent can make possible.

We work on a simple letter of agreement, containing a 90-day cancellation clause, and I'll be happy to send one along as soon as you have had an opportunity to make your decision.

We greatly appreciate your courtesy in giving us such a thorough briefing, and we look forward to what we earnestly hope will be a favorable decision to select us.

My best to Mr. Sachs.

    Cordially,

    (signed)

    Glenn Dresher

NOTES

EXHIBIT 20-6

HAMMER AND ROGERSTEIN

Office of Executive Vice President

March 17, 19--

Mr. Vincent Puleo
Monarch Laundries
210 Lawton Street
Albany, New York 12207

Dear Vince:

This note is just to let you know that it will take a bit longer than planned to send you our informal proposal regarding a public relations program for Monarch.

Bill Francher, who is writing the proposal, has had to make an unexpected trip to London which has set back his timetable a few days. However, I expect that you will be receiving the proposal by the end of next week.

Thanks again for the briefing. It was, as you undoubtedly realize, extremely helpful.

    Best regards,
    (signed and typed)

    Bernard Apfel
    (Address)

NOTES

EXHIBIT 20-7

HAMMER AND ROGERSTEIN

Office of Executive Vice President

March 21, 19--

Mr. Merton Sachs
President
Monarch Laundries
210 Lawton Street
Albany, New York 12207

Dear Mr. Sachs:

I just wanted to thank you for taking so much time to visit us. I am keenly conscious of the complicated requirements that are involved in a program for Monarch Laundries, but if I may say so, it does sound like a tremendous idea and one that is bound to succeed.

Our informal proposal will be going to Vincent Puleo within a few days. I hope you will have a chance to study it as well.

Meanwhile, thanks again for your time and patience.

    Sincerely,
    (Signed and typed)

    Bernard Apfel
    (Address)

NOTES

Case 21

A SEARCH FOR PUBLIC RELATIONS COUNSEL - B*

In analyzing the proposals and the executives of the three public relations counseling firms (See *A Search For Public Relations Counsel-A*), Puleo decided to utilize an elimination process to make his final selection. It was his opinion that Rice Associates rated third, and he suggested to Sachs that they eliminate Rice from consideration. Sachs concurred, Puleo wrote a brief note to Roger Rice (Exhibit 21-1), and Rice replied by return mail (Exhibit 21-2).

Puleo then telephoned Bernard Apfel and Glenn Dresher for appointments to visit each a second time, the former on April 18 and the latter on April 26. He received confirming notes from both.

In making the date with Apfel, Puleo sent his regards to Francher and said that he would be pleased to see him on April 18.

"I'll be glad to pass along your regards, but Bill won't be with us that day," Apfel replied. "Bill is our... well, he writes our proposals because he's so good at this sort of thing, but he won't be working on the account."

"Oh, I see," said Puleo. A moment's pause. "Well, anyway, we'd want to meet the people who will be working on the account. Okay?"

"Of course," replied Apfel, and he was as good as his word when Sachs and Puleo showed up on April 18 for the meeting. Two Hammer and Rogerstein staffers were present, whom Apfel introduced as Kathleen Barnes, a group leader and vice president, and Ralph Schmidt, an account executive.

Puleo judged Barnes to be about 38 and Schmidt about 30. In the ensuing conversation concerning Monarch, it seemed to Puleo (and Sachs

---

* *All names, dates, and places in this case have been disguised.*

later confirmed) that Barnes and Schmidt had had no more than a scant briefing about Monarch, the industry, or the firm's problems.

In preparing for the meeting, and for the later one with Dresher, Puleo had prepared a list of specific questions. Now he asked them of Apfel and in each instance got a quick, to-the-point answer (See Exhibit 21-3 for answers given by Apfel and later by Dresher).

The discussion between Monarch and the Hammer and Rogerstein people lasted through the morning. About 12:30 Apfel invited the group to lunch at an exclusive private club. On the way over, Puleo walked with Schmidt and learned that Schmidt had worked six years for a small city daily and had joined Hammer and Rogerstein only four months earlier. An enthusiastic young man, Schmidt said he welcomed the chance to work on his first account.

Sachs, walking with Apfel and Barnes, learned that Barnes had been with Hammer and Rogerstein for twelve years, and prior to that time had been a newspaper reporter and director of public relations for a hospital. Barnes impressed Sachs as being astute and quick.

When Sachs and Puleo returned from New York, they received letters from Apfel, which they immediately acknowledged (Exhibits 21-4 and 21-5).

In setting up the April 26 visit with Dresher, Puleo asked that the account executive slated for the Monarch account be present, but Dresher was alone in his office when Sachs and Puleo were ushered in. Dresher, responding to a question from Puleo, said that Ralph Nolan would handle their account when it came to Dresher-Placebo Associates and he was available if they wanted him. Puleo said this probably wouldn't be necessary since Dresher hadn't thought it was necessary, and Sachs, Puleo and Dresher discussed the account by themselves. Puleo asked Dresher the same questions he had asked Apfel, and Dresher's replies were as quick and to the point as Apfel's had been (See Exhibit 21-3 for answers given by Dresher).

NOTES

When Sachs and Puleo returned to Albany that evening, Sachs asked Puleo which firm he preferred: Hammer and Rogerstein or Dresher-Placebo Associates.

"I'm satisfied we've explored this sufficiently," Sachs said. "Let's make our decision tonight."

Puleo agreed. "It's a tough one, but it could be worse," he said. "I think either one will do a fine job for us. Frankly, my brain tells me Dresher-Placebo Associates, but my gut tells me Hammer and Rogerstein."

EXHIBIT 21-1
MONARCH LAUNDRIES

(Address)

Mr. Roger Rice
Rice Associates, Inc.
(Address)

April 19,19--

Dear Mr. Rice:

I'm sorry to tell you that we've decided to retain the services of another agency.

The decision was not an easy one for us to make.

We enjoyed meeting you and your associates and we really appreciate the time and effort you spent on us.

Sincerely,
(signed)

Vincent A. Puleo
Assistant to the President

cc: Merton Sachs

NOTES

EXHIBIT 21-2

ROGER RICE ASSOCIATES, Inc.
(Address)

Mr. Merton Sachs April 21, 19--
Monarch Laundries
210 Lawton Street
Albany, New York 12207

Dear Mr. Sachs:

We were disappointed indeed to receive your letter saying that you had selected another agency. We sincerely feel that you are on the right track and that your operation is bound to be successful. We would like to have been a part of it.

If at any future time you should feel like talking with us further, we would be only too happy to meet with you.

                         Cordially,

                         (signed and typed)

                         Roger Rice

NOTES

EXHIBIT 21-3

Puleo's Questions with Answers by Apfel and Dresher
(as Puleo Jotted Them Down During Discussion)

	Question	Apfel Answer	Dresher Answer
1.	Who will be the account executive?	Ralph Schmidt	Ralph Nolan
2.	How will he work with us?	He'll practically be living with you for the first four months.	He'll become part of your family
3.	How will you work?	We sit down with you and jointly work out a plan	We work out a program along with your help
4.	How often do we see your people?	As often as necessary	As much as needed
5.	Do your account execs change often?	No	Of course not
6.	Will the account exec work just for us?	No. You'll have about half of Schmidt's time but don't worry about this	No. Nolan has other accounts, but don't worry, you'll get what you pay for

NOTES

7.	Do we get scheduled reports?	You can get anything you want, but we lay out a plan and meet regularly to check it	You'll have progress meetings with us
8.	How will we be billed?	Monthly in advance on basic fee, and monthly on expenses after incurred	Same general reply
9.	We see vouchers?	If you want them	In extraordinary detail if you want them. In fact, not a penny will be spent without your approval
10.	How involved are you in the hospital field?	Not directly but we're in related fields	We had a hospital supply account and now have related field accounts
11.	When do we start?	Today if you want us to	Right now if you want

NOTES

EXHIBIT 21-4

HAMMER AND ROGERSTEIN
Incorporated

Office of the Executive Vice President

Mr. Vincent A. Puleo April 18, 19--
Assistant to the President
Monarch Laundries
210 Lawton Street
Albany, New York 12207

Dear Vince:

    Notwithstanding the fact that your screening process is as tough as getting into Yale, it was good to see you and Merton Sachs again.
    At the moment we all feel somewhat talked out but if there is anything further that you wish to know, please don't hesitate to get in touch.
    We are awaiting your decision with a great deal of anticipation; but win or lose, I want to express our appreciation for your interest in our organization.

                                       Best regards,
                                       (signed and typed)

                                       Bernard Apfel

P.S.: Since you were nice enough to speak favorably of our Photo Exhibit, I thought you might be especially interested in a booklet we've prepared. It's a complication of articles by our senior people, andwe're rather proud of them.
                      (Address)

NOTES

EXHIBIT 21-5

HAMMER AND ROGERSTEIN
Incorporated

Office of the Executive Vice President

April 18, 19--

Mr. Merton Sachs
President
Monarch Laundries
210 Lawton Street
Albany, New York 12207

Dear Merton:

    Kathleen Barnes, Ralph Schmidt, and I enjoyed our get-together very much. We are all very high at the possibility of working with you.

    There isn't much now about us that you don't already know but if you do need anything else, please give me a call. Meanwhile, thanks again for your obvious interest in hearing us talk about ourselves.

    We look forward to hearing from you.

                                                Best regards,
                                                (signed and typed)

                                                Bernard Apfel

                (Address)

NOTES

Case 22

A SEARCH FOR PUBLIC RELATIONS COUNSEL - C*

After a long discussion regarding the relative merits of Dresher-Placebo Associates and Hammer and Rogerstein (See *A Search For Public Relations Counsel-B)*, Sachs and Puleo agreed they both preferred to retain the Dresher firm; they so notified Glenn Dresher by telephone on April 27. Puleo then notified Bernard Apfel of the decision, and Apfel in turn replied. (Exhibits 22-1 and 22-2)

At Dresher's suggestion, Sachs and Puleo - who were scheduled for another meeting in New York anyway - attended a strategy meeting in Dresher's office on May 2. Present were the two Monarch officials, Dresher, Ev Bushinger, and Ralph Nolan. The meeting lasted all morning and extended through lunch. In the opinion of both Sachs and Puleo, it was very productive. Basic discussion centered around the public relations strategy to be followed in the immediate present and over the long run. Before the meeting ended, it was agreed that Nolan would come to Albany the following week to make a personal tour of the Monarch facilities there and to continue the discussion started at the New York strategy meeting. It was also agreed that the effective date of the Monarch-Dresher contract would be May 8. The contract itself arrived in Puleo's office on May 7, when it was countersigned and a copy returned to Dresher.

When Nolan visited Puleo on May 11, he brought along Steve Kramer, who was introduced to both Puleo and Sachs as a member of the Dresher firm. Puleo in turn introduced Melissa Stangel, the new director of public relations for Monarch as of May 1. Stangel, 30, was the young woman Puleo had been considering for the job for some time. She held a B.S. degree in public relations and had been assistant public relations director of a medical complex in Albany for eight years.

---

* All names, dates, and places in this case have been disguised.

Nolan spent the entire day with Puleo and Stangel, agreeing mutually that Nolan's first job on the account would be to prepare a new brochure underscoring the Monarch "systems" approach as a "fifth option" to existing hospital linen service programs. Nolan told Puleo that he would put together a written plan and would get it to Puleo in the near future. It was also agreed that Nolan would immediately prepare the draft of a letter to be sent out to a specific target audience: administrators of hospitals which, Puleo knew, were considering co-op laundry programs.

Nolan's draft letter arrived in Puleo's office on May 16. It struck Puleo as a poor letter and a disappointing effort. He returned it to Nolan with numerous corrections and suggestions for changes.

NOLAN'S PROGRAM

On May 20 Puleo received from Nolan an eleven-page double-spaced typewritten "Promotional Program for Linen Systems for Hospitals." (Linen Systems for Hospitals was the suggested name Nolan had proposed for Monarch, as a coordinated but separate part of Monarch Laundries)

The program listed four public relations objectives:

1. To create a strong new image of the company as the originator of a unique "systems" approach.

2. To instill in the minds of hospital administrators an appreciation of this unique "systems" approach.

3. To create confidence for the competence and quality of the company and its management.

4. To assist the company's sales force by preconditioning the market and providing tools that will help them sell the "systems" approach to prospects.

NOTES

As "sales objective" the program proposed to increase client hospitals in the company's present sales areas, and to induce hospital groups throughout the United States, which were contemplating the establishment of co-op laundry services, to consider the Monarch approach instead.

The program proposed four "devices and tools":

1) Selection of the name "Linen Systems For Hospitals."

2) Development of a new logo for the new name.

3) Editing and tightening of the sales slide presentation.

4) Preparation of two new sales brochures, one for local and one for national use.

Under "The Local Program," the proposal listed local and regional target publics and suggested the following "basic PR activities": creation of the sales brochures, preparation of articles for professional publications, news releases, and reprint mailing. Suggested supplementary activities included seminars for key hospital personnel, speaking engagements, and assistance in developing trade shows.

Under "The National Program," the proposal listed as the national target audience those hospital groups thinking of "going co-op." It suggested setting up a meeting of those hospital officials with Monarch officials who would utilize the slide presentation, kits, and the new brochures; these groups might also be invited to tour the Albany and Massachusetts plants. Other suggested activities included a basic research study on the merits of co-ops versus Monarch's system, talks before major hospital administrator groups comparing the merits of co-ops versus the "systems" approach, articles in leading hospital journals analyzing the difficulties experienced by co-op groups, and an article in a major business publication identifying the company as the originator of the "systems" concept.

NOTES

In discussion of the proposal with Sachs and Stangel, Puleo and the others agreed that it was somewhat better than the proposal put forth by Rice Associates, but certainly not as good as the one developed by Bill Francher of Hammer and Rogerstein.

KRAMER TAKES OVER

One week after receiving the proposed public relations program, Puleo got a telephone call from Ev Bushinger of Dresher-Placebo Associates informing him that Nolan was no longer with the counseling firm; the account would be handled by Steve Kramer. Puleo's reaction was an ambivalent one. He was not at all happy about having account executives switched on him, but, on the other hand, he had not been satisfied with Nolan's work. When Bushinger suggested that Kramer get up to Albany as soon as possible, a date was arranged for June 7.

At the June 7 meeting - an all-day affair attended by Puleo, Stangel and Kramer - Puleo started to discuss aspects of the Nolan proposal, but Kramer said that proposal was now "out the window" and suggested they disregard it. Puleo asked if there would be another propodal, and Kramer said that, of course, he would set one up and submit it.

At Puleo's suggestion, it was agreed that for the immediate future Kramer would concentrate on: the brochures, a history of the corporation and biographical sketches of the leading executives, assignment of a clipping service, and the development of a logo for the company.

"What about the up-coming national convention of hospital administrators in Denver on August 15?" Puleo asked Kramer. "Should we sign up for a booth, and will you develop it? Will the brochure be ready by then?"

Kramer said they should definitely get into the Denver convention exhibition - there was plenty of time. And he would be glad to work on the booth.

Puleo received the first draft of the brochure copy on July 7 and rejected it outright as poorly conceived, poorly written, choppy, and in

NOTES

many instances ineffective in projecting the Monarch "systems" concept.

"It's as though Kramer didn't even understand what our system is all about," Puleo told Sachs, and the latter agreed. Sachs also expressed perturbation over the fact that the firm had already paid $10,000 to Dresher and seemed to be getting little to show for it. Puleo agreed with Sachs, but suggested that it was perhaps too early to tell.

Telephoning Kramer to express his strong disappointment with the brochure copy, Puleo said he was sending it back. He said he was also disappointed to find that Kramer hadn't seemed to grasp what Monarch's "systems" concept was all about.

"To tell you the truth," Kramer replied, "I didn't write the copy. We have a writer who handles such work, and I guess he missed a good deal. Don't worry, though, we'll work it over again, and I'll get it to you by July 20."

Between July 7 and July 20 Puleo had several visits with Kramer when in New York on company business. On one of these visits he passed Glenn Dresher in the hall and they chatted briefly. Dresher asked how things were going, and Puleo replied "so-so." Dresher suggested they get together while Puleo was there, but he was tied up when Puleo finished chatting with Kramer, and they didn't have a chance to talk further.

Puleo and Kramer did have a chance to discuss work on the logo. At Kramer's suggestion, it was being done by the one-man firm that had put together Monarch's slide-sound presentation. Puleo rejected the logo that Kramer had approved, and Kramer agreed with the one Puleo selected from others submitted. Puleo himself wasn't too satisfied with the logo, but felt it was the best of the group he had seen.

On one of his visits, Puleo asked Kramer what he had in mind for the Monarch booth at the national convention in Denver on August 15.

"Something like this," Kramer replied, and drew a quick rough sketch on a sheet of yellow scratch pad. Puleo said it didn't look like much to him, and Kramer said he would of course rework it and submit it in more polished form.

NOTES

Kramer met his July 20 deadline for submission of the second draft of the brochure. But this one proved as unsatisfactory to Puleo and Sachs as the first. Their chief objection was that the copy was too pedestrian - it didn't have "sparkle." In rejecting the copy, Puleo sent Kramer a three-page letter containing detailed objections and suggestions for improvement.

Kramer came through with a third draft on August 2, and this draft was accompanied by a three-page informal letter saying that Kramer had personally handled the copy this time. Sachs, Puleo, and Stangel all agreed that the copy was an improvement over the first two drafts, but in their opinion it still needed rewriting, more sparkle, and a smoother flow of transitional material.

The letter itself summarized the status of work that had been done to date and work immediately ahead, and in general followed the guidelines set down at the June 7 meeting.

By August 2 no work had been done on the Monarch booth, and at this point Puleo told Kramer to forget the booth and turned over that project to Stangel. Puleo also decided that it was too late to plan to use the new brochure at the August 15 convention exhibit and decided he would use the old one he had on hand.

Discussing Monarch's relationship to date with the Dresher firm, Sachs told Puleo on August 7 that he was very unhappy about the state of affairs.

"We've paid them $18,200 so far and what have we got for it anyway?" Sachs asked. "If you ask me, I think you and Stangel could have done better on your own. Maybe we'd be better off..." Sachs let his thought dwindle off into space.

"I'm not satisfied either, by a long shot," Puleo replied. "On the other hand..." Puleo also let his thought dwindle off. He reviewed the situation in his own mind. He was definitely not happy with the type or amount of service he had received so far from Dresher-Placebo Associates. He could, of course, write a strong letter to Glenn Dresher. He could, of course, lay down the law as strong as he could to Kramer. He could, of course, terminate the contract; in which case he might well consider placing the

NOTES

Monarch account with Hammer and Rogerstein. Finally, of course, he could simply terminate the contract, period. But he knew his own public relations director was new and couldn't really be expected to do the sort of job that a New York City counseling firm could do. He himself was much too tied up in other administrative details to get personally involved in public relations. In fact, he was much too personally involved as it was. He really had a problem, he reflected wryly, as he locked his desk and went home to his family.

EXHIBIT 22-1

MONARCH LAUNDRIES
(address)

April 27, 19--

bcc: Merton Sachs

Mr. Bernard Apfel
Hammer and Rogerstein
(address)

Dear Bernard:

Easier letters I've written.

We've decided to have a go with another agency. I'm sure I must sound like an old fuss-budget, but it sure was difficult to make a decision.

We found it easy to eliminate most of the original agencies we contacted. When we got down to the cream, it got tough. At any rate, for better or worse, we made the decision. This may be a hell of a thing for me to say but if we should find that we made the wrong one, you'll be the first to know.

NOTES

Merton and I enjoyed meeting you and your people and we sincerely appreciate the time and trouble you took with us.

My sincerest regards,

Vincent A. Puleo
Assistant to the President

EXHIBIT 22-2

HAMMER AND ROGERSTEIN
Incorporated

Office of Executive Vice President

April 29, 19--

Mr. Vincent A. Puleo
Assistant to the President
Monarch Laundries
210 Lawton Street
Albany, NY 12207

Dear Vin:

We are disappointed but not downhearted. People who hit it off as well together as we obviously did have a way of getting together from time to time. I have no doubt that one of these days we will be talking to each other again.

Meanwhile, I want to wish you and your agency the best of luck. I honestly think you have a better mousetrap and with the right kind of publicity, public relations, and promotion you will sell it.

NOTES

One final point: Since we are both going to be around for a long time to come, I would like to have the privilege of staying in touch with you from time to time to find out how things are going. I feel a proprietary interest in the future of Monarch and want to keep abreast of what's going on.

> Very best regards,
> (signed and typed)
>
> Bernard Apfel
> (address)

NOTES

Case 23

RUDER & FINN CONFERENCE ON PROFESSIONAL RESPONSIBILITY-A*

Ruder Finn & Rotman, Inc., whose predecessor firm of Ruder and Finn, Inc. was formed in the late 1940s as a two-man operation, is one of the country's largest public relations counseling firms. Over the years the organization has demonstrated its capacity and ability to produce and deliver public relations programs which achieve results and which in turn produce profits for the company. At the same time, its executives have maintained over the years a lively and continued interest in philosophical and ethical questions of the counseling business as evidenced by their articles and speeches on ethics and by their sponsorship of periodic seminars and conferences on the subject.

One such conference was a three-day series of meetings which Ruder and Finn sponsored at the New School for Social Research in New York City on the general subject of "The Concept of Responsibility in Public Relations." Included among the participants were Ruder and Finn executives, staff members, and affiliated associates as well as such nationally known academicians and theologians as Dr. George N. Shuster of Hunter College and Dr. F. Ernest Johnson of the National Council of Churches of Christ in the United States. The sessions were taped and verbatim transcripts were later made available in print form. Excerpts from two of the sessions are reprinted in this case and in the one that follows.

* * *

SESSION WITH DR. F. ERNEST JOHNSON
OF THE NATIONAL COUNCIL OF
CHURCHES OF CHRIST IN THE UNITED STATES

Reprinted with permission of Ruder and Finn.

Moderator: We are here today to talk about what we think is a very important problem in our own field-that of public relations and ethics in a free competitive economy.

I was talking to one of my close friends the other day about our series of seminars on the concept of responsibility in public relations. He looked at me with a sardonic glint in his eyes, and said "I can see it all now. Anguished public relations practitioners in search of their souls." I think not.

First, we are "just plain curious" about what our problems really are. And second, we're not searching our souls, as much as we are indulging in some critical examination of our own business. Why are we doing this now-at this specific time in the history of our profession, and as a matter of fact in the history of R & F? I think there are probably two reasons:

First of all, public relations, with the rising importance of mass media, is becoming a tremendously powerful social force which, of course, can be used either for good or for evil.

At the same time, our profession, our craft if you will, is becoming more mature and more thoughtful. It's a long way that we have come since the time that the press agent has dominated the industry. In many ways, public relations is on the threshold today of becoming somewhat closer to a profession than it has ever been before. I think I should like to read you a few words from a book with which our speaker today is very familiar: It says that "one of the convincing signs of a developing professional sense in public relations is the development of lively self criticism within mass communications."

The scarcity of mutual criticism in communications is one of the features of the industry that outsiders find hardest to explain. We are trying to do something about that here today. We have with us Dr. F. Ernest Johnson, who has a very unusual background and one that is particularly good for the subject which we are discussing today. Dr. Johnson is now the chief study consultant of the department of church and economic life of the National Council of Churches of Christ in the U.S.A. He has been a pastor for many years, he was ordained in the ministry, and he holds degrees from

NOTES

Albion College in Michigan, Union Theological Seminary, and Columbia University...

Now what I propose to do here today is to outline some typical ethical problems with which an agency may be faced. These are case histories, and they will be outlined in some detail. At the end of each of these, Dr. Johnson will have a few words to say about the problem as he sees it. He will try to define the ethical areas of the agency responsibility as they face us, and after Dr. Johnson finishes his presentation, we will then open up the matter for discussion.

But first I thought that we would ask Dr. Johnson to say a few words about the general subject that we are discussing here today - the problem of ethical responsibility in our free competitive economy.

DR. JOHNSON: May I say first that the process that you are engaged in seems to be one of extraordinary significance, which I have personally been interested for a good while, and my organization is very much concerned about it-that is to say, the process of inquiry by a group of people engaged in a particular occupation, tying into the ethical implications of what they are doing. Some of us have become very much concerned because of the tendency to isolate morals from practical pragmatic concern. My theological friends call that moralism - tendency to voice certain moral attitudes - so-called principles. It is then assumed that ethical living is a matter of laying your pattern on your cloth and cutting it.

Increasingly, with the growing complexity of life, and the interpenetration of different subject matters and interests and concerns, the answers to ethical questions have to be sought and given in the context of daily happenings.

In the context of actual problem situations, day by day, you have to make the ethical inquiry, and we are very much interested in stimulating this sort of inquiry. So it seems to me that what you are doing is of the utmost importance...

I have found a tendency among business men to shy away from the use of the word ethics, and to want it understood if they did anything that

NOTES

people thought was good, it was done for business reasons. I don't know why so many successful business men are afraid of being thought of as morally conscious.

I think they're afraid of sentimentality perhaps - and that's all right, but I have a notion that considerations of ethics are just as relevant to the making and marketing of goods, and the furnishings of marketing services. I believe there is just as much relevance in the area of ethical principles, ethical concerns, as in any other. No matter how hardheaded he is, and how tough minded and unsentimental, there are certain things a man won't do - a floor below which he won't go.

And I have a notion that you can generalize a little bit farther and say that, broadly speaking, as a philosophy professor of mine said once, morality begins at the point where one is ready to substitute a remoter for a more immediate end. This does make way for satisfaction - it does recognize self interest - it does recognize the validity of institutional interests, the building up of a business, for instance - but there is a great difference between conducting an enterprise with a view to its future, and conducting it on a basis of immediate quick returns...

MODERATOR: Shall we go right into our case histories now? We have three of them, and I think you will find them interesting.

Only the names and places have been changed; the first one concerns the matter of selecting clients.

Sometimes a client comes to a public relations firm with a very special and pressing problem which involves the need to change something - maybe the public's point of view about his company, his product, or his entire industry. And the change generally implies one of these three things: something is wrong with the product, the company, or the industry; something is not wrong with the product, the company, or the industry, but something is basically wrong with the public's interpretation of these three things; and finally, the company, the industry, or the product have been changed markedly and there is a need to bring this change to the attention of the American people - the general buying public.

NOTES

The factor that we are going to address ourselves to here is the first one - where the product may be shoddy, the company may be inefficient and poorly organized, and possibly the entire industry is backward. Any one of these three cases can be true.

Let us take a look at a specific instance, in which the president of a large direct selling company comes to a public relations agency and tells it these things: First of all, the salesmen for this company visit consumers at home on a nation-wide basis in order to sell their products - they ring door bells, they call up people on the phone, they bring their product forcibly to the attention of the public by direct contact.

Local merchants who have established businesses selling the same products are up in arms over this kind of campaign in which people move into their area in a sort of a blitz campaign.

The would-be client's sales people carry on these campaigns locally and leave rather hurriedly sometimes - after raking in a profit by what might be termed high pressure selling tactics. We learn further that the company, honestly speaking, has a product that sells at a higher cost than local competitive products of the same quality, and that the company salesmen in an attempt to increase their sales, sometimes make false claims, sometimes shove off more of the product than the consumer actually needs, and generally engage in this sort of thing because it's very difficult to control them on a nationwide basis.

Sales management for this company does not have its fingers on the pulse of each salesman. It can't control what every individual salesman does in the field. So very often, what happens is that the consumer buys the product and he sometimes gets stuck. Consequently, local groups stand together against this company and strike out against this door-to-door type of selling through the Better Business Bureau.

At this point the company president comes to us and he says: "Get us out of this mess! We are losing a lot of business. People are starting to talk and the talk is causing us a great deal of trouble." He says further that "you fellows can produce the kind of propaganda that we need to beat this campaign against us. Tell the public how good we are so they will believe in us, and help us get back the business we have lost."

Here I think the question becomes an ethical one for us. Shall we follow the dictates of this company president and circulate what would have to be basic untruths about the product, in order to help this company meet competition for the consumer's dollarf?

In trying to answer that question, I think we have three alternatives open to us.

First of all, we can flatly turn down the business and say we want no part of it. It doesn't sound right.

The second thing we can do is say, yes, we will take the business - we need your business and we'd love to have you with us. We'll do the best we can.

The third thing we can do is accept the job with some reservations.

The decision is finally made after some soul searching by the agency. It elects to accept the job - providing that the client mends his ways - for - as public relations counsel, we can say to him that we don't think we can be effective in promoting something that is untrue, and we don't want to be a party to this in the first place.

We can say to him - clean up your own house before we start talking about how attractive it is. And the client says to us - wonderful, that's exactly what I had in mind. But the story unfortunately is not yet ended. When the client begins to see what we really mean by cleaning up his house, he gets a little bit nervous. It means turning upside down some of the organizational policies that he has built up through the years. It means a reversal in some policies of the company that might not lend itself to increased business, although presumably a better impression of the company by the public would mean more business. And he tells us that as much as he'd like to, we can't do everything at once and we had just better be patient.

At this point, the program is launched. We are already beginning to do things for him. Before we know it, we are doing exactly what we set out not to do. We are puffing up the client's products and giving currency to some basic untruths. And we have never quite got back to the basic ethical

NOTES

question we had raised in the first place so busy are we getting the job done.

This is a case history, and there are three things that we worry about right now.

First of all, the hope of improvement has been held out to us by this client, the hope of his own improvement - his own company's betterment. Can we honestly dedicate ourselves to the client's cause using his possible future improvement as our own ethical out?

Second, should we have forgotten all this "ethics talk" in the first place, and instead depended on the sifting process of the press to separate truth from fiction?

Or third, should we set ourselves up in the first place as judges of morality, of what is right and ethical in a business world where everyone is out to put his best foot forward, and reject such a client from the very outset?

I wonder, Dr. Johnson, if you would have some comments?

DR. JOHNSON: The question is shall we accept this account? I said before that I thought we must assume that there is some ethical rationale for the business order. Dog eat dog is not an ethical version now. If the only aim were profit, then I am somewhat at a loss to see how you can give an answer to a situation or any significance to a transaction.

But everybody has other motives. I think most economists would agree that the maximization of profits is not the sole motive of business. Profit is indispensable - as a matter of fact, you have profit no matter who gets it. Sometimes the profit is divided in the group, but there are motives other than just crude profit motive and, as I see it, the consultant-client relationship is not just one of servicing the client, delivering materials requested by the client. This would be just like the filling station. I think that the consultant - if you are speaking on the level of the profession - is seeking to rise to the professional level. And therefore you have something else to deliver, a successful technique or successful techniques. Now I think that the function is actually, is more like, say the relation of a teacher to

NOTES

students on a high level. Let us say a professor and a graduate student. The process is a reciprocal one. The consultant has something to gain from this; he has his ends to serve. And if you just let him do this - do what he is asked to do - and collect the fee for it, then he is merely a chore boy. He is not really operating at the professional level.

So I think that makes a very great difference. His motives are not quite so crude as we are likely to think, and therefore he has greater freedom. Take the alternatives in our case history.

Turn down the business flatly? It's always a possibility. My guess would be that a firm of consultants that never turned down business flatly on ethical grounds was a pretty crude concern.

Accept the job unequivocally? That doesn't fit the picture either - not as far as my conception of this reciprocal relationship between consultant and client is concerned. For each one has values to be conserved. Both have standards, so I don't think anything is quite unequivocal. If you are going to accept an account look at what you've got to take. The setup of the business, the personnel, organization - all of that is given. But have you got any "given"? You've got a firm, a group of professional people - a reputation that must be conserved. I think this ought to be a two-way street.

So it seems to me that at a professional level, the only "buyable" alternative is to accept the job - only I wouldn't say "with qualifications." I'd say "interpretations."

If you once get yourself accepted on a reciprocal basis, you never have to take a thing just as is. I don't think the consultant is really serving the client in the long run unless there is a reciprocal relationship. He's just not being a consultant.

COMMENT A: This is not an abnormal situation. It is one we face quite commonly. I have faced it with a client we have accepted. And ethics and good business are very compatible. I am assuming now within the context of our discussion, that the agency in question is in a sound condition and will not live or die on the basis of this one account, in which case all bets are off.

NOTES

Now, when involved in an agency-client relationship, much of the profit from a fee is chewed up in about the first six months in getting to know the client and a lot of other semi-productive activities. Thererfore it behooves us to think very carefully before taking on a new client, as to whether we wish to make an investment of it, in a relationship which conceivably might not be a long term relationship.

A relationship which is not based on any kind of respect but is based on a delivery boy - chore boy, if you will - concept, does not appear to me to be one which could mature into a long lasting relationship in an agency operation.

Now this client comes to us with a basic problem and if we agree to do this job for him, we have agreed to debase ourselves in terms of income, not in terms of ethics - I repeat - in terms of income, because we have taken on a job which we know in our own hearts will be uncovered sooner or later by some editor.

We know we've got to live with these editors long after the client is gone. Can we take a chance at putting these relationships with editors, which are our stock in trade - our goods on the shelf - on the block? For one client? I think not.

Here this problem of ethics in our industry relates to the fact that our ethics are under constant scrutiny by the others with whom we deal. And we've got to play it pretty straight. No client is worth the relationship we have built up over the years, and the ethical regard with which we are held by the press.

Now the other alternative is to take this client on with certain qualifications. Here I think it has to be more than qualifications. I think that in this case I would like to see us use ethics as the basis for a good business relationship, because it works out. And in this case it's a matter of honesty. You must be honest with this potential client; you must be honest with yourselves. At the same time in business it is true there are degrees of ethics. I would say that the course of action here is one in which we would take this client unconditionally for a period, in which we will study what the client's problem is, and what they have to do internally to rectify this

NOTES

problem. Put this down in writing and have them sign it. On the basis of that - proceed.

MODERATOR: Are we being realistic, Al?

COMMENT A: Yes. We did just that. In fact this was a client with a similar situation to that which you've outlined in the problem.

COMMENT B: I wonder if it is more a question of practicality than ethics in this case. This man is getting reaction from the Better Business Bureau, so he makes no change - you can't get him to make one but you continue your publicity for him. This publicity is used to help the salesmen sell even more. Result is more pressure, and this results in more reaction from the Better Business Bureau. It gives the client's products a still worse name, and therefore turns out to a complete failure. This is from a practical standpoint.

MODERATOR: What happened was that the thing came to a head, but the client said have patience. He didn't say he wouldn't do what we asked him to do. He said - have patience. But it became apparent that you'd have to have had the patience of Job to attain realization of what we had in mind. So here we were, busy working for this company at the same time. Doing just what we set out not to do. Here is where our problem lay.

COMMENT C: I think a lot of confusion on this entire question could be cleared up. As I see it, the client has a product and we are trying to sell it for him. If we can strip away everything else and measure this as a product, if we accept that it is a worthwhile product, then we can go ahead with it, with the reservations that he will improve his service on it and the salesman would be available to follow through.

However, I am always dubious about taking something on with a future promise of this kind. I think you just get yourself into a corner because whatever you have accomplished there for six months, if the

NOTES

product hasn't been improved, you have aided and abetted bad business and harmed yourself in relation to editors.

MODERATOR: Someone said something before that was very interesting. The suggestion was made that when you are big enough to be selective, and to choose your clients, you have made a big step forward in this business of being ethical. You can afford to be ethical, in a sense, and the good things that come with being ethical come to you. So that the picture presents itself sometimes of a public relations firm which seems forced into something because it is paying the bills for people on the staff, it is paying your office rent, and so forth.

COMMENT D: It seems to me that when you relate the question of the ethics which the agency can afford to exercise to the size of the agency, that at least, by implication, there is a conflict with what Dr. Johnson said a few moments ago about the compatibility of ethics and profit. You are, in effect, I think, implying that ethics is a luxury in which one can indulge after the fundamental economic realities have been coped with.

MODERATOR: I think what Dr. Johnson said has a more far reaching definition of ethics. It begins to be ethical if you can substitute a long range goal for a short range goal.
    You have a conflict between staying alive and being ethical, don't you, and you resolve it in favor of staying alive.

DR. JOHNSON: Of course, my position is sound. There will always be exceptions. People will say, well, if staying in business means doing this, then I'm out. A man once said to me: What does a man do when he can't take it, when he can't be comfortable in himself - he can't do the thing that's prescribed? Then he has to get out! He has to change the situation.
    Now, I think that it's consistent to say, broadly speaking, that there is a positive connection between ethical behavior - behavior that is ethically

NOTES

approvable, and the availability of sufficient funds. There is a correlation there. I think quite definitely.

COMMENT E: I think really what we have here is an economic situation. I mean, certainly the account is not desirable, but if you don't need the business you would be inclined not to touch it. On the other hand, if you need it, why the degree to which you need it would pretty well determine the degree to which you could go along with it.

Maybe never go all the way to the point where it is evident that it just goes on and on and the client has no intention of doing anything about it. Eventually you would drop it, on that basis. If you don't need the business, don't touch it. If you do need it, take a chance on it and go as far as you feel that you can without hurting yourself.

COMMENT F: The other point is that there seems to be some feeling here that because you work for a big company, the corporation can take on an account, but you as an account executive don't even worry about your own morals. I don't feel that that's proper at all. You have to live with yourself as an individual.

While we are discussing it, I don't quite agree with the fact that you could postpone ethics like buying a ticket, you know. I used to work for a man who had very poor ethics. I finally left because he did. He used to say: when they are criticizing me, I'll seek solace. I'll go down to the bank and look at my safe deposit box and count my coupons.

He could find some relief from business but I don't hold with that. I used to find it pretty funny. He had piled up an amount of money which was a comfort to him.

DR. JOHNSON: You are not postponing it. The choice that my professor was talking about is made now. Will you eat your cake right now - do the thing that's going to bring you satisfaction now - or will you take the course that denies yourself, perhaps, for the sake of a result that you will experience later? You don't postpone the choice.

NOTES

COMMENT G: I think in the integral problem you must have a principle: Either you are ethical or not. You cannot say, well, at the moment I need the business and therefore I forget about my principles. Your principles have to lead you all through your life from the very beginning. You cannot afford to start having principles when you are in a very comfortable position. So think if you have to turn it down - even though you are small and it's your only business at the moment - you have to turn it down...

And so I feel in the ethical field too - if you have a principle - you have to follow it and if it hurts you, it hurts you. If you go out of business for that reason, you have to do something else.

COMMENT H: I think there is also another factor that hasn't been considered here. Let's say I have a job to do that I don't like. I have to work to support my family. There is a question of ethics too in my personal responsibilities toward my family. Which comes first? In a case of an employer, where many people are living from that employer and the many families depend on their salaries, which is the first consideration? Should I accept these accounts with which I don't agree, or should I just forget the ethical problems and do what I can to earn my fee?

COMMENT I: You have the responsibility in this case to your family and to the employer for his employees. What is the ethical impact upon all these employees if they are told that their employer has taken an account which goes against his basis ethical standards, and that he is doing something which is wrong in his opinion? Will that not affect the ethical standard of the whole firm? The staff will get its salaries all right, but their whole basic personality and character will be harmed much more than the money that they make is worth.

COMMENT J: I don't think so. I think it's not a question of: "I'm going to be ethical when I have more money. You have to survive first. Otherwise how can you be ethical?"

NOTES

MODERATOR: You can't be ethical without having your business to be ethical with, is that right? (LAUGHTER)

COMMENT K: I just want a little clarification, Dr. Johnson, about what you say about the level of ethical responsibility as it pertains to economics. Do I understand that to be an inference that poor people are less ethical in this field? Somehow, I didn't quite get what you said.

DR. JOHNSON: Let us be sure about the terms. I said that the level of ethical behavior in matters economic, let us say, tends to be higher in a group of people whose circumstances are better. I think that is simply a factual observation, and it reflects only, not that people's impulses vary with their status, but their capacity to resist pressure depends on their economic level. My father, who was a small town minister, used to tell about the struggle he saw a local publisher go through when he was having a very hard time. This small town newspaper needed money. The publisher was offered a bribe to keep something out of the paper. Now he was a man well grounded, and he had the moral guts to say NO. I just won't do it. I can't sell myself for that price.

Well you have a very considerable number of people in that situation. There would be a correlation I think between the financial status and their decision.

COMMENT L: I just wonder if this editor who wouldn't take a bribe though he really needed the money - if he wouldn't take a much larger bribe if he was in a much better financial situation. I can't see where that wealth makes someone more ethical. It might make them less ethical.

DR. JOHNSON: Now then you are saying that correlation may not extend all the way up - quite true, because then you have an entirely different set of factors to deal with. And the fact of great wealth is a terrific moral handicap for the person in a sense. It is an Oriental exaggeration perhaps, a figure of speech, when Jesus said "it is easier for a camel to go through a needle's eye than for a rich man to enter the Kingdom of Heaven." There is, however, an element of truth there: "riches do tend to blunt one's ethical sense."

COMMENT M: I think if a man recognizes that there are ethics and if he has a desire in himself personally or corporately to be ethical, his economic status I don't think is a factor. The ethics are either there or they are not there.

Feeling the mental recognition of ethics and the practice of ethics can be two different things. I think that if the guy in a small shop who is responsible to himself and to his family, and has certain responsibilities which involve a whole set of ethics and morals all by themselves, recognizes that he may in taking on the account of which we were speaking, be using a different set of ethics, this is a step in the right direction. The fact that he recognizes an ethical conflict. However, he still may take on the account because there is not only ethical conflict in taking on the account in his corporate ethics, but there is a conflict between not taking on the account and responsibility to his employees and to his family, which is another set of ethics. So he's got balance in weighing one against the other.

COMMENT N: Well isn't there a very practical matter also involved in the whole discussion. Let's say we have more accounts: We have three clients - a, b, c. Client a is the only one that presents a problem. He is a bad boy and we are doing something for him which we and he also know that is unethical. Now client b and c know that we are also working for client a, and they see what we are doing, because we have to do it in public.

The result is that clients b and c, who are highly ethical companies, will say we won't have anything to do with you any more. And so to keep client a, because we need three companies at least - to go on working - doesn't make sense. We will lose b and c if we don't say "No" to a.

COMMMENT O: This sounds very practical: If I take a, I will not get b and c, because they know that I am working for a. Should my company not

```
NOTES

```

be ethical and get two accounts for whom we can work without any scruples, instead of having one that hurts our conscience and gets nothing else?

I think that we are so surrounded by material things - buildings, houses, that we try when we talk about ethical concepts to give a definite form to, as you say, black and white. There are different shades. And I think even in material things we all know that everything is not completely immobile. Buildings, for example, shiver from one side to the other in the wind. Do you have a break in the storm, or is it better to bend a little bit in order to survive.

DR. JOHNSON: Of course it is a question of whether you can negotiate all the pressure of life and remain quite inflexible. Probalbly not. You are likely to snap off.

COMMENT P: I mean you as an individual have a concept of your own value. You have set yourself a goal - that is the question of surviving - you want to get to that goal. Should you bend or should you break?

DR. JOHNSON: I think it really is the heart of the matter. Living ethically is comparatively simple in a very simple society. It's a much more complicated matter the more complicated society becomes. And size has something to do with it, though size is not as important as other factors - I mean the size of the concern. But - look at this question of self preservation for continuance. Suppose we have a person who is in business with his small family, we'll say. He has no other responsibilities than that. And we'll just assume that he has no young children, and his wife is quite ready to go along and share the consequences. He could be pretty close to inflexible.

Here is the person who takes a position on a university staff, and a lot of nice ethical questions arise, don't they, in the administration of a university? And he has independence - he can be quite inflexible. He can say, now there are certain things I won't do - I don't have to do them and

NOTES

that's that. Take it or leave it. Now then beginning at that level, increasing responsibilities not only family and other dependents, but your business associates - a concern like yours with a large staff and their families - and your clients - complicate the situation very much.

So who is going to be inflexible? Can I be inflexible for others - as a proxy for other people who don't have any say about it? I am really making the policy of a firm by that - the people, the executives working for me. Is it ethical for me to make a decision of that sort at all? Just in deciding for other people, this matter of flexibility, of giving certain amount, doesn't rule one out of the ethical pressure. No one can say that unless you stand absolutely rigidly you are not being ethical. Because if you make clear your position, people understand you, and you are not being hypocritical, you are not pretending. In the circles that I move in, a tremendous amount of time is spent discussing the word "compromise." Some of our realistic moralists say that ethical decisions can't be made on a rigid basis - that you've got to take account of all the consequences and that means compromising in the sense of adjusting.

Unfortunately the word "compromise" is a bad word, it means surrendering principles. But "adjustment" is perhaps more accurate. You have to decide what the consequences are going to be and if on balance, the consequences of a given act seem to be relatively good, as compared with the consequences of the alternative - then I would say it becomes an ethical obligation to take the course even though it's not simon pure - even though there is an element of "evil" in the consequences.

You must take the course which you have every reason to believe will result in the greatest amount of good, the least amount of evil. And that's just what it means to live in the real world.

NOTES

Case 24

RUDER & FINN CONFERENCE ON PROFESSIONAL RESPONSIBILITY-B*

SESSION WITH DR. GEORGE N. SHUSTER HUNTER COLLEGE, NEW YORK CITY

MODERATOR: I am just going to take a couple of minutes to try to outline the problem of Public Service versus Private Interest as it affects people in our type of world. Then I will give you a couple of examples of the kind of things that we are concerned with. Then I am going to ask Dr. Shuster to spend a couple of minutes trying to focus a little bit more attention on the problem from a theoretical point of view. Then I would like to turn this thing wide open and have a riproaring discussion.

I think that perhaps if you wanted to look at the public relations business and draw up an escutcheon for it, that possibly it would have as the motto on the scroll underneath, the phrase that I think a lot of us use in speaking about our business, namely, "He whose bread I eat, his song I sing." I think that is a pretty cynical approach to our business, but I think in large measure it is true and it affects a good deal of our activities and particularly with regard to the conflict between public service and private interest.

The questions that we want to discuss today are these: How can we rationalize the private interests of our clients with the public good? How important is the concept of public service to a man or a company? How much of the public interest should the public relations man attempt to serve in his capacity as counsel to the client? And finally, to what degree must the public relations man heed his own conscience or not heed his own conscience in deference to his clients' wishes?

---

* *Reprinted with permission of Ruder and Finn.*

I want to discuss a couple of examples of the kind of thing that we have faced in the past. Perhaps you can draw upon your own experiences if you know of similar cases as well.

We represented a leading drug manufacturer, one of the first companies to introduce a tranquilizer on the market. We did a tremendous job of introducing this tranquilizer. By means of the techniques at our disposal we tried to make it seem that the tranquilizer was the panacea to end all mental ills; I think the success of our campaign can be measured at least in part by the fact that sales of this product rose in one year from zero to $17 million.

However, after this first heady year of success, further medical research on the part of independent researchers indicated that the drug had some very serious side effects, that it wasn't all that it was cracked up to be on the basis of initial medical research, that it had possibly a very deleterious effect upon certain types of patients, and might not even be a particularly good thing.

What should we advise our clients to do in a case like this? Is it wrong for us to continue to publicize and promote the sale of this drug when we ourselves know that there is a serious question concerning its effect? Do we have an obligation to the client to tell him that we should do something about this, assuming that he is not going to do anything about it because his sales are so good?

Let's say we do believe we have an obligation to our client to do this. What should we do if the client refuses to heed our recommendations? Should we take our hats off the hook and say, "Well, goodbye, you don't want to listen to us. Therefore it is your hard luck. Let somebody else do it." This is keeping in mind, of course, that there are four other people standing in back of you ready to grab the account and do just what it is you refused to do.

The second example: A basic question - is there a conflict between private interest and public service in promoting the sale of liquor, and try to get people to drink more of a certain type of alcoholic beverage, say vodka

NOTES

in this case? Vodka does nothing for you, but a client pays us a fee to promote the sale of vodka.

Of course, one could probably rationalize it easily, but the point is: are there any ethical questions involved in promoting the sale of liquor? And if it is basically wrong, are there any ethical alternatives one should seek to make it right? Is it just a sop of our conscience to be able to recommend to the client that he endow Alcoholics Anonymous in order to do something good with the money he made from the sale of liquor? Or should we simply say, "This is the way the world is" and go ahead and promote the sale of liquor? Again, if it isn't you, it will be five other people.

The third situation, again briefly. We handled the introduction of a new liquid form of aspirin for one of our clients. It really wasn't aspirin. It was another drug that had the same effect as aspirin did. However, it was somewhat safer. Aspirin, as you may know, is one of the leading chemicals in the accidental chemical poisoning of children in the United States today. There are some 17,000 cases of aspirin poisoning every year in this country.

The public relations man's dilemma: Should we take this information concerning the terrible effects of aspirin and use it as a club to beat people over the head so that they will buy more of our client's products instead of aspirin? Should we launch a campaign designed to publicize and promote every case of aspirin poisoning or a death from aspirin poisoning? Are we serving the public interest in a case like this, or are we just serving our client's private interest and using a pseudo-public service approach to get our products sold and our point across? Are we falling into a trap when we do that, or are we merely being ethical, or are we just kidding ourselves and playing somebody else's game and finding it easy to make a lot of money and make the client make a lot of money on what is really an unethical basis?

Those are three examples where the public interest and the private interests of the clients may possibly be in conflict, or where some question concerning ethical questions exists.

NOTES

I would like to ask Dr. Shuster if he would try to put the problem into perspective.

DR. SHUSTER: Thank you very much, Mr. Chairman. I will do my best. This is a task which I approach with a considerable amount of diffidence.

The topic which has been assigned here is a very difficult one, and I am afraid I am going to have to admit that by giving you any advice as to how to solve it is probably beyond my competence.

I think first of all you have to distinguish between what you mean by ethics and what somebody else means by it.

Traditionally our great ethical systems as expressed in literature, religion and philosophy are really based on three problems and their solution.

The first is the problem of incurred guilt which we may call sin or error. The second is the problem of purgation. The third is the problem of sublimation.

Inside the Jewish-Christian system, of course, the process of purgation and the process of sublimation is a process of love, of response in terms of affection to other human beings and eventually to the Creator.

In the oriental system, of course, it is a response which is made in terms of denial.

One always has to bear these systems in mind when we talk about ethics and conduct. This is the great legacy of the human race in terms of our literature and philosophy and religion.

Perhaps we are dealing on a level of what you might call the ethics of prudence, the ethics of everyday life.

Now I am going to state out two positions which to me seem, inside this area, tenable. You may agree. I will state the first as being a position which nobody can take.

During the course of the Nazi regime, I.G. Farben, which was perforce a client of the Nazis, undertook, at their behest, experiments on human beings. These were experiments to which, of course, the human being had not given his consent. These experiments resulted in death, in malformation, in a variety of ills, mental as well as physical.

I would say that no matter how one looks at the problem of ethics this is a positive limit. It would be impossible for any person who believes in decency in any form to subscribe to that.

Now I go to the opposite. I was brought up as a boy thinking that one of the deleterious substances to serve human beings was coffee, that it would keep you awake if you drank too many cups of it. I never expected to live to see the day when the medical fraternity at Harvard would tell you, "it isn't the coffee that is deleterious; it is the cream that you put in it."

If you look at that kind of prudential question and ask yourself, "Well, now, as a public relations expert, am I going to start a campaign against cows or what?" This is an area in which it is impossible to make a decision except in terms of relative evidence. That is clear. If, for example, you were to represent the Standard Oil Company of New Jersey and you said that people go on the highways on Sundays and on weekends and lots of them get killed, therefore we will recommend that we don't sell any gasoline, this would seem to me to be an utterly non-prudential solution because, in the final analysis, all these things are good things and the evil results, the deleterious results that follow, are a result of the inability of human beings to use them properly.

I can only say that I think within this framework the public relations community will have to operate. It seems to me that any decision to separate business conduct or national conduct from standards of prudential ethics is absolutely disastrous in the final analysis.

If you take the position, in terms of national ethics, that too close an identity with national interest in connection with moral objectives is indefensible you are correct because you claim more for them than you can and therefore you indulge in a measure of hypocrisy.

The same thing would be true of business, I think. You cannot claim that business is the Gospel, the Sermon On The Mount, or the final chapters of Isaiah. It would be futile and foolish to do that. On the other hand, I think there is a point at which you have to say, "yes, it is true, this is a

NOTES

football game, but you have got to play this game according to the rules; otherwise the whole of our society will cease to function..."

MODERATOR: I would like to state the opposite point of view in the words of a management consultant named Theodore Levitt. He has been making a big stir these days with articles about the spiritual needs of business. He says:

"It is true, you cannot as a business man serve two masters, God and mammon. As a business man I suggest you serve business and yourself. That is your only function. Saving souls, promoting or preserving spiritual values, elevating taste, cultivating human dignity and consumer self-respect - these high-priority objectives are other people's business if that is what they want to do. The business man's job is to do the things that are the pure, undiluted objectives of business - to satisfy the materialistic and related ego objectives of those who run it. When business gets involved in lofty causes it dilutes its own efforts and ultimately ceases properly to deliver the goods. But perhaps worse, it makes itself or the business executives a sort of self-appointed arbiter - a great white father sanctimoniously and censoriously metering out pre-digested standards of taste, thought, opinion, and material comforts to child-like multitudes whose precious souls must be saved for another world. Aside from this becoming a really powerful threat to our free open society, I am forced to conclude that it represents the height of vanity on the part of its advocates. They are acting very much like lords of the manor."

There you have the two points of view.

COMMENT A: We live in a society where one of the fundamental principles is to sell anything, to sell hula hoops, to sell products which if not used properly can be dangerous, such as aspirins, tranquilizers, and vodka, but the whole economic system is organized for the purpose of selling things, and public relations is only one small element of the apparatus of distributing and selling.

If there is criticism, it seems to me the criticism should be directed

NOTES

towards this whole system and not public relations which is just a small aspect of it.

In almost every case where we try to promote our clients' products, don't we play down the parts that are not particularly good, and don't we push that which will interest the editor and try to get the most favorable story? Wouldn't we be happiest if all the negative implications concerning this particular tranquilizer would just be swept under a little carpet where nobody would have to see it because we would sell more?

DR. SHUSTER: Suppose we take the tranquilizer business. We in education would say it is the function of education to make clear to people, on the basis of scientific analysis, what the virtues and the benefits of these things are. That is the role of education.

Therefore the question is this: Are you going to be satisfied merely with the imposed discipline, that is, the law, or are you going to seek some living, vivid, working relationship with education as a force in American life, and are you, when you talk to your client, going to present that as a possibility? I think that is the question you have to face.

COMMENT B: If a conflict develops between public service and private interests in situations not as clear-cut as tranquilizers, in which the immediate question is, who is going to determine whether it is damaging or not? If it is going to be the public relations man, it isn't automatically going to make the public relations agency a force in society. It is much greater and potentially much more dangerous than the good that might come out of governmental regulation.

COMMENT C: I would like to address myself to some of Dr. Shuster's opening comments and also the point made by Mr. Levitt.

I am not so naive as to think that business men are going to follow the golden rule in the conduct of their economic affairs, although there is one little story that I came upon recently. A theologian who visited two different business groups some place in the midwest asked both groups whether they

NOTES

felt in their daily business affairs that they were able to reconcile the conduct of their business with the golden rule. The first were very unhappy and troubled about it. It was very difficult for them to reconcile business ethics with Christian ethics.

The second group expressed amazement that the question was even raised. They said ther was no question but that they were perfectly able to follow the Golden Rule in their business affairs.

I don't think the business man can, by virtue of the way our economic system is organized. On the other hand, I don't think, going back to the thing that you read of Mr. Levitt's, that the single-minded pursuit of monetary gain for profit, with "The public be damned" kind of attitude, is going to result in anything very meaningful, either. I think if you take that approach, the public is going to be hurt.

I can think, for example, of a very important problem which is not discussed much in this community. That is the problem of commercial bribery which is pretty rampant in business deals and is estimated at a huge sum each year.

The point is that when business men pay kickbacks or commissions or a little Christmas gift which is frequently based upon the amount of business that has been transacted during the year, that is in essence a kickback. When they do this, it is not purely a business matter entirely; it becomes a public problem that affects tax revenues. Ultimately, of course, the consumer will have to pay more for a particular product. This is a hidden, concealed kind of tax which the consumer ultimately pays. We lose millions of dollars in tax revenues every year because of it.

I want to make a point that is analogous to this. I think that in the case of the tranquilizer, either the public relations firm will assume the responsibility involved in knowing that he represents a client that is putting out a product with deleterious side effects. In deference to the public weal and the public good, he will mention this honestly, or this is going to be taken care of in the public interest by some other authority, by governmental agency, through the administration of the Pure Food & Drug Law, through the FTC or some other agency.

NOTES

COMMENT D: I don't think you can say, "My house is clean, and the other fellow takes over." Rather, you have that account and it is your responsibility to the public to present it in a truthful form. It is not only your responsibility to say, "Our tranquilizer is good, or ours is not good." That is the responsibility of the medical profession, to say it should be used in such and such a way. We have our responsibility to present the truth to the public accurately, and not to state that it is a cure-all for all your problems.

COMMENT E: I would like to ask a question: Should we give up the account when we know that if we do there will be five hundred other people who will pick it up? It seems to me you have at a certain point almost to reduce it to a personal kind of thing and divorce your feelings from the business. If you don't, will Joe Blow or somebody else do it? That is what it amounts to.

COMMENT F: Well, she stole my speech. I was going to say that I think the reporter, the journalist, is the man who has the luxury of speaking out the truth, and that we, when we become a publicist automatically give up our right to be completely objective. We have to serve the business or the client. We can persuade the client, if we can, to follow the ethical precepts which we believe in, and, failing that, we have a choice of giving in or getting out.

The way you can live with this I think is to go back to what was said, namely, to devote time and effort to working with other groups in the society in order to change some of the rules by which we live so that the problems in the business world become less.

COMMENT G: I think the public is attuned enough to public relations and advertising that a mild misrepresentation does not really do any serious damage. I think if you start splitting hairs, we are never going to have any common ground. I do think there is a difference between a product that can be misused and a product that is essentially dangerous.

I would like to touch on a public relations practice which all of us

NOTES

subscribe to, which is a practice that we can discuss and possibly come to an agreement on. That is the "buying and selling" of the press, the extent to which we "buy and sell" reporters, editors and photographers.

It ranges all the way from a luncheon in which we attempt to sell the reporter or editor a story, to a complete press junket on which you take the reporters and editors and pay their expenses, pay their meals, and hope they will write a favorable story about what they have seen.

It is true that the primary responsibility is ours, but a major part of the responsibility may be the responsibility of the journalist himself, the editor.

Wherein do these responsibilities conflict, and what shall we do about it? How far shall we go in our attempt either to buy or persuade the journalist, the press?

COMMENT H: The Commission on the Freedom of the Press attempted to deal with this question and actually did formulate its responses. These were in essence that any press which offered itself for sale was a venal press. This was not a popular statement, so far as the editors and managers were concerned. As a matter of fact, most of them didn't even read the report.

But I agree wholeheartedly that you cannot isolate one segment of the society and say, "You are solely responsible." You have to look at practices in toti. Then I think you have to be very reasonable about them.

I come back once more to the question that you raised. If your tranquilizer is actually a medicine which in itself, viewed objectively, apart from the use to which it is put by an individual, is bad, then I think you have the moral obligation to realize the objective, intrinsic evil that there is in the tranquilizer. However, if the objective, intrinsic evil is in the person who may use it and therefore becomes subjective, I don't think you have the responsibility for him at all. I think that is his.

COMMENT I: That is a little bit easy. What about a worthless product? What about a placebo that is being offered on the market, that doesn't do any harm but is taking people's money for doing nothing, like a gadget for

---

NOTES

an automobile which is supposed to make it run 40 miles on a gallon but which really doesn't.

DR. SHUSTER: It is a confounded lie and if you promulgate it of course you are telling one. Whether or not you are going to look upon this as a grave offense depends somewhat upon your approach to the whole problem of public relations. For example, take a problem in literary terms which is comparable. Take comic magazines, for example. Everybody knows that they probably serve no useful purpose even though they may not serve a necessarily deleterious one. This is part, I would say, of the whole fringe area of how the public spends its time. I don't think you have much of a responsibility for that. I would say unless it is objectively in itself evil and that in terms of the prudential ethics which apply in this society, I would not have too many qualms about that kind of operation...

Then when you look at the other and you say, what is this chap over here going to do with it, it is like your aspirin. It is our job as educators to tell parents that aspirin potentially speaking is dangerous to children if you don't keep it under control. I think society has the duty to make that clear. But it does not deprive aspirin of its very essential function as a beneficial drug with no evil effects observable on adults. So I certainly would say that I would advertise aspirin or something like that with a completely clear conscience. I have very grave doubts, however, about the tranquilizer.

COMMENT J: What I had to say was on another topic. It may be possible to "buy" a reporter with a lunch or "buy" him with a case of whiskey for Christmas or with a junket to Paris. It certainly may be true that the press is subject to the pressures of its advertisers and radio and TV even more so, but that does not relieve us of our obligations in the matter. If it is wrong for us to plug a tranquilizer and if the press may do these things which we regard as unethical, that does not mean that we should...

Isn't it part of our obligation to tell the drug company or the manufacturer of the tranquilizer that we cannot ignore the possible dangerous consequences of this drug, that it is to his interest to recognize

NOTES

this and to encourage people to consult their physicians before using it? In other words, wouldn't we be falling down on our job unless we advise the client of the possible consequences of the side effect?

COMMENT K: What do we do though? We say what we should do but what do we do in actual practice? I will be frank enough to admit it, very frankly if I had that situation I wouldn't mention until the last possible minute the fact that this drug could lead to problems.

NOTES

An Excerpt For Discussion

S. Africa: A Thorny Ethics Problem*

By Jack Bernstein

Chief executive officers of 52 of the best-known U.S. corporations, most of which have operations in South Africa, have banded together to support efforts seeking an end to apartheid.

States, cities, counties and universities have voted to divest or restrict nearly $50 billion of investments in companies doing business in South Africa.

Covington and Burling, the largest law firm in Washington, has severed its relationship with South African Airways. The firm has denied, not very credibly, that it has succumbed to pressure by boycotting students.

Et cetera, et cetera, et cetera.

So what to do is the thorny question facing pr people whose organizations or clients are involved in South Africa.

Stanley Rubenstein, chairman of Rubenstein, Wolfson & Co., which represents the South African Chamber of Mines, an association of the country's largest employers, laments the situation but stresses that his agency's relationship is based on business and economic, not social, considerations.

"We've always felt that apartheid is wrong and has to go, but we're not wise enough to know how to go about it," he says. "We're convinced, however, that anything that can be done to avoid violence should be done, and that peaceful change can only take place in a viable economy."

Rubenstein, Wolfson, he maintains, is working with private business interests that seek an economic vitality that will benefit the entire population.

---

* Reprinted with permission from the Nov. 18, 1985 issue of *Advertising Age*. Copyright, Crain Communications Inc., 1985.

"The withdrawal of U.S. interests and those of other nations will cause the South African economy to wither, which, in turn, will result in chaos," Mr. Rubenstein asserts.

"The Covington and Burling decision is wrong. The boycotting students who apparently inspired the action are making a judgment before hearing the case. They would be better served if they would go to work for just such a firm and try to influence change.

"We agonized over the situation and some of the younger members of our staff have questioned the propriety of our relationship with the Chamber of Mines and its marketing arm, International Gold Corp., which goes back to 1976," he says.

"But we came out convinced of South Africa's need for economic viability and that if we can communicate effectively with our client, which is seeking to achieve that goal, then we are making a useful contribution."

John Scanlon, who has gained a degree of celebrity as pr counselor to CBS and the *Boston Globe* in two high-visibility court cases, considers "untouchable" any agency of the South African government or a business that is government-controlled.

"Under no conditions would I represent such an entity," says Mr. Scanlon, an exec vp at Daniel J. Edelman Inc., a major Chicago-based pr agency. "With respect to private enterprise," he says, "each situation must be evaluated individually and would be contingent on whether the organization's commitment to change was real and demonstrated in fact, and not just mouthing to mask a desire to continue business as usual."

Mr. Scanlon gives short shrift to the claim by some that everyone is entitled to a pr defense just as they are to a legal defense. "I don't see the right to pr written in the Constitution," he says. "If I think something is morally wrong, then I'm not going to do anything to promote or defend it."

Legendary pr counselor Edward Bernays is strongly in Mr. Scanlon's camp. "No decent pr firm would touch South Africa any more than it would take the Ku Klux Klan or [John] Birch Society as clients," he says. He, too, has little patience with the argument that an entity is entitled to pr

NOTES

representation, noting how in years past his agency turned down entreaties by representatives of Hitler, Franco and Somoza.

"A doctor must treat a criminal because the medical profession's code of ethics mandates it. The same is true of the legal profession," Mr. Bernays says. "But pr must be guided by the public interest and social good, and has no such obligation."

Mr. Bernays describes as "cockeyed reasoning" the belief that pr can help achieve economic and social gains for South Africa. "You don't commit a crime to do good," he says. "There is no excuse for a pr agency to engage in anti-ethical acts."

How do black pr people feel about it? Connie Seals, a pr counselor in Chicago, holds the view that everyone is indeed entitled to pr help. She emphasizes, however, that pr people have an obligation to make certain they will have some influence on their clients' policies. "This would certainly be the case with any client involved in South Africa," she says.

Ms. Seals spent 10 years with the Chicago Urban League. In 1973 she left her post as director of communications and became executive director of the Illinois Commission on Human Relations. Three years ago she established her own company, C-BREM Communications Corp. She is currently chairman of the minority affairs committee of PRSA.

"If I thought I could effect changes in the policies of the KKK or the Birch Society, and my intent to do so was recognized and understood up front, then I'd sign on," she says. "But you've got to have your role ironed out in the beginning. You can't go in blind and hope for the best. Of course, ethics and personal conviction enter into such a decision. That's why it's important that the contract be written carefully so if it is breached you can pull out."

Stanley Scott, vp-director of public affairs, Philip Morris Cos., sees the "racist system of apartheid as a morality issue, most definitely." Whether a pr person takes on a client with South African involvement is, however, a personal decision, says Mr. Scott, who is black. Philip Morris, he notes, has no operations in South Africa, so neither he nor the company has been confronted with such a decision.

NOTES

David Finn, chairman of Ruder, Finn & Rotman, the nation's largest independent pr agency, is unequivocal when asked about working for South African interests. "Nope," he says. "We've been approached a number of times, and we're just not interested."

Mr. Finn also takes issue with the argument that by getting involved you can work for change from within. "That's a slippery slope of ethics that pr people can slide down. It's a rationalization, because you know you're not going to bring about a change. The client wants you for what you can do to advance his cause, not to effect change."

With respect to being available to one and all, Mr. Finn is adamant about never working for someone or something that you can't support wholeheartedly. "There's a world of difference between pr counsel and legal counsel," he says. "There's a tradition of law, a system of law, judges and juries. Pr deals with public sentiment and public opinion. How can you retain your own integrity if you represent an organization or issue with which you disagree?

"It's risky and dangerous to say you can represent either side," Mr. Finn says. He notes that the issue of ethics is so sticky and multifaceted, his agency has had an ethics committee and an outside adviser - a theologian, philospher or sociologist - for about 25 years. He points out, however, that the question of serving South African interests never got to the committee. "I made that decision myself."

There are practical, as well as moral and ethical, considerations that must be taken into account before entering into a new client relationship, says Craig Lewis, exec vp at Adams and Rinehart, a large New York-based pr agency.

Former chairman of Earl Newsom & Co., the distinguished counseling agency that merged with Adams & Rinehart in mid-'83, Mr. Lewis says, "Our approach to a controversial situation was to determine whether or not the story we were being asked to tell was a viable one. If it was a story you could not tell effectively, or one that the American public wouldn't accept, then our advice to the prospect was to save the money.

NOTES

"Pr agencies not only have the right but the obligation to choose their clients carefully," Mr. Lewis says. "This goes beyond likes or dislikes; you have to evaluate whether or not you can be effective for them. Of course, if what a prospective client stands for is morally repugnant to you, then the chance of you being able to do an effective job are pretty slim.

"So, with respect to South Africa, if an agency of the governement came to us, the decision would be pretty clear."

NOTES

Part 4. Appendix

PRSA Code Of Professional Standards With Official Interpretations

APPENDIX

PUBLIC RELATIONS SOCIETY OF AMERICA
Code of Professional Standards
For the Practice of Public Relations

This Code, adopted by the PRSA Assembly, replaces a similar Code of Professional Standards for the Practice of Public Relations previously in force since 1954 and strengthened by revisions in 1959, 1963 and 1977.

DECLARATION OF PRINCIPLES

Members of the Public Relations Society of America base their professional principles on the fundamental value and dignity of the individual, holding that the free exercise of human rights, especially freedom of speech, freedom of assembly and freedom of the press, is essential to the practice of public relations.

In serving the interests of clients and employers, we dedicate ourselves to the goals of better communication, understanding and cooperation among the diverse individuals, groups and institutions of society.

We pledge:

To conduct ourselves professionally, with truth, accuracy, fairness and responsibility to the public;

To improve our individual competence and advance the knowledge and proficiency of the profession through continuing research and education;

And to adhere to the articles of the Code of Professional Standards for the Practice of Public Relations as adopted by the governing Assembly of the Society.

ARTICLES OF THE CODE

These articles have been adopted by the Public Relations Society of America to promote and maintain high standards of public service and ethical conduct among its members.

1. A member shall deal fairly with clients or employers, past and present, with fellow practitioners and the general public.

2. A member shall conduct his or her professional life in accord with the public interest.

3. A member shall adhere to truth and accuracy and to generally accepted standards of good taste.

4. A member shall not represent conflicting or competing interests without the express consent of those involved, given after a full disclosure of the facts; nor place himself or herself in a position where the member's interests is or may be in conflict with a duty to a client, or others, without a full disclosure of such interests to all involved.

5. A member shall safeguard the confidences of both present and future clients or employers and shall not accept retainers or employment which may involve the disclosure or use of these confidences to the disadvantage or prejudice of such clients or employers.

6. A member shall not engage in any practice which tends to corrupt the channels of communication or the processes of government.

7. A member shall not intentionally communicate false or misleading information and is obligated to use care to avoid communication of false or misleading information.

8. A member shall be prepared to identify publicly the name of the client or employer on whose behalf any public communication is made.

9. A member shall not make use of any individual or organization purporting to serve or represent an announced cause, or purporting to be independent or unbiased, but actually serving an undisclosed special or private interest of a member, client or employer.

10. A member shall not intentionally injure the professional reputation or practice of another practitioner. However, if a member has evidence that another member has been guilty of unethical, illegal or unfair practices, including those in violation of this Code, the member shall present the information promptly to the proper authorities of the Society for action in accordance with the procedure set forth in Article XIII of the Bylaws.

11. A member called as a witness in a proceeding for the enforcement of this Code shall be bound to appear, unless excused for sufficient reason by the Judicial Panel.

12. A member, in performing services for a client or employer, shall not accept fees, commissions or any other valuable consideration from anyone other than the client or employer in connection with those services without the express consent of the client or employer, given after a full disclosure of the facts.

13. A member shall not guarantee the achievement of specified results beyond the member's direct control.

14. A member shall, as soon as possible, sever relations with any organization or individual if such relationship requires conduct contrary to the articles of this Code.

OFFICIAL INTERPRETATIONS OF THE CODE

Interpretation of Code Paragraph 2 which reads, "A member shall conduct his or her professional life in accord with the public interest."

> The public interest is here defined primarily as comprising respect for and enforcement of the rights guaranteed by the Constitution of the United States of America.

Interpretation of Code Paragraph 5 which reads, " A member shall safeguard the confidences of both present and future clients or employers and shall not accept retainers or employment which may involve the disclosure or use of these confidences to the disadvantage or prejudice of such clients or employers."

> This article does not prohibit a member who has knowledge of client or employer activities which are illegal from making such disclosures to the proper authorities as he or she believes are legally required.

Interpretation of Code Paragraph 6 which reads: " A member shall not engage in any practice which tends to corrupt the channels of communication or the processes of government."

1. Practices prohibited by this paragraph are those which tend to place representatives of media or government under an obligation to the member, or the member's employer or client, which is in conflict with their obligations to media or government, such as:

a. the giving of gifts of more than nominal value;
   b. any form of payment or compensation to a member of the media in order to obtain preferential or guaranteed news or editorial coverage in the medium;
   c. any retainer or fee to a media employee or use of such employee if retained by a client or employer, where the circumstances are not fully disclosed to and accepted by the media employer;
   d. providing trips for media representatives which are unrelated to legitimate news interest;
   e. the use by a member of an investment or loan or advertising commitment made by the member, or the member's client or employer, to obtain preferential or guaranteed coverage in the medium.

2. This Code paragraph does not prohibit hosting media or government representatives at meals, cocktails, or news functions or special events which are occasions for the exchange of news information or views, or the furtherance of understanding which is part of the public relations function. Nor does it prohibit the bona fide press event or tour when media or government representatives are given an opportunity for on-the-spot viewing of a newsworthy product, process or event in which the media or government representatives have a legitimate interest. What is customary or reasonable hospitality has to be a matter of particular judgment in specific situations. In all of these cases, however, it is or should be understood that no preferential treatment or guarantees are expected or implied and that complete independence always is left to the media or government representative.

3. This paragraph does not prohibit the reasonable giving or lending of sample products or services to media representatives who have a legitimate interest in the products or services.

Interpretation of Code Paragraph 13 which reads, " A member shall not guarantee the achievement of specified results beyond the member's direct control."

This Code paragraph, in effect, prohibits misleading a client or employer as to what professional public relations can accomplish. It does not prohibit guarantees of quality or service. But it does prohibit guaranteeing specific results which, by their very nature, cannot be guaranteed because they are not subject to the member's control. As an example, a guarantee that a news release will appear specifically in a particular publication would be prohibited. This paragraph should not be interpreted as prohibiting contingent fees.

AN OFFICIAL INTERPRETATION OF THE CODE AS IT APPLIES TO FINANCIAL PUBLICATION

This interpretation of the Society Code as it applies to financial public relations was originally adopted in 1963 and amended in 1972 and 1977 by action of the PRSA Board of Directors. "Financial public relations" is defined as "that area of public relations which relates to the dissemination of information that affects the understanding of stockholders and investors generally concerning the financial position and prospects of a company, and includes among its objectives the improvement of relations between corporations and their stockholders." The interpretation was prepared in 1963 by the Society's Financial Relations Committee working with the Securities and Exchange Commission and with the advice of the Society's Legal Counsel. It is rooted directly in the Code with the full force of the Code behind it and a violation of any of the following paragraphs is subject to the same procedures and penalties as violation of the Code.

1. It is the responsibility of PRSA members who practice financial public relations to be thoroughly familiar with and understand the rules and regulations of the SEC and the laws which it administers, as well as other laws, rules and regulations affecting financial public relations, and to act in accordance with their letter and spirit. In carrying out this responsibility, members shall also seek legal counsel, when appropriate, on matters concerning financial public relations.

2. Members shall adhere to the general policy of making full and timely disclosure of corporate information on behalf of clients or employers. The information disclosed should be accurate, clear and understandable. The purpose of such disclosure is to provide the investing public with all material information affecting security values or influencing investment decisions. In complying with the duty of full and timely disclosure, members shall present all material facts, including those adverse to the company. They shall exercise care to ascertain the facts and to disseminate only information which they believe to be accurate. They shall not knowingly omit information, the omission of which might make a release false or misleading. Under no circumstances shall members participate in any activity designed to mislead, or manipulate the price of a company's securities.

3. Members shall publicly disclose or release information promptly so as to avoid the possibility of any use of the information by any insider or third party. To that end, members shall make every effort to comply with the spirit and intent of the timely disclosure policies of the stock

exchange, NASD, and the Securities Exchange Commission. Material information shall be made available to all on an equal basis.

4. Members shall not disclose confidential information the disclosure of which might be adverse to a valid corporate purpose or interest and whose disclosure is not required by the timely disclosure provisions of the law. During any such period of non-disclosure members shall not directly or indirectly (a) communicate the confidential information to any other person or (b) buy or sell or in any way deal in the company's securities where the confidential information may materially affect the market for the security when disclosed. Material information shall be disclosed publicly as soon as its confidential status has terminated or the requirement of timely disclosure takes effect.

5. During the registration period, members shall not engage in practices designed to precondition the market for such securities. During registration the issuance of forecasts, projections, predictions about sales and earnings, or opinions concerning security values or other aspects of the future performance of the company, shall be in accordance with current SEC regulations and statements of policy. In the case of companies whose securities are publicly held, the normal flow of factual information to shareholders and the investing public shall continue during the registration period.

6. Where members have any reason to doubt that projections have an adequate basis in fact, they shall satisfy themselves to the adequacy of the projections prior to disseminating them.

7. Acting in concert with clients or employers, members shall act promptly to correct false or misleading information or rumors concerning clients' or employers' securities or business whenever they have reason to believe such information or rumors are materially affecting investor attitudes.

8. Members shall not issue descriptive materials designed or written in such a fashion as to appear to be, contrary to the fact, an independent third party endorsement or recommendation of a company or a security. Whenever members issue material for clients or employers, either in their own names or in the name of someone other than the clients or employers, they shall disclose in large type and in a prominent position on the face of the material the source of such material and the existence of the issuer's client or employer relationship.

9. Members shall not use inside information for personal gain. However, this is not intended to prohibit members from making bona fide investments in their company's or client's securities insofar as they can make such investments without the benefit of material inside information.

10. Members shall not accept compensation which would place them in a position of conflict with their duty to a client, employer or the investing public. Members shall not accept stock options from clients or employers nor accept securities as compensation at a price below market price except as part of an overall plan for corporate employees.

11. Members shall act so as to maintain the integrity of channels of public communication. They shall not pay or permit to be paid to any publication or other communications medium any consideration in exchange for publicizing a company, except through clearly recognized paid advertising.

12. Members shall in general be guided by the PRSA Declaration of Principles and the PRSA Code of Professional Standards for the Practice of Public Relations of which this Code is an official interpretation.

About The Author:

Raymond Simon, professor emeritus of public relations at Utica College of Syracuse University, has had four decades of teaching and practical experience in public relations. He is the author of four textbooks which have been used at more than 300 colleges and universities in this country and abroad.

A former trustee of the Foundation for Public Relations Research and Education, Professor Simon is an accredited member of the Public Relations Society of America and authored one of the PRSA's early accreditation examinations. Graduates who have studied under Professor Simon are found among leading public relations counseling firms and departments, including Burson-Marsteller, General Motors, General Electric, United Technologies, Westinghouse, Alcoa, and the John Hancock Life Insurance Company. In 1976 he received the PRSA's Outstanding Educator Award, and he has twice been selected by his institution as its distinguished teacher of the year.

Professor Simon resides in New Hartford, N.Y. with his wife Lyn and their two daughters, Melissa and Karen. His hobbies are swimming, Fanny Farmer lollipops, poker, and watching basketball.